C000258105

The Unification of Germany and the Challenge of Nationalism 1789–1919

ALAN FARMER AND ANDRINA STILES

FOURTH EDITION

HODDER
EDUCATION
AN HACHETTE UK COMPANY

The Publishers thank OCR for permission to use a specimen exam question on page 230 from OCR's A Level History A specification H505 © OCR 2014. OCR have neither seen nor commented upon any model answers or exam guidance related to these questions.

The Publishers would like to thank Robin Bunce, Nicholas Fellows and Sarah Ward for their contribution to the Study Guide.

The Publishers would like to thank the following for permission to reproduce copyright material:

Photo credits: p37 Barricades in Berlin during the 1848 German Revolution (engraving) (b/w photo), German School, (19th century)/Private Collection/Archives Charmet/Bridgeman Images; **p41** The National Assembly in the church St Paul, Frankfurt, convened in May 1848 (colour lithograph), May, E.G. (fl.1848)/Historisches Museum, Frankfurt, Germany/Archives Charmet/Bridgeman Images; **p51** BPK; **p66** Bettmann/Corbis; **p73** Library of Congress, LC-USZ62-122505; **p82** Bettmann/Corbis; **p99** Library of Congress, LC-USZC2-2786; **p111** Bettmann/Corbis; **p137** Punch Limited; **p149** Corbis; **p157** Library of Congress, LC-USZ62-89797; **p207** Bettmann/Corbis; **p215** Library of Congress, LC-USZ62-103826; **p219** Mary Evans Picture Library/Weimar Archive.

The Publishers would like to acknowledge Wiley for permission to use extracts from the following book: M. Kitchen, *A History of Modern Germany 1800–2000*, Blackwell, 2006.

Acknowledgements: Cambridge University Press, J.C.G. Röhl, *Kaiser Wilhelm II*, 2014; J.C.G. Röhl, *The Kaiser and his Court: Wilhelm II and the Government of Germany*, 1995. Connoisseur Edition, C.D. Warner, editor, *Library of the World's Best Literature: Ancient and Modern*, 1896. German History in Documents and Images, germanhistorydocs.ghi-dc.org. Ginn & Co., J.H. Robinson, editor, *Readings in European History*, 1904; J.H. Robinson, editor, *Readings in European History: A Collection of Extracts from the Sources*, 1906. Hamish Hamilton, A.J.P. Taylor, *Bismarck: The Man and the Statesman*, 1955. History Man, historyman.co.uk. Hodder & Stoughton, Andrina Stiles, *The Unification of Germany 1815–90*, 1986; Andrina Stiles and Alan Farmer, *The Unification of Germany 1815–90*, 2001. Longman, M.S. Anderson, *The Ascendancy of Europe 1815–1914*, 1972; J. Hiden, *The Weimar Republic*, 1996; D. Thompson, *Europe Since Napoleon*, 1962. Macdonald Library, H. Kurtz, *The Second Reich: Kaiser Wilhelm II and his Germany*, 1970. Macmillan, Prince Hohenlohe, *Memoirs of Prince Chlodwig of Hohenlohe-Schillingsfuerst*, 1906. McClure Company, Carl Schurz, *The Reminiscences of Carl Schurz*, 1913. National Library of New Zealand, paperspast.natlib.govt.nz. Oliver & Boyd, Frank Eyck, *The Revolutions of 1848–49*, 1972. Oxford University Press, J. Steinberg, *Bismarck: A Life*, 2011. Torch Press, Thomas J. McCormack, editor, *Memoirs of Gustave Koerner, 1809–1896*, volume 1, 1909. Vintage Books, W.L. Langer, *European Alliances and Alignments 1871–90*, 1950. William Collins, Max Hastings, *Catastrophe: Europe Goes to War 1914*, 2013.

Every effort has been made to trace all copyright holders, but if any have been inadvertently overlooked the Publishers will be pleased to make the necessary arrangements at the first opportunity.

Although every effort has been made to ensure that website addresses are correct at time of going to press, Hodder Education cannot be held responsible for the content of any website mentioned in this book. It is sometimes possible to find a relocated web page by typing in the address of the home page for a website in the URL window of your browser.

Hachette UK's policy is to use papers that are natural, renewable and recyclable products and made from wood grown in sustainable forests. The logging and manufacturing processes are expected to conform to the environmental regulations of the country of origin.

Orders: please contact Bookpoint Ltd, 130 Milton Park, Abingdon, Oxon OX14 4SB. Telephone: +44 (0)1235 827720. Fax: +44 (0)1235 400454. Lines are open 9.00a.m.–5.00p.m., Monday to Saturday, with a 24-hour message answering service. Visit our website at www.hoddereducation.co.uk

First published in 2007 by
Hodder Education
An Hachette UK Company
Carmelite House, 50 Victoria Embankment,
London EC4Y 0DZ

Impression number	10	9	8	7	6	5	4	3
Year		2019	2018	2017	2016			

Cover photo © akg-images
Produced, illustrated and typeset in Palatino LT Std by Gray Publishing, Tunbridge Wells
Printed and bound by CPI Group (UK) Ltd, Croydon CR0 4YY

A catalogue record for this title is available from the British Library

ISBN 978 1471839030

Contents

Dedication

Keith Randell (1943–2002)

The *Access to History* series was conceived and developed by Keith, who created a series to 'cater for students as they are, not as we might wish them to be'. He leaves a living legacy of a series that for over 20 years has provided a trusted, stimulating and well-loved accompaniment to post-16 study. Our aim with these new editions is to continue to offer students the best possible support for their studies.

CHAPTER 1

Germany 1789–1848

At the end of the eighteenth century there seemed little likelihood of a united German nation coming into existence. Germany, in so far as it existed, was a ramshackle empire, made up of hundreds of petty principalities, free cities and ecclesiastical and aristocratic estates. However, by 1815, largely as a result of the French Revolutionary and Napoleonic Wars, thousands of Germans longed passionately for a unified Germany. Nationalist enthusiasm continued post-1815. This chapter will examine the factors that led to the rise of German nationalism by focusing on the following themes:

★ The impact of the French Revolution and Napoleon

★ Reform and repression 1815–40

★ Economic developments 1815–48

★ Germany 1840–8

Key dates

1789	Start of the French Revolution	1830	July	Revolution in Paris
1806	End of the Holy Roman Empire	1832	May	Nationalist festival at Hambach
1813	Battle of Leipzig	1832	June	The Six Articles
1814–15	Vienna peace settlement	1834		*Zollverein* came into operation
1815	German Confederation established	1840		Frederick William IV became King of Prussia
1817	Wartburg Festival			
1819	Carlsbad Decrees	1846		Schleswig-Holstein affair
1820	Congress of Troppau	1847		Hippenhelm meeting

1 The impact of the French Revolution and Napoleon

▶ *What was Napoleon's impact on Germany?*

Historian Thomas Nipperdey (1996) begins his monumental history of nineteenth-century Germany with the phrase, 'In the beginning was Napoleon'. The French emperor's influence on German development was considerable.

The situation in Germany in 1789

In 1789 Germany did not exist as a country in the sense of being a unified political state. Indeed, the term 'Germany' had little political significance.

The political situation

In 1789 some 22 million Germans were divided into 314 states, varying in size from the 300,000 km² (115,533 square miles) of the **Habsburg** monarchy to the 85 km² (33 square miles) of Schwartzburg-Sonderhausen. Another 1400 towns, cities and territories had a degree of autonomy. Each state had its own ruling class, its own traditions, its own laws and its own nobility determined to maintain their prerogatives.

Since 1512 the multitude of states had been loosely united within the Holy Roman Empire, whose nominal emperor was the Habsburg emperor of Austria. According to the French writer Voltaire, the Holy Roman Empire was neither holy, Roman nor even an empire. It certainly lacked any real power. What power it had was essentially Austrian power.

The Holy Roman Empire did have a permanent Imperial **Diet**, a gathering of representatives of the various states nominally chaired by the emperor, who was bound by its decrees. However, the conflicting interests of the states rarely achieved a unified position. The empire had no central political administration, no common tax system and no standing army. While the Imperial *Diet* could call up an army, there was no guarantee (or much likelihood) that the states would send the predetermined quota of troops or pay their financial contributions for the army's upkeep.

Germany lacked clear natural frontiers, especially in the east and south. Nor was it possible to define Germany's extent on ethnic grounds. The Holy Roman Empire included land peopled by French, Dutch, Danish, Polish and Czech speakers. It also excluded sizeable territories with a predominantly German population – not least Prussia, the only other German state apart from Austria that counted for anything in international affairs.

Germans in the south German states were overwhelmingly Catholic. Those in the north were mainly Protestant. Religious hostility between Protestants and Catholics made political unification difficult.

The economic and social situation

German economic and social development lagged far behind that of Britain and Western Europe. Development was retarded by several factors:

- The **feudal system** of economic and social order survived almost intact in many states. This meant that there were strict divisions of society: a large class of peasantry, a small number of urban workers, an even smaller middle class and a privileged aristocracy.

- Over 80 per cent of Germans lived and worked on the land. In the west, most of the so-called free peasants were burdened by rent, **tithes** and labour dues. East of the River Elbe most peasants were still **serfs**.
- There were great varieties in currencies and weights and measures, innumerable customs barriers and internal taxes, and poor communications, all of which restricted commercial growth.
- Most skilled workers in the towns belonged to powerful guilds. Determined to retain their privileges, the guilds prevented free competition and blocked economic progress.
- The aristocracy owned most of the land and held all the key posts in the various courts, armies and administrations.

Napoleon's impact on Germany

Historian Martin Kitchen (2006) argued, 'The old [German] empire was destroyed by blood and iron, just as some seventy years later the new empire was to be created by the use of force.' French force destroyed the old Germany and provided the initial stimulus to the movement towards German unification. Ironically, traditional French policy had been to keep Germany divided.

The impact of the French Revolution

In 1789 France rose up in revolt against the *ancien régime*. The power of the French monarchy, the Church and aristocracy was reduced. Many educated Germans initially approved of developments in France, particularly calls for liberty, equality and **fraternity** and for representative government. They were less supportive of developments in 1793 when King Louis XVI was executed and thousands of people followed him to the guillotine in the Reign of Terror. By 1793 Austria, Prussia and many other German rulers, anxious to stop the spread of revolutionary ideas, were at war with France – a war which they failed to win. Some German radicals, still supportive of the Revolution, welcomed French military successes against Austria and Prussia.

The Napoleonic settlement

The hotchpotch of German states lacked the ability and unity to resist the military ambitions of Napoleon Bonaparte, French leader from 1799 and French emperor from 1804. Having defeated both Austria and Prussia in 1805–6, Napoleon controlled most of central Europe. In **Karl Marx's** words, he set about **'cleansing the** German **Augean stables'**.

- France annexed the territory on the left bank of the Rhine in 1803.
- French policy (in 1803 and 1806) ensured that a host of small German states were absorbed by their larger neighbours. The total number of states was reduced to 39. Baden increased four-fold as a consequence of the Napoleonic settlement while Bavaria now included 80 previously autonomous political entities.

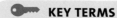

KEY TERMS

Tithes A tax paid to the Church; in theory, a tenth of a person's earnings.

Serfs Peasants who are forced to remain on the land and work for a landowner.

Ancien régime The old feudal order in France.

Fraternity Brotherhood and companionship.

Cleansing the Augean stables A difficult and dirty task. (According to Greek legend, it was one of the labours of the hero Hercules.)

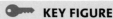

KEY FIGURE

Karl Marx (1818–83)

German philosopher, economist and revolutionary who is generally regarded as the founder of communism.

- In 1806 Bavaria, Württemberg Baden and thirteen other south German states were formed into the Confederation of the Rhine – a third German power to offset Prussia and Austria.
- Prussia (in 1807) lost all its land west of the Elbe, much of which became part of the Kingdom of Westphalia. Prussia's Polish territories became the Grand Duchy of Warsaw.
- In 1806 the Holy Roman Empire was formally dissolved.

German opposition

For several years Germany was subject to Napoleon's will. However, in 1809 Austria resumed war with Napoleon. Count Philip Stadion, Austria's first minister, hoped to mobilise popular German sentiment and inspire a war of liberation. The romantic notion that the people would arise and overthrow France was naïve. Only the Tyrol, an area annexed by Bavaria in 1805, caused the French much trouble. Here Andreas Hofer led a guerrilla campaign in the mountains, defeating French and Bavarian forces in a series of engagements. But this was a regional revolt, not a fully fledged German uprising. Hofer was eventually captured and executed.

Austria received little support from the other German states. Its regular army was crushed by Napoleon in June 1809 at the Battle of Wagram. In the Peace of Schönbrunn, Austria ceded further territories and was forced to pay crippling **reparations** to France. Austria now sought to appease Napoleon, who married the emperor's daughter.

The development of German nationalism

French domination soon contributed to a sense of common cause and an emerging German **nationalism**.

French impositions

French rule alienated many Germans. Most were affected by sharply rising prices, by heavy taxes and by French controls. The German economy, subordinated to French needs, was seriously disrupted by Napoleon's **continental blockade** that tried to exclude British goods. Germans also loathed military conscription. In 1808, for example, the Confederation of the Rhine was forced to provide Napoleon with 119,000 soldiers. Resentment thus built up against the French invaders, who squeezed all they could from Germany.

Spain and Portugal

In 1808 the Spanish and Portuguese rose in revolt against French rule. Their efforts to win independence from Napoleon were an inspiration for many Germans.

KEY TERMS

Reparations Money that a country is forced to pay to the victor after defeat in war.

Nationalism The belief in – and support for – a national identity and the desire for the nation's success.

Continental blockade Napoleon's trade boycott of British goods. Introduced in 1806, its aim was to force Britain to make peace with France.

German intellectuals

From the late eighteenth century a number of German intellectuals, stressing the importance of a common language and common cultural traditions, had supported national unity.

German philosophers – Johann Herder, Johann Fichte and George Hegel – developed the view that the German people were a unique *volk* who should belong to the same state (see Source A). More accessible to most Germans were the writings of Ernst Arndt, a poet and pamphleteer, who urged the creation of a German fatherland.

Emulating France

To some Germans France was a useful model – a politically self-confident nation that had come to dominate Europe. Liberal Germans also approved of many French reforms. In many German states:

- The Napoleonic Code was introduced, ensuring equality before the law and an end to aristocratic and Church privileges.
- There was increased middle-class involvement in government and in administration.
- Feudal restrictions came to an end.
- Church lands were secularised.

SOURCE A

From *Address to the German Nation* (1808) written by German philosopher Johann Gottlieb Fichte, www.historyman.co.uk/unification/Fichte.html.

The first original and truly natural boundaries of states are beyond doubt their internal boundaries. Those who speak the same language are joined to each other by a multitude of invisible bonds by nature herself, long before any human art begins: they understand each other and have the power of continuing to make themselves understood more and more clearly; they belong together and are by nature one and an inseparable whole.

Prussia 1806–13

After devastating defeats by Napoleon at Jena and Auerstedt in 1806, the Prussian state virtually collapsed. It only survived because of the intervention of Russian Tsar Alexander I and Napoleon's calculation that a buffer state between France and Russia might be desirable. Nevertheless, Prussia lost much of its territory, had to pay huge reparations to France, endured a French army of occupation and had to agree to limit its army to 42,000 men.

Under the leadership of Baron vom Stein and then Karl August von Hardenberg, chancellor from 1810 until his death in 1822, a body of administrators set out to revive Prussian power by overhauling its institutions. Essentially, their reforms were designed to strengthen the Prussian state in order to free the kingdom

KEY TERM

Volk The German word translates as people or folk but the concept goes beyond that, implying that the (German) *volk* are almost mystically united and are superior to other groups.

What were the 'multitude of invisible bonds' that Fichte refers to in Source A?

from French domination. The aim was to give Prussians some rights, freeing them from the restrictions of a hierarchical society, so that they were able to develop their talents and contribute to the common good. Hardenberg advised Prussian King Frederick William III in 1807, 'we must do from above what the French have done from below':

- Serfdom was abolished and peasants were liberated from the remnants of the old feudal order. Peasants were now free subjects before the law, able to own property and to marry as they wished, and free to move and to practise any trade or profession.
- In 1810 the power of the Prussian guilds was broken.
- Church lands were secularised.
- Military reformers Gerhard Scharnhorst and Carl August von Gneisenau reorganised the army. The officer corps was purged. Henceforward, commissions were to be awarded by competitive examination. Universal military training was introduced, with training in a professional army on a rolling programme. Men served for 30 months then joined the *Landwehr* – a reserve force. (This system ensured that the Prussians were able to keep their treaty with France while in reality evading its restrictions.) Soldiers were no longer subjected to inhuman punishment.
- The government was overhauled to provide a more efficient central authority. The civil service was thrown open to men of all classes.
- Wilhelm von Humboldt, Prussian minister of education, introduced major reforms in the education system. Determined that education should not be the preserve of a small elite, Humboldt introduced elementary schools for all children. Those who were able could go on to secondary schools. Humboldt also introduced state certification requirements for teachers, and established the University of Berlin, in 1810.
- Towns were given elected municipal councils.

Stein had envisaged the creation of an elected national assembly but this was a step too far for the Prussian king and aristocracy. Nevertheless, the reforms, according to historian Kitchen, were 'astonishing and rapid'. They ensured that Prussia would become the most modernised state in Germany.

The War of Liberation

In 1812 Napoleon invaded Russia with an army of over 600,000 men, a third of whom were German. The campaign was a disaster. Napoleon lost over 500,000 men. This weakened his grip on Europe. The heavy losses angered Germans.

Popular anti-French opinion encouraged King Frederick William III of Prussia to ally with Russia against France in January 1813. Responding to patriotic enthusiasm, Frederick William called for a people's war of liberation. In June, Austria also declared war on France. In October, the three allies defeated

KEY TERM

Landwehr A reserve army, made up of men who are partially but not necessarily fully or recently trained.

Napoleon at the Battle of Leipzig (sometimes called the Battle of Nations) – Europe's greatest and costliest land-battle of the nineteenth century. (Both sides lost 60,000 men.) Within a few months the allied armies invaded France, occupied Paris and forced Napoleon to abdicate.

This so-called War of Liberation has often been seen by historians as the first collective action of the German nation. Certainly, for some Prussian patriots, the war was a struggle of the German people against a foreign tyranny, a struggle that they hoped would result in the rebirth of a German empire. A 'free corps' of German student volunteers, led by the Prussian officer Adolf von Lützow, captured popular imagination. The black-clad troops, under their black, red and gold banner, seemed akin to a German army. Baron vom Stein, who had become an advisor to Russian Tsar Alexander I, drafted the text of the Proclamation of Kalisch, which outlined allied war aims. They included the re-establishment of a reformed German empire with a **constitution** that would reflect the 'quintessential spirit of the German people' and the freedom of the German princes and people.

Prussian troops played a crucial role when Napoleon returned from exile in 1815. A Prussian army, led by Gebhard von Blücher, and an Anglo-Allied army, led by the Duke of Wellington, defeated Napoleon at the Battle of Waterloo. The battles of Leipzig and Waterloo offered all Germans a rallying point of pride and enthusiasm.

Later romantic **nationalist** myths about the war bore little relation to reality, however. Most Germans were indifferent to calls for a popular rising against France. Moreover, King Frederick William of Prussia and other German princes remained suspicious of a national movement which might 'overheat' the people and get out of control. Most Prussian leaders were Prussian – not German – nationalists. Thus, Germany's future was decided, not by German patriots, but by the particular interests of Prussia and Austria.

The Vienna peace settlement

Nationalists' hopes that a powerful united Germany would arise from Napoleon's defeat were dashed at the Congress of Vienna. In 1814–15 German unification was not a practical proposition. Too many deep-seated divisions stood in the way of national unity. Perhaps the most important was the rivalry between Austria and Prussia. These two states were obvious rival candidates for the control of any united Germany. However, at this stage, they were content to exist side by side in what Austrian Foreign Minister Metternich called 'peaceful dualism'. Both were among the **Great Powers** who drew up the peace treaty at the Congress of Vienna in 1815. Not surprisingly, both benefited substantially from the Vienna peace settlement.

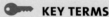 **KEY TERMS**

Constitution A set of rules by which a state is governed.

Nationalist Someone who favours or strives after the unity, independence, interests or domination of a nation.

Great Powers Europe's strongest nations in 1814–15 were Britain, Russia, Austria, Prussia and France. The first four countries had allied together to defeat France.

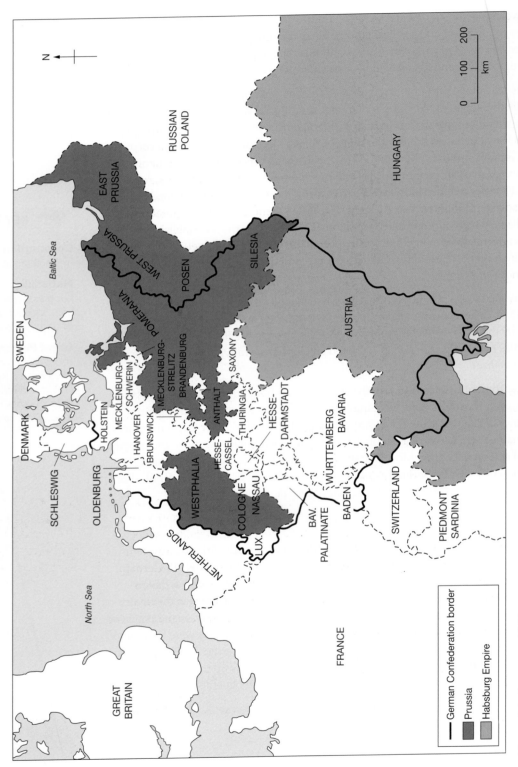

Figure 1.1 Germany in 1815.

Austrian gains

Most of Austria's territorial gains came in Italy, not Germany. Austria secured Lombardy and Venetia in northern Italy, while Habsburg rulers were restored to the central Italian duchies of Parma, Modena and Tuscany.

Prussian gains

Prussia gained considerable territory, including part of Saxony, the Rhineland, Westphalia and Pomerania (see Figure 1.1 on page 8). Prussia's population was more than doubled to 10 million. The sudden increase in size brought problems. The Catholic Rhinelanders resented being annexed to Protestant Prussia, from which they were separated by more than 80 km (50 miles) and with which they had little in common. Prussia was similarly reluctant to take the Rhineland. It would have preferred to take the whole of Saxony and/or more Polish territory. Moreover, Prussia was now lumbered with the task of defending Germany's borders against any resurgence of French military might. Nevertheless, the Congress of Vienna considerably strengthened Prussia's role in Germany.

Metternich's influence at Vienna

Although Prussia emerged as the big German winner from Vienna, this was not apparent at the time. This was largely because Austria's political influence at the Congress (and thereafter) was greater than that of Prussia. The most important influence on the future of the German states in 1814–15 was that of Prince Metternich, Austria's chief minister. Metternich's aim was the maintenance of Austria's traditional authority over the German states. He was not concerned with German political unity, and his negotiations at Vienna ensured that Germany would become a loose confederation of states under Austrian control.

The German Confederation

In June 1815 the German Confederation, comprising 39 states, was established by the Congress of Vienna. Its declared aim was to maintain 'the external and internal security and the independence and integrity of the individual states'. It thus sought to uphold the ***status quo*** in individual states through a system of mutual assistance in times of danger, such as internal rebellion or external aggression. The Confederation was not concerned with promoting a united Germany. In fact, its aim was exactly the opposite, for none of the rulers of the separate states wished to see their independence limited by the establishment of a strong central German government.

The boundaries of the Confederation were modelled on those of the old Holy Roman Empire rather than on ones that would encourage the development of a German nation-state. Areas peopled by Poles, Czechs, Danes and French were included and provinces with largely German-speaking populations were

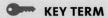

KEY TERM

Status quo The existing condition or situation.

excluded. States such as Luxemburg, Hanover and Holstein, which were ruled by foreign monarchs (the Dutch king ruled Luxemburg, the British king Hanover and the Danish king Holstein), were within the Confederation while parts of German-speaking Austria and Prussia were not.

The *Bundestag*

The Confederation had only one **executive** body, the *Bundestag* or Federal Council, which met at Frankfurt am Main. This was a permanent conference of representatives, who were not elected but were sent by their governments with instructions how to act. It was to be presided over by the Austrian representative, in recognition of the imperial power traditionally held by the Habsburg emperors. Given that the agreement of every state government was required before any measure could be passed, little was ever achieved. Representatives were more concerned with safeguarding the interests of their own states than working for the Confederation as a whole.

The weakness of the Confederation

The Confederation had very little control over the 39 individual states, apart from being able to prevent them making foreign alliances which might threaten the security of the Confederation, or concluding separate peace agreements in the event of the Confederation being involved in war. The constitution of the Confederation, the Federal Act, had empowered the *Bundestag* to organise a federal army and to develop commercial and economic co-operation between the states, but local jealousies and fiercely guarded independence meant that nothing of importance was done to unify the Confederation militarily or economically. The defence of the Confederation depended on the continued co-operation of Austria and Prussia.

The Confederation thus disappointed those Germans who hoped for greater national unity. It has also been criticised by historians who see it as being essentially the Holy Roman Empire mark II – an organisation which had no place in the age of emergent nation-states. However, the Confederation at least provided a framework within which German states coexisted, albeit uneasily.

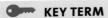

KEY TERM

Executive The power or authority in government that carries laws into effect.

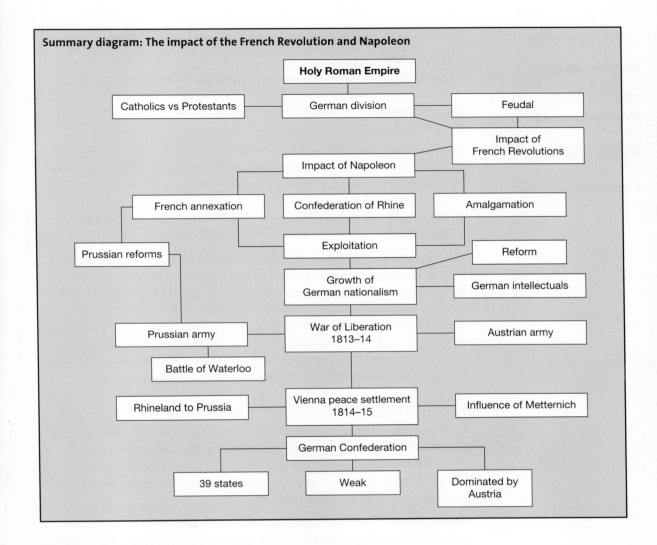

Summary diagram: The impact of the French Revolution and Napoleon

② Reform and repression 1815–40

▶ *Why was the period from 1815 to 1840 a period of repression?*

The years 1815–48 are often called the *Vormärz* or pre-March (a prelude to the March revolutions in Berlin and Vienna in 1848; see page 36). Associated with the Austrian statesman Metternich, the *Vormärz* is usually seen as a period of reaction and repression. But liberal and nationalist views survived the repression and had growing support.

German constitutions

Absolute rule was restored in most German states in 1815. All but four were **dynastic** states: monarchies, **duchies** and **principalities**. However, one of the Articles of the Federal Act laid down that the ruler of each state should sooner or later give his subjects a 'Constitution of Regional Estates', that is, some kind of parliament. The response varied:

- Some rulers totally ignored the Article.
- Most north German states allowed the 'estates' to meet. These 'estates' were traditional representative bodies, not always elected, and usually composed largely of nobles.
- In southern and central Germany there was more compliance with the Federal Act.

Between 1818 and 1820 Bavaria, Baden, Württemberg and Hesse-Darmstadt introduced constitutions that created elected assemblies. These assemblies had the power to make laws and control taxation, powers which could not be ignored. However, suffrage was based on strict property requirements, which meant that only a small portion of the male population could vote. Moreover, the assemblies had limited influence. The monarchs continued to appoint their own ministers and retain real power. Nevertheless, most governments did their best to avoid confrontation with the assemblies.

Developments in Austria and Prussia

Little was done to encourage democratic reform in Austria. The Austrian kings, Francis I (1804–35) and his mentally retarded successor Ferdinand I (1835–49), wished to maintain their absolute power. The old provincial *Diets* were eventually revived, but only as a means of preserving the existing social order. They were dominated by the local aristocracy.

Austria, virtually bankrupt in 1815 and chaotically administered, was in need of reform. But those in power (Metternich dominated foreign affairs, his rival Franz Kolowrat dominated domestic affairs), fearing upheaval, prevented any major changes after 1815. Austria remained an inefficient police state in which the aristocracy retained its privileges.

In Prussia, King Frederick William III (1797–1840) showed little interest in liberal reform. After 1815 Prussia was a patchwork of disparate territories, divided culturally, religiously and economically. The country was divided into provinces, each with a president, appointed by the central government in Berlin. Each province enjoyed a high degree of independence and each maintained its own distinct identity. Although Frederick William III did agree to set up provincial estates with limited advisory powers in 1823, these were controlled by large landowners. Prussia remained a state without a constitution until 1848.

Monarchical rule

The majority of German rulers, following the lead of Austria and Prussia, clung obstinately to their absolute power. Noble families continued to wield huge influence. However, many states emerged from the years of war with better organised and stronger **bureaucracies**. This was the result of French occupation, imitation of French methods, or simply financial necessity. The bureaucracies were active in a host of areas: economic, legal and educational. They ensured, for example, that educational provision in Germany was the best in Europe.

The influence of Metternich

Metternich believed that the maintenance of international peace was directly linked with the prevention of revolution in individual states. What happened inside one state was of concern to other states, and entitled them to intervene if they considered it necessary. The social order had to be defended against the forces of destruction. For Metternich these forces were liberalism and nationalism. If these – in his view – revolutionary ideas spread, they could lead to the overthrow of absolute monarchy and the end of the **multinational Austrian Empire**. He, therefore, opposed any constitutional change, however modest.

German liberalism and nationalism

Many liberal Germans opposed Metternich's conservatism. Most liberals wanted:

- parliamentary rule
- freedom of speech
- freedom of the press
- freedom of worship
- freedom to form political associations and hold political meetings.
- a united Germany.

Liberals were almost exclusively well-educated, well-to-do members of the middle class who, fearful of the excesses of the French Revolution, had no wish to bring about radical changes in the structure of society. Few supported a universal **franchise**. They believed that only men of property should be entitled to the vote. Most were opposed to violence and hoped to achieve their aims by intellectual argument and peaceful persuasion.

Virtually all German liberals were nationalists. They wanted to establish a strong German state. However, there was little agreement about how this state would be organised and what would be the relative roles of Austria and Prussia.

It is difficult to know how far liberal and nationalist ideas filtered down from the educated minority to the rest of the population. For many ordinary

🔑 KEY TERMS

Bureaucracies Systems of administration.

Multinational Austrian Empire The Austrian Empire contained people of many different nationalities. Although a relatively small minority, the Germans were the dominant ethnic group within the Empire.

Franchise The right to vote.

Germans, nationalism had arisen simply as a resentment of French rule. Once French occupation ended, nationalist sentiment declined. Local patriotism and regionalism remained strong.

In some cases well-meaning liberals set up study groups in German cities, hoping to attract the support of workers. Moreover, groups were sometimes formed by workers themselves. These groups tended to be more radical. Their politics often became democratic rather than liberal, centred on the **sovereignty** of the people rather than on the sovereignty of parliament, on a republic rather than a monarchy, and on violence rather than on peaceful means to obtain their ends. But however enthusiastic these groups were, they involved only a small proportion of urban workers and hardly any agricultural workers.

Student movements

In the years after 1815 thousands of young middle- and upper-class Germans, hoping to give practical form to their romantic sense of national identity, joined student societies and campaigned for a united Germany and abolition of absolutist forms of government.

In October 1817 some 500 nationalist students converted the Wartburg Festival from a celebration of the tercentenary of **Luther's stand against the Pope** and the fourth anniversary of the victory of Leipzig into a demonstration against the princes (see Source B). Metternich was horrified when he received reports of the

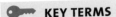

KEY TERMS

Sovereignty Supreme power.

Luther's stand against the Pope In 1517 this German religious leader protested against a number of practices of the Catholic Church, leading to a bitter religious divide. Martin Luther's followers became known as Protestants.

SOURCE B

? Do you think the artist who drew Source B was sympathetic with the students? Explain your answer.

This print published in 1817 shows a procession of students on their way to the Wartburg Festival.

Wartburg Festival. Convinced that the student societies posed a serious threat, he requested that universities should be placed under close supervision. But he met resistance from several German states who resented any encroachment on their sovereignty that such a step would inevitably involve.

The Carlsbad Decrees

In 1819 a member of an extreme student society murdered August von Kotzebue, a German dramatist who was also one of the Russian tsar's informers on German affairs. This murder prompted Metternich to take action. After consulting the Prussian king, he summoned representatives of the German states to meet him at Carlsbad. Their decisions were ratified by the *Bundestag* as the Carlsbad Decrees. The Decrees:

- provided inspectors for universities
- ensured that student societies were disbanded
- threatened radical university lecturers with dismissal
- introduced press censorship
- set up a commission to investigate 'revolutionary' movements
- allowed the Confederation to intervene in any state that refused to implement these measures or which was threatened by revolution.

Implementation of the Decrees varied in severity from state to state. In Austria and Prussia a number of professors were dismissed and radical student leaders imprisoned. It seemed that **reactionary** forces had triumphed. It also seemed that the sole purpose of the Confederation was to crush radical dissent. Metternich tried to go further still, stopping the movement for constitutional reform and revoking some of the more progressive south German constitutions. His efforts were frustrated by opposition from Württemberg, Bavaria and Saxony-Weimar.

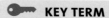 **KEY TERM**

Reactionary Opposing political or social change and wanting to revert to past conditions.

The Congress of Troppau

Metternich supported the idea of European Congresses – meetings of the Great Powers to discuss and settle international disagreements and maintain peace. At the Congress of Troppau in 1820 discussion centred on revolutions which had broken out in Spain, Portugal, Piedmont and Naples. Tsar Alexander I, in sympathy with Metternich's reactionary beliefs, put forward a proposal that Russia, Austria and Prussia should act jointly, using force if necessary, to restore any government which had been overthrown by violent action. The proposal was accepted and in the Protocol of Troppau, Russia, Austria and Prussia – the Holy Alliance – announced that they 'would never recognise the rights of a people to restrict the powers of their king'. This ran directly contrary to the ambitions of liberals and nationalists everywhere, and was particularly disappointing to those in the German states. Both Prussia and Austria were firmly ranged on the side of reaction.

Clemens von Metternich

1773	Born into nobility in the Rhineland
1794	Family moved to Vienna to escape a French invasion of the Rhineland
1809	Became foreign minister of Austria
1814–15	Played a key role at the Vienna peace settlement
1821	Became Austrian chancellor
1848	Forced to resign; fled to England
1859	Died

Metternich was a complex personality. Vain and arrogant, he was also extremely able. In 1819 he said: 'There is a wide sweep about my mind. I am always above and beyond the preoccupations of most public men; I cover a ground much vaster than they can see or wish to see. I cannot keep myself from saying about twenty times a day: "O Lord! How right I am and how wrong they are."'

Although confident in his own abilities and ideals, he was pessimistic about the future: 'My life has coincided with a most abominable time … I have come into the world too soon or too late. I know that in these years I can accomplish nothing … I am spending my life underpinning buildings which are mouldering into decay.'

He was totally opposed to democracy. He wrote: 'It is true that I do not like democracies. Democracy is in every case a principle of dissolution, of decomposition. It tends to separate men, it loosens society. I am opposed to this because I am by nature and by habit constructive. That is why monarchy is the only government that suits my way of thinking … Monarchy alone tends to bring men together, to unite them in compact, efficient masses, and to make them capable by their combined efforts of the highest degree of culture and civilisation.'

Metternich believed that popular challenges to legitimate authority would result in chaos, bloodshed and an end to civilisation. His single-mindedness prompted contemporaries to speak of a 'Metternich System' and historians have subsequently found this a useful concept to help to analyse his actions. Some think his 'System' was based on a complex philosophy. Others, like A.J.P. Taylor, have doubted whether there was a 'System', believing that Metternich was simply a traditional conservative with no profound philosophical beliefs. His main aims were simply to maintain the Austrian Empire, maintain the traditional order in Europe and maintain himself in office.

Repression in the 1820s

As well as the weapons of diplomacy and threats of force, Metternich used those of the police state to maintain the existing political and social conditions. A special office was set up in Vienna to open, copy and then reseal foreign correspondence passing through Austria. This gave Metternich an enormous amount of information and it was backed up by reports from his network of spies throughout Europe and by the work of his secret police. His efforts to turn the Confederation into a police state were only partially successful. Repression and press censorship varied in severity from state to state. Nevertheless, Metternich was generally successful in keeping Germany (and indeed Europe) quiet throughout the 1820s.

Liberal reform in the 1830s

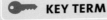 **KEY TERM**

July Revolution in Paris
In 1830 the reactionary King Charles X of France was overthrown and replaced by the more liberal Louis-Philippe.

The **July Revolution in Paris** of 1830 sparked off a series of uprisings across Europe. Demonstrations and riots also took place in several south German states. The demands were for a constitution as laid down in the Federal Act of 1815; or, if a constitution already existed, for its liberalisation.

- In Brunswick the Duke was driven out and his successor was forced to grant a more liberal constitution.
- In Saxony and Hesse-Cassel more liberal constitutions were obtained.
- In Bavaria, Baden and Württemberg liberal opposition parties gained parliamentary seats and greater freedom of the press allowed criticisms of the government.
- In Hanover the government granted a constitution in 1832.

The growth of German nationalism in the 1830s

In the early 1830s there was a profusion of folk festivals, especially in southwest Germany. The numbers who attended such festivals suggest that the idea of establishing a German nation-state had considerable support. In 1832 some 30,000 people – artisans, peasants and students – met at the Hambach Festival in the Palatinate to talk, listen to nationalist orators and (in some cases) plan revolution (see Source C). Those attending waved black, red and yellow German flags and drank toasts to the notion that power should lie with the people.

Metternich was thrown into a panic. In 1832, with Prussian support, he persuaded the *Bundestag* to pass the Six Articles. These increased the *Bundestag*'s control over the internal affairs of individual states, and, in particular, its control of the universities and the press. The *Bundestag*'s member states agreed to send military assistance to any government threatened by unrest, and half the Bavarian army marched to the Palatinate to subdue the province. Karl Heinrich Brueggemann, a radical student leader, was arrested, sent to Prussia and condemned to death. (He was later pardoned.)

In 1833 armed students attacked the *Bundestag*'s main gatehouse hoping to trigger a general revolt. The rising was quickly defeated and the *Bundestag* set up a special commission to round up student agitators. In Prussia, over 200 students were arrested and given lengthy jail sentences. Membership of a student association was now regarded as high treason. Many middle-class liberals sympathised with the authorities in their pursuit of men who were perceived to be dangerous radicals. Some German radicals fled abroad. Others went underground in Germany. Some writers joined a 'Young Germany' movement dedicated to establishing a united Germany.

In 1834 Metternich summoned representatives from the Confederation to meet him in Vienna to discuss the need for yet sterner action against subversive elements. Press censorship was intensified and new controls were placed on universities. Liberals and nationalists were powerless against Metternich's domination:

- The *Bundestag* was little more than an Austrian tool.
- As long as Prussia remained Austria's ally and equally reactionary, there was little hope of a change in the situation.

? Why might Metternich have been horrified by Koerner's account in Source C?

SOURCE C

An account by Gustave Koerner, a revolutionary journalist, who was present at the Hambach Festival, quoted in Thomas J. McCormack, editor, *Memoirs of Gustave Koerner, 1809–1896*, volume 1, The Torch Press, 1909, pp. 191–2.

From various platforms eloquent speeches were made … representing the sad condition of Germany, its insignificance in the council of European nations, its depression in trade and commerce, all owing to the want of national union, the division into thirty-eight States large and small, with their different laws, different weights and measures, different currencies and most of all to the custom-house lines surrounding every State. The orators complained of the pressure which Austria and Prussia exercised over the German Diet at Frankfort, compelling even liberal-minded princes to the adoption of unconstitutional and illegal measures. Brueggemann, whose speech was one of the most eloquent, addressed the meeting as the representative of the German youth which, in spite of criminal persecution, he asserted had kept the idea of the liberty and unity of the Fatherland alive.

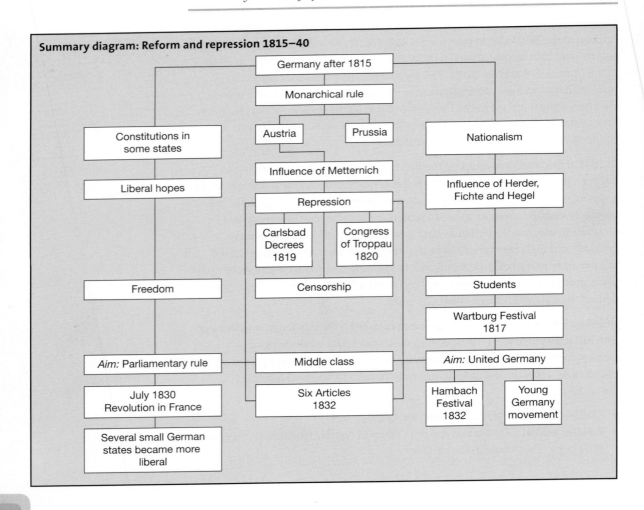

Summary diagram: Reform and repression 1815–40

Economic developments 1815–48

▶ *Why did economic developments encourage German unification?*

Few liberal-nationalists in the period 1815–48 could have foreseen that the political unification of Germany would eventually be brought about by Prussia, one of the most reactionary of the German states. Nevertheless, one of the foundations of German unification was laid by Prussia before 1840. That foundation was the **Zollverein**.

The Prussian Customs Union

After 1815 the 39 German states managed their own economies. Innumerable customs barriers and internal **tariffs** restricted trade. Even within single states there were large numbers of tolls. Variations in currency values within the Confederation were an added problem.

 KEY TERMS

Zollverein The Prussian Customs Union.

Tariffs Import duties, intended to raise money or protect domestic industry and agriculture from foreign competition.

SOURCE D

Karl Friedrich Nebenius, a Baden minister, writing in 1819, http://en.wikipedia.org/wiki/Zollverein.

The 830 toll barriers in Germany cripple domestic trade … In order to trade from Hamburg to Austria, from Berlin to the Swiss Cantons, one must cut through the statutes of ten states, study ten tolls and toll barriers, ten times go through the toll barriers and ten times pay the tolls. Who but the unfortunate has to negotiate such bodies? … Where three or four states collide, then one must live his whole life under evil, senseless tolls and toll restrictions. That is no Fatherland.

Why did Nebenius in Source D regard toll barriers as a problem?

In 1818 Rhineland manufacturers complained to the Prussian king about the problem of internal customs duties and about competition from unrestricted foreign imports on which no duty was charged. As a result, in the same year, the Prussian Tariff Reform Law brought into being the Prussian Customs Union. The law did away with the plethora of internal customs duties and replaced them with a tariff to be charged at the Prussian frontier.

The Customs Union was not quite what the Rhinelanders had sought: they had hoped for a high protective tariff, particularly against British goods. Instead, the tariff was low: nothing at all on raw materials, an average of only ten per cent on manufactured goods and twenty per cent on luxury goods such as sugar or tea. The Prussian government opposed high tariffs on the grounds that they would:

- encourage smuggling, which was already widespread
- result in a tariff war: other countries would respond by raising duties on Prussian exports.

Later, Prussia did introduce customs duties on raw materials, especially iron and cotton yarn, as it tried to protect home industry from foreign competition.

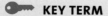

KEY TERM

Free trade Unrestricted trade without protective import duties.

Nevertheless, it also worked to extend **free trade**, first within Prussia and then within other states in the Confederation. The aim was to get rid of as many internal trade barriers as possible so that goods could move more freely. This meant wider markets for home-produced goods at cheaper prices.

Prussian Finance Minister Friedrich von Motz was determined to extend the Prussian Customs Union. He believed that customs duties were symbolic of political divisions: if the duties were abolished, political unity would follow. It proved a difficult task to get the patchwork of states in north and central Germany to agree. Nevertheless, most states, impressed by Prussia's economic success or forced by economic pressure, eventually agreed to join the Prussian Customs Union. In 1828 Hesse-Darmstadt also joined, enabling the union to establish a foothold south of the river Main. However, a few northern states, including Hanover and Hesse-Cassel, which stood between the eastern and western Prussian provinces, stubbornly resisted all Prussia's efforts to win them over.

Other customs unions

By 1830 there were two other important customs unions. One was between Bavaria and Württemberg; the other, known as the Middle German Commercial Union, was made up of Hanover, Brunswick, Saxony and several smaller states. This union was not so much concerned with encouraging its own trade as damaging that of Prussia.

Prussia was geographically well placed to control north–south routes through north Germany and to generate a large income out of duties charged on foreign goods carried along these routes. The Middle Union worked to protect and keep open the existing roads from the North Sea ports to the central German cities of Frankfurt and Leipzig and to build a series of new roads which would go round the states of the Prussian Customs Union. In this scheme they were thwarted by Prussian Finance Minister Motz, who:

- encouraged the building of roads joining Prussia directly with Bavaria, Württemberg and Frankfurt
- extended Prussian trade along the Rhine through a customs agreement with the Dutch.

The *Zollverein*

In 1830 Hesse-Cassel, one of the smaller but vitally important states of the Middle Union, ran into financial difficulties and revolutionary upheaval. In 1831, to the horror of its Middle Union partners, it joined the Prussian Customs Union. The Middle Union, which was already in trouble, collapsed soon afterwards, while the Prussian Customs Union went from strength to strength.

In 1834 Bavaria and Württemberg joined the Prussians. This new enlarged Customs Union – the *Zollverein* – now covered eighteen states with 23 million people. In 1836, when Baden and Frankfurt joined, it included 25 states with a population of 26 million. By 1844 only Hanover, Oldenburg, Mecklenburg, the **Hanseatic towns** and Austria were not members. The organisation and supervision of the *Zollverein* was carried out by a specially appointed body, the *Zollverein* Congress. All *Zollverein* member states had a common system of tariffs and abolished all internal customs barriers.

In the next few years a start was made on unifying both the currency and the system of weights and measures in the *Zollverein* states.

There were some difficulties:

- The *Zollverein* administration did not always work smoothly.
- As any member state could veto a proposal at the *Zollverein* Congress, decisions were often held up or not made at all.

Nevertheless, the *Zollverein* experiment was generally successful, certainly from Prussia's perspective. The member states worked together and Prussia achieved a position of economic leadership within the Confederation.

Prussia's aims

Successive Prussian finance ministers realised that doing away with internal customs duties, first within Prussia, and then between Prussia and neighbouring states, would increase trade and bring prosperity. However, as early as 1830, even before the *Zollverein* was formed, Motz pointed out to his king that such a free trade organisation would not only bring prosperity but also isolate Austria. This isolation would eventually weaken Austria's political influence within the Confederation.

Motz and other Prussian ministers realised that those states which found financial advantage in an economic union under Prussian leadership might well take a favourable view of similar arrangements in a political union. Moreover, the *Zollverein* was itself a force for unity and therefore a focal point for nationalist sentiments. Accordingly, Prussia, despite its reactionary political sympathies, came to be regarded by many northern states as the natural leader of a united Germany.

Austrian isolation

Austria refused to join the *Zollverein* because it disagreed with the policy of free trade. Austria's policy was **protectionist**. It already had large markets within the **Austrian Empire** for home-produced goods, and therefore wanted high import duties to protect its industries and markets from cheap foreign imports. Joining the *Zollverein* would have meant reducing import duties to the same level as the other states, and this it would not consider. Austria gave Prussia a great opportunity when it refused to join. Prussia took this opportunity, established a position of leadership and made sure that Austria would stay outside. By 1848, while Austria still retained political control of the Confederation, Prussia had the economic leadership.

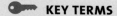

KEY TERMS

Hanseatic towns A league of German commercial cities mainly on the Baltic Sea coast.

Protectionist Favouring the protection of trade by having duties on imports.

Austrian Empire Included much of what is today Austria, Hungary, Poland, the Czech Republic, Slovakia, Croatia and northern Italy.

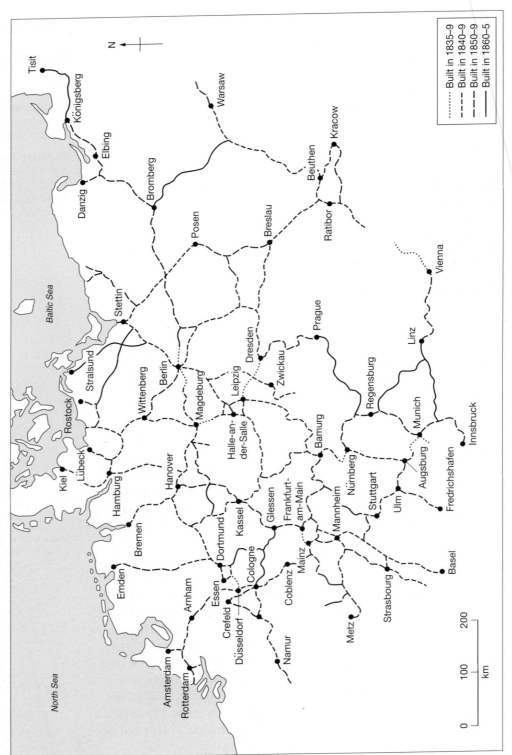

Figure 1.2 German railways 1835–65.

Railway development

A precondition of the free movement of goods was an efficient transport system. The road construction programme, begun in Germany by Napoleon, continued. There was also considerable investment in canal construction, efforts to improve the navigability of Germany's main rivers and development of steam ships on those rivers. But the coming of railways was the most crucial development.

According to German patriotic novelist Wilhelm Raube, writing in the late nineteenth century, 'The German empire was founded with the construction of the first railway.' This was built in 1835. It connected Nuremberg and Fürth and was only 6 km (4 miles) long. In 1839 the Leipzig–Dresden railway line opened. By 1840 there were 462 km (287 miles) of track. The 1840s saw a great expansion: in 1846 alone some 1100 km (690 miles) of track were laid. Lacking a national capital, the rails looped in webs, linking towns and markets within regions, regions within larger regions and so on (see Figure 1.2). The growing railway network did the following:

- made it cheaper to transport goods
- encouraged economic activity by creating demand for commodities
- made Germans more mobile, thereby contributing to the breakdown of local and regional barriers
- created a tremendous demand for iron and steel and encouraged coal production: workers in these industries trebled in the two decades after 1835. The Ruhr area, which had large deposits of iron, soon became Germany's main industrial centre.

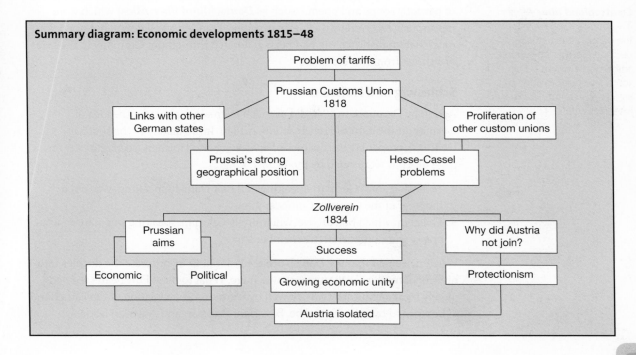

Summary diagram: Economic developments 1815–48

Germany 1840–8

> ► *How strong was German nationalism in the 1840s?*

Metternich's repressive policies did not quell the numbers of Germans who supported nationalism and called for political change.

The growth of nationalism

Growing numbers of Germans were attracted by the emotional appeal of nationalism. This appeal was encouraged by poetry, music, history and philosophy. German artists painted canvases of Germany's heroic past. German architects tried to build in a German style (although there was some uncertainty about what that style should be). After 1815 there were a remarkable number of national associations and festivals in Germany. German nationalism was also fuelled by several foreign crises which appeared to threaten Germany as a whole (see below). This made many Germans, who normally thought of themselves as Bavarians, Hessians or members of other states, discontented that Germany could not speak with a single, strong voice.

The 1840 crisis

Nationalist feelings were particularly widespread in 1840 when it seemed possible that France would invade the German states along the Rhine in an attempt to change the 1815 settlement and the Rhine frontier. The German press threw its weight behind the nationalist upsurge and there was a flurry of patriotic songs and poems (such as ***Deutschland über Alles***) which were rapturously received by the German public. France backed down, but not before much nationalistic feeling had been generated throughout Germany in the face of a threat from the 'old enemy'.

Schleswig and Holstein

Action by Denmark in 1846 did as much to create support for the idea of German unification as French action in 1840. Immediately to the south of Denmark proper lay the duchies of Schleswig and Holstein (see Figure 1.1 on page 8). They were ruled by the Danish king:

- Schleswig, half German-speaking and half Danish-speaking, was not a member of the German Confederation.
- Holstein, which had an overwhelmingly German-speaking population, was one of the Confederation's member states.

When it seemed that the Danish king was about to incorporate the duchies into his kingdom, the German outcry was huge. What to most Europeans seemed merely legal technicality was viewed by Germans as a violation of the Fatherland to be resisted by force if need be. Bavarian, Prussian and Austrian leaders

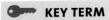 **KEY TERM**

Deutschland über Alles
This means 'Germany above the others'. It eventually became Germany's national anthem, the words being set to a popular melody by eighteenth-century composer Joseph Haydn.

all spoke against the Danish action. This strength of feeling was enough to persuade the Danish king to abandon his plans.

SOURCE E

A memorandum written by Prince Hohenlohe, a liberal-minded Bavarian in 1847, quoted in Prince Hohenlohe, *Memoirs of Prince Chlodwig of Hohenlohe-Schillingsfuerst*, Macmillan, 1906, p. 41.

In the history of every nation there is an epoch in which it comes to full self-consciousness and claims liberty to determine its own destiny. … We Germans have reached this stage. … No one will deny that it is hard on an energetic thinking man to be unable to say abroad 'I am a German' – not to be able to pride himself that the German flag is flying from his vessel, to have no German consul in cases of emergency, but have to explain 'I am a Hessian, a Darmstadter, a Buckeburger: my fatherland was once a great and powerful country, now it is shattered into nine and thirty splinters'.

What does Source E suggest about the nature of German patriotism?

The growth of liberalism

Throughout the 1840s liberal doctors, civil servants, teachers and lawyers regularly held national meetings to discuss matters of common concern. (There was a certain irony in that civil servants were among the most outspoken critics of the states which, for the most part, they continued loyally to serve.) The 1840s were to bring new and hopeful developments for liberals.

The southwestern states

- In 1846 liberals in Baden managed to obtain a relaxation of press censorship, and reforms of the police and judicial system.
- In Hesse-Darmstadt there were strong liberal parliamentary campaigns for changes in electoral rules and for a free press.
- In Bavaria the liberals were helped by an unexpected change of policy on the part of the eccentric King Ludwig I. His passion for his mistress Lola Montez led him to propose that she should be given a title and land and be introduced to court. When his reactionary ministers criticised him, he replaced them with liberal ones.

Developments in Prussia

Developments in Prussia seemed promising to many liberals. King Frederick William III, who had ruled as an absolute monarch for over 40 years, died in 1840. Although he had agreed to the establishment of provincial *Diets* in 1823, he had avoided granting a constitution and throughout his reign had close ties with reactionary Austria. But while Prussia, post-1815, remained authoritarian, it was not quite a police state.

Frederick William III was succeeded by his son Frederick William IV, an intelligent, cultured, but very unstable man whose policies were to fluctuate widely throughout his reign. Sometimes he behaved as a reactionary absolutist, sometimes as a **constitutional monarch**. In many ways he was a man of compromise who sought to be popular and to heal political divisions within Prussia. He started by acting as many liberals wished:

- He released many political prisoners.
- He relaxed censorship.
- In 1842 he arranged for the Prussian provincial *Diets* to elect representatives to meet as an advisory body on a temporary basis in Berlin.
- He extended the powers of the provincial *Diets* and allowed them to publish reports of their debates.

Encouraged by this, liberals in the Rhineland agitated for a constitution and the calling of a single *Diet* for all Prussian territories. The **Junkers** watched the activities of the new king with anxiety and even considered a coup to replace him with his brother, William.

Frederick William, finding himself under political attack from both left and right, reimposed press censorship in 1843. However, in 1847 he called a meeting of the United *Diet* in Berlin to vote on a loan for building a railway to link East Prussia and Berlin. The 600 delegates, appointed by the provincial *Diets*, were all men of substance: more than half of them were aristocrats. They were prepared to support the railway, but insisted on a guarantee that the United *Diet* should meet on a regular basis. Frederick William promptly dissolved the *Diet*. The king's action only strengthened the determination of Prussian liberals to push for constitutional change.

German newspapers

In the 1840s the pace of political debate picked up and public opinion grew bolder. More books were published. Newspapers and political journals flourished. The fact that Germans were the most literate people in Europe helped. Popular journals played a crucial role in arousing interest in issues such as Schleswig-Holstein in 1846. In 1847 liberal and nationalist sentiments found expression in the foundation at Heidelberg of a newspaper with the prophetic title of *Die Deutsche Zeitung* (*The German Newspaper*).

The Hippenhelm meeting

In 1847 liberal representatives of the southwestern states met at Hippenhelm. They demanded the following:

- an elected national assembly
- the liberation of the press
- open judicial proceedings with juries
- the end of feudal restrictions
- reduction of the cost of the Confederation's **standing army** and the creation of a **national guard**
- reform of the system of taxation.

Conclusion

The *Zollverein's* example of economic co-operation between the German states encouraged liberals and nationalists. It made their dreams of a politically united Germany seem more attainable. By the late 1840s there was a growing call for the setting up of a new nation-state. The greatest support for nationalism and liberalism came from the middle classes. Most liberal-nationalists envisaged a **federation** of states under a constitutional monarch. Suspicious of full democracy, they wanted to limit the vote to the prosperous and well educated. Radicals, by contrast, favoured universal manhood suffrage and pressed for a German republic.

It is wrong, however, to overestimate the degree of political consciousness attained by Germans on the eve of the 1848 revolutions. Among the middle classes probably a minority were liberal-minded and even fewer were politically active. Most liberals were concerned with developments in their own states, not in the situation across Germany as a whole. Small in number and far from united, they were also isolated from the mass of the people.

In truth, nationalists, liberals and radicals had not achieved much by 1848. As long as Metternich remained in power and Prussia remained Austria's ally, there seemed little chance of changing the situation. German nationalism as a mass phenomenon tended to be reactive, erupting in response to perceived threats and then subsiding again. Although nationalist organisations grew at an impressive rate in the 1840s, loyalty to individual states and dynasties remained strong. There was still a major division between the Catholic south and the Protestant north. There were also cultural differences between the more industrialised and liberal west and the agrarian, autocratic east.

 **KEY TERM**

Federation A group of states joined together in some form of union.

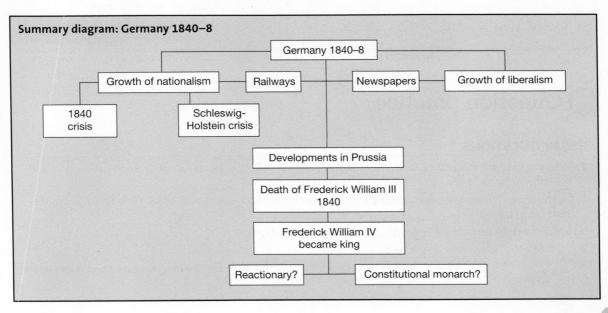

Summary diagram: Germany 1840–8

Chapter summary

In 1789 Germany comprised a multitude of states that were loosely linked by their membership of the archaic Holy Roman Empire. The French Revolution and Napoleonic conquests laid the basis for the movement towards unification. This movement, reinforced by economic and social pressures, grew in popularity after 1815, despite Metternich's attempts at repression. The development of the *Zollverein* and the building of German railways contributed to the breakdown of local and regional barriers. By the 1840s the emotional appeal of nationalism was experienced by increasing numbers of Germans. Nevertheless, the prospect of German unification did not seem imminent in the 1840s given the power of Austria and Prussia, both of which opposed anything which smacked of liberalism or nationalism.

 # Refresher questions

Use these questions to remind yourself of the key material covered in this chapter.

1 Why was Germany not a meaningful concept in 1789?

2 What impact did Napoleon have on Germany?

3 Was Germany a meaningful concept in 1815?

4 How did the Vienna peace settlement affect Germany?

5 How important was the German Confederation?

6 How strong were German nationalism and liberalism in the period 1815–40?

7 How democratic were German states in the years 1815–40?

8 How successful were Metternich's repressive policies?

9 To what extent did economic developments encourage German unity?

10 What was the importance of the *Zollverein*?

11 How strong were German nationalist and liberal movements by 1848?

 # Question practice

ESSAY QUESTIONS

1 How accurate is it to say that Metternich had successfully held back the forces of German nationalism and liberalism prior to 1848?

2 'Austrian and Prussian strength made German unification impossible prior to 1848.' How far do you agree with this statement?

3 To what extent had the *Zollverein* encouraged German unification?

SOURCE ANALYSIS QUESTIONS

1 How much weight do you give the evidence of Source 1 with regard to the success of the *Zollverein*? Explain your answer using the source, the information given about it and your own knowledge of the historical context.

2 Why is Source 2 valuable to the historian studying the views of liberal Germans in the 1840s? Explain your answer using the source, the information given about it and your own knowledge of the historical context.

3 How far could the historian make use of Sources 1 and 2 together to investigate the strength of the movement for German unity in the 1830s and 1840s? Explain your answer using both sources, the information given about them and your own knowledge of the historical context.

SOURCE 1

From *A Report on the Prussian Commercial Union*, written by John Bowring, a British MP, in 1840.

The objects proposed by the Zollverein *were the removal of all restrictions to communication and transit, the abolition of all internal customs-houses, the establishment of a common tariff and system of collection, and the repartition of the receipts on all imports and exports according to the population among all the members of the League …*

The Zollverein, *by directing capital to internal, in preference to external trade, has already had a great influence in improving the roads, the canals, the means of travelling, the transport of letters – in a word, in giving additional impulse to inland communications of every sort. The isolation of the several German states, with separate fiscal interests, and often hostile legislation, prevented those facilities from being given to intercourse which are alike the evidence and the means of civilisation. On every side beneficial changes are taking place. Railways are being constructed in many parts of the German territory – steam-boats are crowding the German ports and coasting along the German shores – everything is transported with greater cheapness and rapidity.*

SOURCE 2

From *Die Deutsche Zeitung* (*The German Newspaper*). The paper is reporting a meeting of liberal representatives of the southwestern states at Hippenhelm in October 1847.

1 From the assembly of the Confederation, in its present form, nothing profitable can be expected with regard to the prospects for national unification. It has not carried out its duty, as laid down in the acts of the Confederation, in respect of representative governments, free trade, etc. The press is censored, the procedures of the Confederate Assembly are cloaked in darkness, out of which decrees are announced from time to time, which place obstacles in the path of all liberal development.

2 The only bond of common German interests, the customs union, was not created by the Confederation but by agreements reached between the individual German states.

3 The question must be raised as to whether improvements can be gained by achieving the representation of the people in the Confederate Assembly and thus as to whether this should be an aim of those loyal to the Fatherland. However, there are no prospects for the realisation of this aim.

4 *The aim of German unification, with a German policy and common direction and protection of national interests, will be more easily achieved once public opinion has been won over in support of the extension of the customs union to a German society. The customs union already directs a whole series of common interests and has established treaties with outside states. Through its further development the customs union will act as an irresistible pole of attraction for the participation of the remaining German states and will also bring about unification with the Austrian states and thus lead to the establishment of true German power.*

CHAPTER 2

Germany in revolution 1848–9

In 1848 France, the German Confederation, Habsburg lands including both Austria and Hungary, and large parts of Italy experienced revolution. One striking feature of the 1848 revolutions, both in Germany and elsewhere, was the rapidity of the success they enjoyed. Another was the fact that all – equally rapidly – failed. The revolutions are complex affairs. Some historians claim that general, European-wide, factors explain the cause, course and failure of the revolutions. Others stress that revolutionaries in different areas had very different grievances and demands. Even within specific countries, there was often little cohesion among the revolutionaries and what cohesion there was soon collapsed. This chapter will consider the German revolutions through the following sections:

★ The causes of the German revolutions

★ The Frankfurt Parliament

★ The situation in Prussia 1848–9

The key debate on *page 53* of this chapter asks the question: Why did the German revolutions fail?

Key dates

1848	March 5	Declaration of Heidelberg	1848	Nov.	King Frederick William re-established control in Berlin
	March 13	Metternich fell from power		Dec.	New Prussian constitution
	Mid-March	Riots in Berlin	1849	March	Frankfurt Parliament agreed on a constitution
	Late March	King Frederick William made concessions to liberals		April	King Frederick William rejected the offer of the German crown
	March 31	Meeting of the *Vorparlament*		June	Frankfurt Parliament dispersed
	May 18	Meeting of Frankfurt Parliament			

1 The causes of the German revolutions

▶ *What were the main causes of the German revolutions?*

In Europe, 1848 was a year of dramatic, violent events, of hope and of failure. It was a year of death as a cholera epidemic swept across Europe, causing such loss of life that for a while society in some areas was totally disorganised. It was the year that Karl Marx's **The Communist Manifesto** was published. This did not have the drama of the cholera epidemic and attracted little attention at the time, but in twenty years its message had spread across Europe and beyond to become, a century later, the basis of the political system of nearly half the world. In the spring of 1848, revolutionaries, to the delight of Marx, seemed to carry all before them across Europe.

Why did revolutions in France, Germany, Prussia, Austria, Hungary and Italy all happen in the same year? Historians used to think that the French troubles, beginning in Paris in February 1848, led to copycat revolutions in other countries. Now, a generally accepted view is that the revolutions took place at about the same time because conditions across Europe were very similar. These conditions – economic, social and political – are seen as giving rise to revolutions. The sections of this book that follow focus on Germany. However, much of what is said applies to many parts of Europe.

Economic and social problems

Most historians agree that the German revolutions resulted, at least in part, from a social and economic crisis. However, the precise nature of this crisis and its effects on different classes have generated much debate.

Increasing population

Since the middle of the eighteenth century, Germany's population had grown dramatically, doubling in the century up to 1848. The rise was probably due more to a declining death rate than to an increasing birth rate. The result was that some areas found it difficult to sustain their populations. Thus, people left the land and drifted to the towns in search of work or went to other parts of the world, hoping to better themselves. Of the 250,000 who left Germany in the 1840s, most went to the USA.

Problems in the countryside

The vast majority of Germans still lived and worked on the land. Those people who remained in the countryside found life hard. In eastern Prussia much of the land belonged to the *Junkers* and was worked by landless peasants. Even in the parts of Germany where the peasants had become **tenant farmers** rents were high and it was difficult to make a living.

The vast majority of the rural population were poverty-stricken agricultural workers who possessed little if any land. Feudal injustices continued in many areas.

The impact of urbanisation

Town populations massively increased: Berlin, for example had 172,000 people in 1800 and by 1848 it had more than 400,000. In most towns there were insufficient jobs and housing to cope with the influx of migrants from the countryside. Given the surplus labour, wages were low. Living and working conditions were often appalling. Even in good times workers were poorly clothed and fed. Inadequate sanitation encouraged diseases like typhoid and cholera. Many newcomers, unable to find work, depended on charity or turned to crime. Strikes and riots among the urban working class, over working conditions and pay, multiplied in the 1830s and 1840s. Towns had concentrations of discontented people who were better able to organise and far more likely to act together than their rural counterparts. It is worth noting that the 1848 revolutions in Germany were overwhelmingly urban.

The impact of industrialisation

Industrialisation was relatively slow to develop in Germany. High costs, shortage of capital and an ample supply of cheap labour reduced the coming of machines. In 1846, 97 per cent of German looms were still operated by hand. Nevertheless, across Germany skilled craftsmen (and their apprentices) feared the coming of industrialisation and with good cause. They were aware that they could not compete with mechanical production.

The economic crisis 1846–7

In 1846 and 1847 the corn harvests were disastrous and the situation was made worse by a serious outbreak of **potato blight**. Potatoes were the main item of diet for most German peasants, and failure of the crop meant starvation. There was distress and unrest, and food riots broke out. There had been poor harvests before, but the increased population made the position worse.

Urban workers also suffered from the sharp rise in food prices. In Berlin, there was a short-lived 'potato revolution'. Barricades were erected, shops were looted and the crown prince's palace was stormed before soldiers restored order.

Across Germany, the rise in food prices led to a reduction in consumer spending on items other than food. Consequently, craft and industrial production suffered a fall in demand. Employers responded by laying off workers. There was thus a rapid increase in unemployment, particularly in the textile industry. Even those in work found their wages cut. The result was that the standard of living of most workers fell alarmingly. Consequently, in both towns and countryside, there was growing unrest. Workers and peasants demanded an improvement in their living standards.

Class consciousness

Historians remain divided about whether 'class consciousness' was developing among industrial workers. This was a key issue for **Marxist historians** who believed that historical change grew out of conflicts between classes. Karl Marx argued that as industrialisation developed, so each class evolved its own consciousness. He believed that the **proletariat** was inevitably opposed to

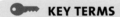

KEY TERMS

Potato blight A destructive disease of the potato caused by a parasitic fungus.

Marxist historians Historians who accept the ideas of Karl Marx and believe that history is essentially about class conflict.

Proletariat The exploited industrial workers who (Marx claimed) would triumph in the last great class struggle.

the **bourgeoisie**. Marx, and Marxist historians since, argued that the 1848 revolutions were caused by the effect of industrialisation on the working class. Certainly, in Germany it was often workers who fought and died in the streets behind the barricades. However, Marx's thesis was very much a simplification of the situation and the events for several reasons:

- It was not only the workers who made the German revolutions. Others – peasants and the liberal middle classes – played an important role.
- In 1848 the real proletariat, the industrial working class who possessed nothing but their labour, scarcely existed in Germany outside the fevered imagination of Marx. Industrial workers made up only a small fraction of manual labour. Most urban workers were artisans and skilled craftsmen who had little in common with factory workers who threatened their livelihood. In towns such as Cologne and Bonn, skilled craftsmen had their own trade organisations, and kept themselves apart from unskilled factory workers, whom they despised and feared.
- The most radical urban workers were the apprentices. Fearful of machines and exploited by their masters, they had their own grievances.
- Such were the differences in interests, status and income among urban workers, the concept of a united proletariat working class is inappropriate.

The intellectual challenge

The economic crisis helped to shake the prestige and self-confidence of many existing regimes. Most lacked the financial and bureaucratic resources – and also possibly the will – to intervene effectively to alleviate the social distress and improve economic conditions. The calibre of rulers was not high and many monarchs and their ministers attracted a great deal of personal unpopularity, particularly from the growing number of educated middle-class people such as lawyers, doctors, journalists, teachers and civil servants.

In 1848 power lay where it always had, with the nobility who owned the land, filled senior government jobs and officered the army. They guarded their privileges jealously against any infiltration by the middle classes. Middle-class Germans were critical of systems which largely excluded them from participation in the political process, and in which they were restrained from free expression of their grievances by the censor and the secret police. Many of the dissatisfied middle classes wanted the establishment of some form of parliamentary system and the guarantee of basic civil rights.

Middle-class Germans also wanted to see the creation of a German nation-state, governed by a popularly elected assembly. By 1847 patriotism was running high.

Conservative strength

By no means did all Germans sympathise with reform or nationalist movements. 'Authority not majority' was the rallying cry of conservatives, most of whom regarded the urban middle classes as a major threat. Conservatives believed that liberals and radicals, with their demands for constitutions, were at odds with the mass of Germans who simply wanted peace and quiet. Conservative attacks on the bourgeoisie won support from artisans and peasants who were losing ground as Germany became a more industrial society. Many conservatives also denounced nationalism, which they regarded as a flagrant violation of legitimate, time-honoured and sovereign rights, the brainchild of the godless bourgeoisie. Conservatives feared that liberal and radical demands for freedom and democracy would lead to chaos and terror.

The situation in early 1848

In 1848 few Germans expected revolution. There was still widespread loyalty to the established dynasties. Moreover, the economic situation was beginning to improve slightly. Nevertheless, economic distress in the major cities, which continued over the winter of 1847–8, helped to foment revolution. The urban and rural poor, however, did not have a clear set of aims and were often untouched by the radical, liberal and nationalist ideologies of the middle classes.

On 24 February 1848 King Louis-Philippe was overthrown and a republic was established in France. The French revolutionaries' proclamation of the idea of the sovereignty of the people called into question all established authority. The revolution in France had an enormous impact in many parts of Europe – not least Germany. There was not one revolution in Germany in 1848 but several. Events in one area impacted on others but there was never a single organised revolutionary movement.

Events in Baden

On 27 February, there was a mass meeting in Mannheim in Baden. Liberals demanded freedom of the press, freedom of assembly, trial by jury, a militia and a German national parliament. On 1 March a deputation presented these demands to the Grand Duke of Baden. The deputation was accompanied by a vast crowd, some of whom were armed. While the grand duke initially refused to negotiate, he also turned down an offer of military assistance from Prussia. He then proceeded to form a new ministry, which included liberal leaders. This new government began to implement most of the original liberal demands.

In April, radical republicans tried to lead a peasant and worker rising in Baden, marching on Freiburg with some 6000 armed supporters. Federal troops, mainly Prussian, had little difficulty in crushing the ill-organised rebellion. Most liberals and some radicals denounced the rebels for betraying the revolutionary cause by robbing it of its democratic legitimacy.

Metternich's fall

News of events in France helped to spark revolution in Austria. On 13 March there were mass demonstrations in Vienna. The situation quickly got out of hand, especially in working-class areas where there was widespread looting. Metternich fled to Britain and the army, whose loyalty was suspect, was withdrawn from the capital. The city was left in control of radical students and their working-class supporters.

Metternich's fall had a profound effect on the Austrian Empire and on Germany:

- Austrian rule was soon under attack in northern Italy, Hungary and Prague.
- Given the apparent collapse of authoritarian rule, in some places, peasants attacked their landlords, stormed castles and destroyed feudal records.
- Elsewhere, artisans used the opportunity of the breakdown of law and order to destroy new machines that they saw as a threat to their livelihood.

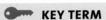 **KEY TERM**

Universal suffrage
A system that allows everyone over a certain age to vote.

In May 1848 Austrian Emperor Ferdinand agreed to summon a constituent assembly, elected by **universal suffrage**, to draw up a new constitution. The Austrian government, which moved to Innsbruck, was reformed to include a few liberals. A radical Committee of Public Safety was formed in Vienna. Faced with serious revolts in Italy, Hungary and Bohemia, Austria was too engrossed in its own affairs in the spring and summer of 1848 to exert its customary influence on Germany.

Revolution in Prussia

On 13 March 1848 a demonstration by workers, mostly self-employed craftsmen, took place in the palace square in Berlin. The demonstrators threw stones at the troops and the troops replied by opening fire (see Source A). Deputations of leading citizens called on King Frederick William IV and asked him to make political concessions. Fighting continued in a confused way during the next two days. The original demonstrations, begun as a protest about pay and working conditions, quickly turned into a general, if vague, demand for 'the maintenance of the rights irrefutably belonging to the people of the state'.

On 16 March, news of revolution in Vienna and the dismissal of Metternich reached Berlin, and popular excitement rose even further. Frederick William accepted the idea of a new German constitution and agreed to recall the United *Diet* (see page 26) and to end censorship.

On 18 March a large crowd collected outside the royal palace. The king appeared on the balcony and was loudly cheered. He then ordered the troops to clear the crowds. In the ensuing jostling, two shots were fired either in panic or by accident. Students and workers immediately set up barricades and serious fighting erupted. More than 230 people died as troops tried to win back control of the city.

SOURCE A

A contemporary illustration of street fighting in Berlin in 1848.

What does Source A suggest about the threat posed by the Berlin rioters?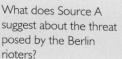

Frederick William's action

The king, who all his life hated bloodshed and, most untypical for a Prussian leader, disliked the army and all military matters, determined to try and defuse the situation by making a personal appeal for calm. At 3.00a.m. he wrote a letter 'To my dear Berliners'. Copies were quickly printed and were put up on trees in the city centre early on the morning of 19 March. It promised that the troops would be withdrawn if the street barricades were demolished.

Troops were indeed withdrawn, largely due to a misunderstanding, so that the king was left in his palace guarded only by Berlin citizens who formed a **Civic Guard**. He had little option but to appear on the balcony and salute the bodies of the dead rioters. Berliners hoped that Frederick William might become a constitutional monarch and that he might also support the German national revolution. On 21 March he rode through the streets of Berlin wearing the black, red and gold armband of the liberal-nationalists. He was greeted with tumultuous applause and declared: 'I want liberty: I will have unity in Germany.' In the following days, Frederick William granted a series of general reforms, agreeing to the election of an assembly to draw up a new constitution for Prussia, and appointing a liberal ministry.

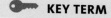 **KEY TERM**

Civic Guard A military force composed of ordinary people, not professional soldiers.

Frederick William's motives

Did Frederick William submit to the revolution from necessity, join it out of conviction, or, by putting himself at its head, try to take it over? Given his unstable character, he may well have been carried away by the emotion of the occasion and felt, at least for a short time, that he was indeed destined to be a popular monarch.

But the king's apparent liberalism did not last long. As soon as he had escaped from Berlin and rejoined his loyal army at Potsdam, he expressed very different feelings. He spoke of humiliation at the way he had been forced to make concessions to the people and made it clear that he had no wish to be a 'citizen' king. However, he took no immediate revenge on Berlin and allowed decision-making for a time to pass into the hands of the new liberal ministry.

The situation in Germany by April 1848

By late March 1848 most German rulers had lost their nerve, giving in easily to demands for more representative government. Almost everywhere, elections were held, liberal ministries appointed and constitutional changes set in train. For a time, the revolutionary fire seemed irresistible because no one was fighting it. Although Bavarian King Ludwig was forced to abdicate, in most states the old rulers survived and watched developments.

Austria and Prussia apart, there was relatively little violence. Meetings, demonstrations and petitions, not armed risings, were the chief weapons of the middle-class revolutionaries who hoped to work with, not destroy, the princes.

In many areas, the revolutions were essentially urban. But in the southwest and in Thuringia, there were peasant uprisings. These were directed against the great landowners, their administrators, Jewish money-lenders and cattle dealers. Deeds were burnt, taxes left unpaid, committees of public safety formed. These peasant uprisings had little in common with the urban revolts. Their aims and methods were quite different. Indeed, in some instances new liberal governments, appalled by the destruction of private property in the countryside, sent in troops to restrain the peasantry.

The new liberal governments, at least, sympathised with the peasants' demands that aristocratic privileges should be abolished and that the last vestiges of feudalism should be removed. Once that was achieved, peace and stability were generally restored in the countryside.

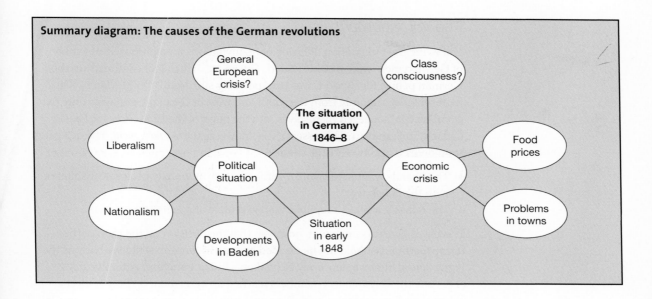

Summary diagram: The causes of the German revolutions

The Frankfurt Parliament

▶ *Why did the Frankfurt Parliament fail?*

In early March 1848, at a meeting in Heidelberg, 51 representatives from six states (Prussia, Bavaria, Württemberg, Baden, Nassau and Frankfurt) discussed changes to Germany's political institutions. They did so before revolutions had made an impact on the individual German states. On 5 March their decisions were published in the Declaration of Heidelberg.

SOURCE B

Part of the Declaration of Heidelberg, quoted in Frank Eyck, *The Revolutions of 1848–49*, Oliver & Boyd, 1972, p. 48.

The meeting of a national representation elected in all the German lands according to the number of the people must not be postponed, both for the removal of imminent internal and external dangers, and for the development of the strength and flowering of German national life! … A main task of the national representation will in any case be common defence … and external representation, whereby great sums of money will be saved for other important needs, while at the same time the identity and suitable self-administration of the different states remains in existence.

The Heidelberg politicians could agree on little more than that a ***Vorparlament*** should be formed from the various *Diets* to meet in Frankfurt and set the ground rules for an all-German election.

According to Source B, what were the main aims of the men who drew up the Declaration of Heidelberg?

 **KEY TERM**

Vorparlament Usually translated as 'pre-parliament', but it is better thought of as 'preparatory parliament', which was preparing the way for the real parliament.

The *Vorparlament*

Following the Declaration of Heidelberg, invitations for a proposed 'assembly of German men' were quickly issued. This move, which looked directly to the German people for support, was unexpectedly successful. On 31 March, 574 representatives, mainly from the south and west of Germany and with only two from Austria, squeezed themselves into the pews of the *Paulskirche* (St Paul's Church) in Frankfurt. This assembly is known as the *Vorparlament*. The delegates soon divided into two hostile camps:

- The liberals wanted to create a parliamentary monarchy in close consultation with the *Bundestag*.
- The radicals wanted a republic with executive and legislative powers.

There was general agreement, however, that the decision on the form of the future Germany should not be decided by such an unrepresentative body as the *Vorparlament* but by a new body elected on a broad franchise. After five days of debate, the *Vorparlament* members reached an agreement on how to elect a national parliament that would draw up a constitution for a united Germany. It was decided that the parliament:

- would meet in Frankfurt
- should consist of one representative for every 50,000 inhabitants
- should be elected by citizens, who were of age and 'economically independent'.

It was left to individual states to decide who was an independent citizen. Most states decided on a residence qualification, some on ownership of property. Although the *Vorparlament* did not actually say so, it was assumed that only men could vote, so women (who had played an active role in demonstrations) were excluded from the franchise, along with servants, farm labourers and anyone receiving poor relief. This last category alone excluded large numbers: in Cologne, for example, nearly a third of the population was on poor relief.

The election of the Frankfurt Parliament

The elections, arranged at short notice and in all 39 states, were carried out peacefully and successfully. Probably some 85 per cent of men were able to vote. However, in most of the states the elections were indirect. The voters elected delegates who then chose representatives. The Parliament, which met in Frankfurt in May 1848, did not represent the population as a whole. Most of those elected were prominent figures in the local community. Of the 596 members, the vast majority were middle class. There were large numbers of teachers, professors (the Frankfurt Parliament was often dubbed the 'Professors' Parliament'), lawyers and government officials. It was probably the best-educated German Parliament ever: over 80 per cent of the members held university degrees. There were a few landowners, four craftsmen and one peasant.

SOURCE C

The Frankfurt Parliament, painted in 1848.

How far does Source C suggest that the Parliament was a significant body?

The Parliament was essentially moderate and liberal. It intended to establish a united Germany under a constitutional monarch who would rule through an elected Parliament. Only a small minority of its members were radical, revolutionary or republican. Reactionary conservatives were similarly scarcely represented.

The various political factions were soon named after the inns where they met: conservative-liberals in the 'Café Milani', moderate-liberals in the 'Casino', left-liberals in the 'Wurttemberger Hof', democrats in the 'Deutscher Hof' and radicals in the 'Donnersberg'. Of these, the 'Casino' faction was easily the largest with about 130 members, including most of the distinguished professors.

The work of the Frankfurt Parliament

It had been a great achievement to have had the Frankfurt Parliament elected, convened and ready to begin work in little over a month. For the moment, the Parliament filled a power vacuum that had been created by the revolutions:

- Austria was absorbed in suppressing uprisings throughout its multinational empire.
- Prussia was in a state of disarray after events in March 1848.
- The Frankfurt Parliament started with the advantage that the *Bundesrat* of the Confederation, with representatives appointed by new liberal governments, had agreed to its own demise and nominated the Parliament as its legal successor.

The key issue was whether the Parliament would be able to draw up a national constitution that would be accepted by all Germans. In addition, it hoped to agree a series of 'Basic Rights and Demands', such as:

- freedom of the press
- fair taxation
- equality of political rights without regard to religion
- German citizenship for all.

The Parliament began by considering the relationship between itself and the individual states. The Confederation had been an association in which the states had a very large degree of independence from federal control. The Frankfurt Parliament's intention was that the new Germany should have much stronger central government, with correspondingly greater control over the actions of the states. It quickly decided that any national constitution it framed would be sovereign, and that while state parliaments would be free to make state laws, these would only be valid if they did not conflict with that constitution. So by the end of May the Frankfurt Parliament had declared its authority over the states, their parliaments and princes. Now it remained to draw up a constitution and to organise a government.

Most members of the Parliament accepted that the logical approach would be to agree a constitution and then to set up a government according to its terms. But it was another matter to find a majority of members who favoured any one procedure for carrying out these tasks, or who agreed on the type of constitution that should be established. Without the discipline imposed by well-organised political parties and without the leadership provided by outstanding individuals, the Frankfurt Parliament became a 'talking shop' in which it was difficult to reach agreement on anything.

The Provisional Central Power

Once it became clear that it would not be possible to reach rapid agreement on a constitution, steps were taken to establish a provisional government to rule in the meantime. But so little was agreed about the specific ways in which its powers were to be carried out that the 'Provisional Central Power', established at the end of June, was largely ineffectual. It provided for an imperial **regent** of the empire, to be elected by the Parliament. He was to govern through ministers, appointed by him and responsible to Parliament, until such time as a decision about the constitution could be reached. An elderly Austrian archduke, John, was elected as temporary regent. He was an unusual archduke, married to the daughter of a village postmaster, and with known liberal and nationalist sympathies. He duly appointed a number of ministers but, as they did not have any staff or offices or money, and their duties were not clearly defined, they could do little.

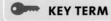 **KEY TERM**

Regent A ruler invested with authority on behalf of another.

The Fifty Articles

By the autumn it seemed less and less likely that the Frankfurt Parliament would be able to create a viable united Germany. Nevertheless, the Parliament did not give up and continued its interminable debate over the constitution.

In December, the Fifty Articles of the fundamental rights of the German citizens were approved and became law. For the Parliament to have reached this degree of agreement was an unexpected achievement. The Articles included:

- equality before the law
- freedom of worship
- freedom of the press
- freedom from arrest without warrant
- an end to discrimination because of class.

The problem of 'Germany'

Apart from the constitution, other problems beset the Parliament. One concerned the territorial extent of 'Germany'. The existing boundaries of the Confederation did not conform to any logical definition of 'Germany'. Parts of Prussia and the Austrian Empire were included while others were not. Those parts that were within the Confederation contained many Czechs and Poles while some of the excluded provinces had an overwhelmingly German-speaking population.

The Austrian Empire, which comprised a host of different nationalities and in which Germans were a minority, was a major problem. Should all the Austrian Empire be admitted into the new Germany? Should only the German part of it be admitted? Should none of it be admitted?

The Parliament was divided between the members who wanted a *Grossdeutschland*, which would include the predominantly German-speaking provinces of the Austrian Empire, and those who favoured a **Kleindeutschland**, which would exclude Austria but include the whole of Prussia. The *Grossdeutschland* plan would maintain the leadership of Germany by Catholic Austria, while the *Kleindeutschland* plan would leave Protestant Prussia as the dominant German state. The Parliament was unable to decide between the two proposals and debate dragged on inconclusively.

In October 1848 the Parliament voted for a *Grossdeutschland* but one which would incorporate only Austria's German lands. Austria refused to accept this solution. Its new conservative prime minister, Prince Felix of Schwarzenberg, declared the indivisibility of the Austrian Empire. It thus became clear to the Frankfurt Parliament that it could only achieve national unity by adopting a *Kleindeutschland* solution.

It had been an article of faith among most European liberals that all people would live in peace and harmony once they had thrown off the yoke of

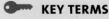 **KEY TERMS**

Grossdeutschland A greater Germany that would include the German-speaking provinces of the Austrian Empire.

Kleindeutschland A little Germany that would exclude Austria.

oppression. The events of 1848–9 were to destroy these naïve illusions. Relations between the peoples of central Europe deteriorated as conflicts broke out between Hungarians , Czechs, Croats, Poles, Italians and Germans.

In general, the Frankfurt Parliament had little sympathy for non-Germans within Germany. Not wishing to see a diminution of German power, it opposed the claims of Poles, Czechs and Danes for territory seen as part of Germany, namely Posen, Bohemia and Schleswig-Holstein. The Parliament applauded many of the actions of Austria in re-establishing control in Prague and northern Italy in the summer of 1848.

The weakness of the Frankfurt Parliament

From the start the Frankfurt Parliament lacked legal legitimacy since it had not been initiated by the German Confederation. Consequently, several major European powers including France and Russia declined to recognise the Parliament. The Parliament also lacked real muscle. Unable to collect taxation, it had no financial power. Nor did it have an army. The only army in any way capable of acting as a national army in 1848 was the Prussian one. Prussian General von Peucker was appointed minister of war, but he agreed to accept the post only on condition that he would not be expected to act in any way contrary to the wishes of the King of Prussia. Von Peucker did try to persuade the rulers of Bavaria and Austria, the only other states that had armies of any significance, to join with Prussia if 'exceptional circumstances' should make it necessary to field a national German army, but he failed. Without an army loyal to it, the authority of the Frankfurt Parliament remained theory rather than fact. It was wholly dependent on the goodwill of the member states of the Confederation, and their loyalty to the Parliament was far from guaranteed.

Lack of popular support

The Parliament was not in tune with the views of a large segment of the working class. German artisans established their own assemblies in 1848, the two most important being those meeting in Hamburg and Frankfurt. The Industrial Code put forward by the Artisan Congress in Frankfurt, as well as regulating hours of work and rates of pay, proposed to retain the restrictive practices of the old guild system. The Frankfurt Parliament delegates were mainly liberal. Regarding political freedom and economic freedom as inseparable principles, they rejected the Industrial Code out of hand. Many workers thus lost faith in the Frankfurt Parliament.

Divisions within the Frankfurt Parliament

The Frankfurt Parliament was seriously divided. The radical minority, who wanted to do away with the princes and replace them with a republic, found themselves in conflict with the majority of liberal members, who wanted a moderate settlement which would safeguard both the rights of individual states and those of the central government, and with a minimum of social change. There was also a small conservative group who wanted to preserve the rights of individual states and ensure that neither the Frankfurt Parliament nor the central government would exercise too much control.

These groups were simply loose associations within which there were many shades of opinion. In addition to the three main groups there were a large number of independent, politically uncommitted members. On top of this there were divisions between Protestants and Catholics and between those who wanted a *Grossdeutschland* or *Kleindeutschland* solution.

Not surprisingly, for much of the time it proved impossible to resolve the differences between the members sufficiently to reach any decision.

Heinrich von Gagern

The Parliament was handicapped by its unwise choice of leader, Heinrich von Gagern, who served as its president from May to December 1848. He was a distinguished liberal politician, sincere and well meaning, but without the force of character needed to dominate the assembly.

Schleswig-Holstein

Events in Schleswig-Holstein showed the Parliament's weakness. Denmark's decision to absorb the two provinces brought a noisy protest from Frankfurt. Lacking an army of its own, it had to look to Prussia to defend German interests. Prussia did occupy the two duchies in April–May 1848 but King Frederick William, aware of Russian, French and British opposition and doubting the wisdom of war with Denmark, agreed, in August, to the Treaty of Malmö. The Frankfurt deputies regarded the Prussian withdrawal from Schleswig-Holstein as a betrayal of the German national cause. They initially rejected the Treaty of Malmö, but, aware they could do nothing to change the situation, finally accepted it by a narrow majority. Public support for the Frankfurt Parliament declined sharply after this vote.

The radical challenge

Radicals, both within and outside the Frankfurt Parliament, continued to demand widespread political and social reform. Some 200 delegates, representing radical associations from across Germany, met in Frankfurt in mid-June. They agreed to form a national democratic and republican movement, based in Berlin. They gained considerable support from urban workers. The acceptance of the Malmö armistice by the Frankfurt Parliament brought matters to a head.

On 18 September 1848, a radical mob stormed the St Paul's Church (*Paulskirche*) in Frankfurt where the Parliament met. The building was defended by Austrian, Prussian and Hessian troops, and some 80 people were killed, including two conservative deputies. Archduke John placed Frankfurt under martial law. This violence discredited the radicals in the eyes of many Germans. Moderate liberals, horrified by the prospect of further violence, joined forces with the conservatives to combat the radicals. They regarded law and order as more important than freedom and equality.

The radicals refused to give up the struggle. At the second Democratic Congress, held in Berlin in October 1848, they pronounced the Frankfurt Parliament illegitimate and demanded new elections. However, by this time the **counter-revolution** was in full swing. Moreover, the radicals were hopelessly divided into various rival factions.

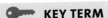

KEY TERM

Counter-revolution
A subsequent revolution (usually by conservative forces) counteracting the effect of a previous one.

German rights

In December 1848 the Parliament declared the basic rights of the German people. These included freedom of movement, equal treatment for all Germans, abolition of class-based privileges and feudal burdens, freedom of religion and conscience, abolition of capital punishment, freedom of assembly, freedom of the press and independence of judges.

A German Constitution

On 28 March 1849 a constitution for a German Empire was finally agreed (by 267 votes to 263). According to the *Paulskirche* constitution:

- There were to be two houses, the lower house to be elected by a secret ballot among men over the age of 25 and of 'good reputation', the upper house to be made up of the reigning monarchs and princes of the Confederation.
- The two houses would have control over legislation and finance.
- There was to be an emperor who had considerable power. However, he would only be able to hold up legislation for a limited time.
- The new Germany was to be a 'little' rather than a 'greater' Germany. But the constitution was designed to allow Austria to join at a later date if it so wished.

The failure of the Frankfurt Parliament

On 28 March 1849 the Frankfurt Parliament voted, half-heartedly (290 votes in favour, 248 abstentions) to elect Prussian King Frederick William as Emperor of Germany. However, Frederick William refused to accept the title on the grounds that it was not the Parliament's to offer. He distrusted 'the gentlemen of Frankfurt' who had, he believed, taken it on themselves to speak for a united Germany without any legal authority. He was not prepared to be Emperor of Germany if it meant putting himself and Prussia under the Frankfurt Parliament's control. He regarded himself as a king by the grace of God and refused to accept a crown 'from the gutter', a crown 'disgraced by the stink of revolution, defiled with dirt and mud', a crown which he saw as a 'dog collar with which they want to chain me to the revolution of 1848'. Moreover, he was aware that if he accepted the crown, this would have serious foreign policy implications and might even lead to war with Austria and Russia.

Prussia's rejection of the *Paulskirche* constitution was a signal to the other German princes that the political scales had tipped against the liberals. While 29 smaller states did accept the constitution, all the kingdoms, with the exception of Württemberg, rejected it. In the face of these disappointments, many members of the Parliament, including all those from Austria and Prussia, lost heart and went home. The remnants, about 150 of them, mostly radical democrats from south German states (many of whom had initially opposed the new constitution), made a last attempt to recover the situation. They called for the election of the first new German Parliament, or *Reichstag*. The call fell on deaf ears. The moment was past, the high hopes were gone.

The Parliament, driven out of Frankfurt by the city government, now moved to Stuttgart, the capital of Württemberg. There it was forcibly dispersed by the king's soldiers in June 1849. So ended the Frankfurt experiment.

Why did the Frankfurt Parliament fail?

The Frankfurt Parliament has been harshly treated, particularly by Marxist historians. Marx's friend and colleague Friedrich Engels described it as 'an assembly of old women' and blamed it for not overthrowing the existing power structures. However, it is unfair to condemn the Parliament for failing to do something that it did not want to do. Most of its members had no wish to be violent revolutionaries.

Another charge levelled against the Parliament is that its members were impractical idealists who wasted valuable time (six months) discussing the fundamental rights of the German people. Unable to agree on a new constitution, it failed to grasp the opportunity of filling the power vacuum in Germany in 1848. In reality, however, there probably never was a real possibility of creating a unified German nation in 1848–9. Had the members of the Frankfurt Parliament acted as decisively as their critics wanted, they would probably have been dispersed far earlier than they were. Dependent on the willing co-operation of the individual states, the Parliament lacked the power to enforce its decrees.

The attitude of Austria and Prussia was crucial. Constitutional government and national unity could be achieved only on their terms. Austria had no wish to see a more united or democratic Germany: she hoped to dominate Germany by keeping it weak and divided. The best, perhaps only, chance of the Frankfurt liberals lay in working out an agreement with Prussia. The chaos in Austria in 1848 gave Prussia a unique chance to play a dominant role in German affairs. Prussia did not grasp this opportunity. This was a failure not just on the part of King Frederick William, but also on the part of the Prussian liberal ministry (see pages 49–50). Both king and ministry ultimately failed because they were not at all anxious to succeed. Frederick William, like most of his subjects, was unwilling to see Prussia merged in a united Germany, at least in the way envisaged by the Frankfurt Parliament.

In fact, the authority of the Frankfurt Parliament was never accepted wholeheartedly by most of the individual states. When the ruling princes feared that they were about to lose many of their powers or even their thrones because of revolutions within their territories, they were prepared to support the Parliament. They feared that by opposing it, they would stir up even more opposition. But once the rulers had re-established their authority, their enthusiasm waned. Attractive as might be the idea of a united Germany in theory, in practice the princes had no wish to see their powers limited by liberal constitutions and a strong central authority.

When Austrian Emperor Franz Joseph regained control of all his territories in 1849, all hope of the Frankfurt Parliament experiment ended. The Austrian government opposed all revolutionary change. Once effective Austrian opposition was established, no other ruler dared to be seen to be taking the lead in establishing a German Empire.

Summary diagram: The Frankfurt Parliament

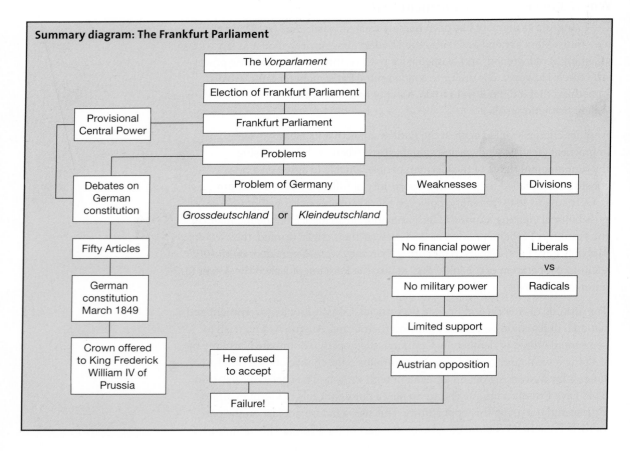

The situation in Prussia 1848–9

▶ *Why were developments in Prussia so important to the outcome of events in Germany in 1848–9?*

In 1848–9 the hopes of the Frankfurt Parliament lay with Prussia, and King Frederick William IV.

King Frederick William IV

Frederick William was a strange and complex character, sensitive, cultured and charming, but moody and unpredictable and so unstable that later in life he was to be declared insane. A fervent believer in the **divine right of kings**, he had a mystical idea of kingship and its privileges and duties. However, at the beginning of Frederick William's reign in 1840 it seemed that he might be a reforming monarch (see pages 25–6). But angered by opposition, Frederick William returned to restrictive policies. For most of the 1840s, he was a friend and ally of Metternich and dedicated to maintaining the old order in Europe. Then, in March 1848, it seemed he might swing back to supporting more liberal ideas.

The liberal ministry and the Prussian Parliament

In March 1848, Frederick William IV appointed a liberal ministry and agreed to the election of an assembly to draw up a new constitution for Prussia. The liberal ministry was hardly revolutionary. Its members were loyal to the crown and determined to oppose social revolution. Riots and demonstrations by workers in Berlin were quickly brought under control – by the army rather than by the bourgeois Citizens' Militia. Meanwhile the ministry, supporting German claims to the duchies of Schleswig-Holstein, declared war on Denmark (see page 45). It also supervised elections to a Prussian Parliament on the basis of male suffrage.

The new Parliament met in May. Although it was dominated by liberals, a third of its members were radicals and there was no agreement about the nature of the new constitution. Its main achievement was to abolish the feudal privileges of the *Junker* class. On 26 July the Berlin Parliament finally published a draft constitution. It was a moderate, liberal document that proved unacceptable to both conservatives and radicals. Frederick William IV typically vacillated, taking steps in the direction of the reactionaries and then steps back in the direction of compromise. The Parliament's position began to harden as it called for parliamentary control over the judiciary and police, the abolition of aristocratic titles and the king's right to rule by the grace of God. The mob continued to be restless and there were sporadic outbursts of violence.

 KEY TERM

Divine right of kings The notion that kings are God's representatives on earth and thus entitled to full obedience from their subjects.

Conservative reaction

Determined to defend their interests, Prussian landowners and nobles formed local associations. In August 1848 the League for the Protection of Landed Property met in Berlin. This '*Junker* Parliament', as it was dubbed by the radicals, pledged itself to work for the abolition of the Prussian Parliament and the dismissal of the liberal ministry. The conservatives' main hope was the army. Most army officers were appalled at the triumph of the liberals.

In Potsdam, Frederick William was surrounded by conservative advisers who urged him to win back power. The conservatives – *Junkers*, army officers and government officials – were not total reactionaries. Most hoped to modernise Prussia but insisted that reform should come from the king, not from the people. The tide seemed to be flowing in their favour. By the summer, most Prussians seemed to have lost their ardour for revolution and for German unity. The liberal ministry was increasingly isolated.

In August the king resumed control over foreign policy and concluded a ceasefire with the Danes, to the disgust of the Frankfurt Parliament. Riots by workers in Berlin in October ensured that the middle classes drew closer to the traditional ruling class. Habsburg success in Vienna in October (see page 54) also encouraged the king to put an end to the Prussian Parliament and to dismiss the liberal ministers.

In November 1848 Frederick William appointed his uncle Count Brandenburg to head a new ministry. The reactionary Otto von Manteuffel became minister of the interior. Almost at once Brandenburg ordered the Prussian Parliament out of Berlin. The Citizens' Militia was dissolved and thousands of troops moved into Berlin. **Martial law** was proclaimed. All political clubs were closed and all demonstrations forbidden. There was virtually no resistance to the counter-revolution in Berlin. The army made short work of industrial unrest in the Rhineland and Silesia.

The Prussian Parliament, still unable to agree a constitution, was dissolved by royal decree in December. On 5 December Frederick William proclaimed a constitution of his own which, to the extreme annoyance of the conservatives, was not dissimilar to that proposed by the National Assembly. This was a shrewd move by Frederick William, easing tensions.

The Prussian constitution

The Prussian constitution of December 1848 was a strange mixture of liberalism and absolutism:

- The constitution guaranteed the Prussians freedom of religion, of assembly and of association, and provided for an independent judiciary.
- There was to be a representative assembly, with two houses. The upper house would be elected by property owners, and the lower one by male suffrage.

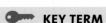 **KEY TERM**

Martial law The exercise of military power by a government in time of emergency, with the temporary suspension of ordinary administration and policing.

- Voters were divided into three classes, according to the amount of taxes they paid. This ensured that the rich had far more electoral power than the poor.
- In an emergency, the king could suspend civil rights and collect taxes without reference to Parliament.
- Ministers were to be appointed and dismissed by the king, and were to be responsible only to him and not to Parliament.
- The king could alter the written constitution at any time it suited him to do so.
- The king retained control of the army.

The constitution thus confirmed the king's divine right to rule while limiting his freedom to act. A genuine parliament, albeit subservient to the crown, had been created – from above. While Frederick William would not accept that his subjects could limit his power, he was prepared to limit his own powers. The new proposals were well received in Prussia, and ministers made no secret of the fact that they hoped it would be a better model for a united Germany than the Frankfurt Parliament. They had ambitions to make Prussia the leading state in Germany, and Frederick William the leading monarch.

Prussian action in 1849

In 1849 there were major uprisings in Saxony and the Rhenish Palatinate in support of the *Paulskirche* constitution. In Baden, the Grand Duke of Baden had

SOURCE D

German cartoon, entitled 'Panorama of Europe', which appeared in August 1849.

> Explain the significance of the large figure with a broom in the centre of Source D.

to flee the country after a mutiny of the Rastatt garrison. The rebels declared a Baden government and formed a revolutionary government. Prussian troops, under orders from the German Confederation, set about crushing the revolutions. The leaders and main participants, if caught, were executed or imprisoned. The successful suppression of the revolutions increased Prussia's standing in German politics. Prussia also won the gratitude of the family of the Grand Duchy of Baden, its first important ally in southern Germany.

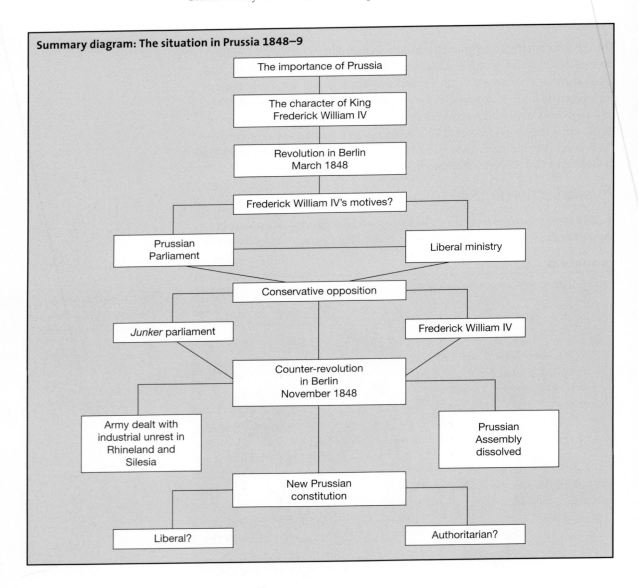

Summary diagram: The situation in Prussia 1848–9

- The importance of Prussia
- The character of King Frederick William IV
- Revolution in Berlin March 1848
- Frederick William IV's motives?
  - Prussian Parliament
  - Liberal ministry
- Conservative opposition
  - *Junker* parliament
  - Frederick William IV
- Counter-revolution in Berlin November 1848
  - Army dealt with industrial unrest in Rhineland and Silesia
  - Prussian Assembly dissolved
- New Prussian constitution
  - Liberal?
  - Authoritarian?

Key debate

▶ *Why did the German revolutions fail?*

In 1849 the German Confederation set about undoing most of the liberal achievements of 1848. Constitutional reforms in many individual states were revoked and new constitutions introduced that were far less liberal than those in effect before 1848. Radicals all over Germany were arrested and imprisoned. Some were executed. By mid-1849, it was clear that the German revolutions had failed. Different historians explain the failure in different ways. Historian M.S. Anderson emphasises the importance of social division.

EXTRACT I

From M.S. Anderson, *The Ascendancy of Europe 1815–1914*, Longman, 1972, p. 102.

… the revolutions suffered from the narrowness of their social base. In particular the dislike felt by the peasant for educated urban revolutionaries who pursued objectives which he did not understand and was not expected to understand showed itself almost everywhere. For a moment one of the greatest of the submerged social resentments of the eighteenth and first half of the nineteenth centuries, that of the countryside for the increasingly dominant and apparently exploiting town, showed itself with unusual clarity.

Historian Martin Kitchen stresses the importance of military force.

EXTRACT 2

From M. Kitchen, *A History of Modern Germany 1800–2000*, Blackwell, 2006, p. 83.

There had been an uprising in Prague on June 12 [1848] of unemployed workers and a poverty-stricken rabble led by a motley crew of socialists, democrats and students, who protested against the decision of the Slav Congress to press for a federal Austria in which the Germans no longer would have a monopoly of political power … The military commander in Prague, Prince Alfred von Windischgratz, waited for a couple of days before striking with full force. It was all over by June 16, by which time 400 people had been killed. The Germans in Bohemia applauded Windischgratz's savage suppression of the Czech radicals. Wealthy Czechs were relieved to see the end to a dangerous threat to their property, and heralded the victory of Austrian troops over Czech nationalists as a victory of the Habsburg Empire over German nationalism. The radicals in Vienna read the situation in much the same way. They were delighted to see the Czechs take a beating, but also knew that this was a significant victory for Vienna over Frankfurt and that their revolution was now very much on the defensive … It was in Vienna not Frankfurt that the future of Germany would be decided.

Historian David Thompson provides another explanation.

EXTRACT 3

From D. Thompson, *Europe Since Napoleon*, Longman, 1962, pp. 197–8.

Among the major forces of counter-revolution must be included fate itself, in the form of cholera. The year of revolutions was also the year of plague in Europe. Filling people with fear akin to the modern terror of cancer … , this particular epidemic had begun in China in 1844 and reached Russia by 1847, and in the fall of 1848 began to spread rapidly and devastatingly westward across Europe … Producing hundreds of deaths each day, it struck especially at the towns, the very centres of revolution … . Among the living it physical exhaustion and a dispirited apathy that quenched the fires of revolt … The year of revolutions was bounded by calamity, and the embers that had been partly kindled by hunger were partly quenched by disease.

? Which explanation outlined in Extracts 1, 2 and 3 do you find most convincing and why?

But Kitchen, Anderson and Thompson would probably agree that a number of factors were also important.

The situation in Austria

According to Kitchen, the fate of the German revolution was largely dependent on the outcome of the power struggle in Austria. In the summer of 1848 Austrian forces crushed major risings in Prague and in northern Italy. In October 1848, 2000 people died in Vienna as government forces regained control of the Austrian capital from radicals. In December the mentally defective Austrian Emperor Ferdinand was persuaded to abdicate in favour of his 18-year-old nephew Franz Joseph. By mid-1849 his forces had regained control of all the Austrian Empire including Hungary. Dissolving the Austrian Constituent Assembly, he subjected all parts of the Empire to rigid control from Vienna. Martial law was enforced in regions deemed to be infected with liberalism.

By 1850 it seemed as if the events of the previous two years had never been; nothing had changed in most of the states. In 1851, as though to complete the restoration of the old order, Metternich returned from exile to Vienna to live as a revered 'elder statesman'.

The situation in Prussia

In Prussia the liberals were effectively defeated by late 1848 (see page 50). King Frederick William IV committed himself to the conservatives. Police powers were increased and local government powers reduced. The 'three-class suffrage' for the Prussian lower house ensured that there was no real democracy. It was Prussian troops who put down revolutions elsewhere in Germany in 1849.

The failure of revolution across Europe

By 1849 the hopes of the revolutionaries, so high in the spring of 1848, had died. By 1849 the forces of reaction were once again in the ascendant. The three dynastic empires of Austria, Prussia and Russia continued to dominate central and eastern Europe. Most of the reasons for the failure of the German revolutions relate specifically to the situation in Germany. But the fact that revolutions failed across Europe in 1848–9 had a major impact on Germany.

Limited revolution

In Germany active revolution was comparatively rare. In Prussia it was restricted to riots in Berlin and unrest in the Rhineland and Silesia. In the small states of the southwest, poverty-stricken peasants attacked their landlords, castles were stormed and property was destroyed. Most revolutionary activity in Germany did not involve armed uprisings. Meetings, peaceful demonstrations and petitions were the chief weapons of the revolution.

In 1848 most German rulers gave in to demands for more democratic governments, fearing that otherwise they might be overthrown. But almost everywhere, the old rulers retained control of their armed forces and waited for an opportunity to regain power. Growing disunity among the revolutionaries gave them that opportunity.

Revolutionary divisions

There were wide differences in the political aims of liberals and radicals. While the former wanted constitutional government in all states and a united Empire with a national parliament, the latter worked for complete social and political change within a republican framework. Nor were the nationalists united. There was no agreement on the form the new Germany should take: a unified state or a federation, a monarchy or a republic, *Grossdeutschland* or *Kleindeutschland*?

Moreover, different social groups in Germany had very different interests. While popular movements were at the root of the revolutions, it was the propertied classes who seized power. Once middle-class liberals had secured the election of their own assemblies, most were as afraid of social revolution as the conservatives.

Working-class movements and the organisation of the radical left were not sufficiently well developed to force social change in their favour. Most workers had a purely practical revolutionary aim: the improvement of their working and living conditions. Unlike their 'intellectual', usually self-appointed, leaders, they were not concerned with – or even aware of – political ideologies that supposedly promoted their cause. Nor were they united. Master craftsmen, apprentices and unskilled workers had little in common.

Karl Marx played only a minor role in the revolutions. Hastening back to Germany, like hundreds of other revolutionary exiles in 1848, he was disappointed by the apathy shown by the working class and correctly observed that the revolutions had staff officers and non-commissioned officers, but no rank and file. The proletariat failed to live up to Marx's high and wholly unrealistic expectations. Far from forming the vanguard of social revolution, urban workers preferred to smash machines rather than smash the forces of conservatism. Artisans and their apprentices, threatened by the machines, were far more active than most of the proletariat.

Rural apathy

Germany was still essentially agrarian in 1848. The 1847 and 1848 harvests were reasonably good. Consequently, the rural populations were not in a desperate economic situation in 1848–9. This may explain the unenthusiastic support for revolutionary movements among peasants and their role in suppressing revolution by serving as loyal military conscripts. Across Germany, the peasantry, the vast majority of the population, lost interest in the revolution once the last remnants of feudalism had been removed. Indeed, many peasants felt hostility towards, rather than affinity with, the urban revolutionaries, and had little interest in liberal, democratic ideas or the national question. The failure of the peasantry to support the revolutions was of crucial importance.

Loss of support

Within a few months much of the active support for national unity and a national parliament had disappeared. This loss of support was encouraged by the slow progress made by the Frankfurt Parliament. But, in general, national consciousness failed to develop among the mass of Germans. Local loyalties remained strong and proved an important obstacle in the way of national unity.

Conservative strength

In the end the revolutions failed because the enemy was stronger and better organised and above all possessed military power. The story might have been very different in Berlin, for example, if there had not been a well-trained army available – and loyal – to the king. Given their military advantages, their determination and often their ruthlessness, the princes were clear favourites to win in the end. Constitutional government and national unity could be achieved only on their terms, not through the well-intentioned but ineffectual efforts of a liberal parliament, or by the uncoordinated actions of popular revolt. Once order was restored in the Austrian Empire and Austrian policy was still based on dominating Germany by keeping it weak and divided, there was no possibility of any moves towards a more united Germany being allowed to take place. Germany would be unified only when the military might and moral authority of the Austrian Empire had been overcome.

Were the revolutions a complete failure?

The 1848–9 revolutions were a severe setback for liberalism, but not a total failure. At least the remnants of feudalism had been swept away. Parliamentary government of a sort had been introduced in Prussia. Attempts to turn back the clock after 1849 were only partially successful. Many influential Germans were determined to continue the fight for greater freedom, more democracy and a German nation-state. After 1848 virtually all the monarchical regimes in Germany accepted the need to modernise. Conservatives also accepted the need to show an interest in the social problems of the lower classes if they were to ensure support for their policies and/or regimes. Moreover, the 1848–9 revolutions had helped to stir national consciousness across Germany.

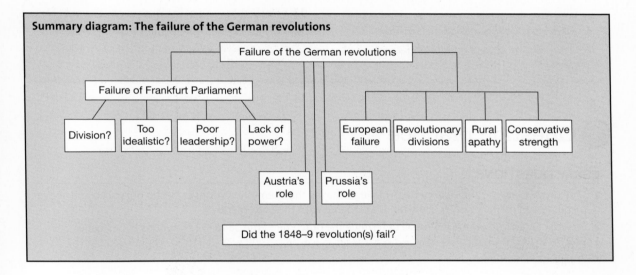

Summary diagram: The failure of the German revolutions

Chapter summary

In 1848 revolution affected Germany as it affected many parts of Europe. The German revolutions were sparked by events in France and by economic and social unrest in the towns and countryside. Metternich's fall from power had a profound impact on most Germans. German leaders, including those of Austria and Prussia, were initially forced to make concessions to the revolutionaries. The establishment of the Frankfurt Parliament gave hope to nationalists and liberals that a greater Germany was about to be established. However, a conservative reaction, led by Austria and Prussia, ensured the failure of both the Frankfurt Parliament and the revolutions generally. Divisions among the revolutionaries and rural apathy contributed to revolutionary failure.

Refresher questions

Use these questions to remind yourself of the key material covered in this chapter.

1 To what extent was there a general European revolutionary movement in 1848?

2 What were the main economic and social problems in Germany in the late 1840s?

3 To what extent was class consciousness developing in Germany?

4 What were the main political problems in Germany?

5 What sparked the revolutions in Germany?

6 How and why was the Frankfurt Parliament created?

7 What were the main concerns of the Frankfurt Parliament?

8 What problems did the Frankfurt Parliament face?

9 Why did the radicals pose a threat to the Frankfurt Parliament?

10 Why did the Frankfurt experiment fail?

11 Was King Frederick William IV a liberal or a reactionary?

12 Why did the Prussian liberals fail?

13 How democratic was the Prussian constitution?

14 Why did the German revolutions fail?

 # Question practice

ESSAY QUESTIONS

1 'The revolutions of 1848–9 in Germany failed because the enemy was stronger, better organised and above all possessed military power.' How far do you agree with this statement?

2 To what extent did events in Prussia determine the outcome of the 1848–9 revolutions in Germany?

3 How accurate is it to say that King Frederick William IV of Prussia was responsible for the failure of the Frankfurt Parliament?

INTERPRETATION QUESTION

1 Evaluate the interpretations in both of the passages and explain which you think is a more convincing explanation of the causes of the March Revolution of 1848 in Germany.

PASSAGE A

From 'Questions on German history: ideas, forces, decisions from 1800 to the present'. *Historical Exhibition in the Berlin Reichstag*, 1984, published by the German Bundestag, p. 108.

In 1847–8 social and political tension increased, against the background of a European economic crisis, and led to uprisings, with the exception of Russia and England, in all European countries against the existing order: in France against the selfish policies of the upper middle class; in Italy and Germany against the territorial fragmentation, against the remaining features of the feudal system and the absolutist state governments; in Eastern Europe there were rebellions against foreign domination and social injustice. In Germany the uprising was propelled by a strong national movement which combined the demands for national unity with those for social and political reforms. These demands found expression in the desires of people from all classes for a German parliament and a constitution. In the first phase of the Revolution the revolutionary forces succeeded in winning concessions from the governments – successes which were almost completely nullified by later developments and the onset of a counter-revolution.

PASSAGE B

From M. Kitchen, *A History of Modern Germany 1800–2000*, Blackwell, 2006, p. 74.

An increasingly self-confident bourgeoisie was the standard bearer of the new industrial society that was developing in Germany and which set the tone in the years between 1815 and 1848. They faced the intractable forces of the old order, the harsh repression of the Metternichian system, and the irksome supervision of the bureaucratic and authoritarian state. The dynamism of the new clashed with the immobility of the old, giving rise to frustration and radicalism on both sides. There was little pragmatism on either side, there were wide divisions within the ranks, and a latent tendency towards the impractical and the doctrinaire.

These political and ideological divisions were made all the more acute by pressing social problems as Germany went through the painful and disruptive process of industrialisation. The economy failed to provide for the needs of a rapidly rising population. Proud artisans had their livelihoods destroyed by power-driven machinery. Crop failures resulted in famine and disease. Millions were wrenched free of old social structures and were lost at sea in an unfamiliar and threatening world. Old certainties were shattered and new remedies had yet to be suggested for the individual lost in an increasingly pluralist society. Small wonder then that many grew impatient with the liberals' self-absorbed legalism and sought a radical and even revolutionary solution.

SOURCE ANALYSIS QUESTIONS

1 Why is Source 1 valuable to a historian studying the reasons for the failure of the Frankfurt Parliament? Explain your answer using the source, the information given about it and your own knowledge of the historical context.

2 How much weight do you give the evidence of Source 2 for an enquiry into the reasons for the failure of the 1848 revolutions? Explain your answer using the source, the information given about it and your own knowledge of the historical context.

SOURCE 1

From a speech made to the Frankfurt Parliament by Johann Gustav Droysen, 1848. Droysen was a member of the Frankfurt Parliament and secretary of the committee that was drawing up a constitution in 1848. He was one of the first members of the Parliament to leave when King Frederick William IV of Prussia refused the crown in 1849.

We cannot conceal the fact that the whole German question is a simple alternative between Prussia and Austria. In these states, German life has its positive and negative poles. In Prussia, all the interests are national and reforming. In Austria, all the interests are dynamic and destructive. The German question is not a constitutional question, but a question of power. The Prussian monarchy is now wholly German, while that of Austria cannot be. We need a powerful ruling house. Austria's power meant lack of power for us, whereas Prussia desired German unity in order to supply the deficiencies of her own power. Already Prussia is Germany in the making. She will merge with Germany.

SOURCE 2

From Carl Schurz, *The Reminiscences of Carl Schurz*, The McClure Company, 1913, p. 134. At the time of the 1848 revolutions, Schurz was a student at the University of Bonn and was editor of a newspaper that promoted democratic reform. He left Germany in 1849.

The political horizon, which after the revolution in March 1848 looked so glorious, soon began to darken. In South Germany, a republican uprising took place but was speedily suppressed by force of arms. The bulk of the liberal element did not desire anything beyond the establishment of national unity and a constitutional monarchy on a broad democratic basis.

The national parliament at Frankfurt elected in the spring showed a dangerous tendency to engage in more-or-less fruitless debates. This wasted time which was sorely needed for prompt and decisive action to secure the legitimate results of the revolution against hostile forces.

Our eyes turned anxiously to developments in Berlin. Prussia was by far the strongest of the purely German states. It was generally felt that the attitude of Prussia would be decisive in determining the fate of the revolution. For a while the Prussian king, Frederick William IV, seemed to be pleased with the role of leader of the national movement, which the revolution had made him assume. His volatile nature seemed to be warmed by a new enthusiasm. He took walks on the streets and talked freely with the people. He spoke of constitutional principles of government to be introduced as a matter of course. But when the Prussian constituent assembly had met in Berlin and began to pass laws, and to design constitutional provisions, and to interfere with the conduct of the government in the spirit of the revolution, the king started listening to more conservative voices.

What troubled me most was the visibly and constantly growing power of the reactionary forces and the frittering away of the opportunities to create something real and durable, by the national parliament in Frankfurt and by the assembly in Berlin.

CHAPTER 3

Austro-Prussian rivalry 1849–68

After the failure of the 1848–9 revolutions it seemed that Austrian power had revived. Austrian policy was still based on dominating Germany by keeping it weak and divided. Thus, Germany would be unified only after Austrian strength had been broken. The only country that could do that was Prussia. In the 1850s Prussia was regarded by virtually all international statesmen as the least important of the major powers. But appearances were deceptive. In 1862 Otto von Bismarck was appointed minister-president of Prussia. Four years later Prussia defeated Austria in the Seven Weeks' War and established the North German Confederation. How much of Prussia's success was due to Bismarck? How much was due to other factors? The chapter will consider these (and other) questions by examining:

★ The position of Austria after 1848

★ The position of Prussia after 1848

★ Bismarck: the man and his aims

★ Austro-Prussian conflict

★ Prussian ascendancy

★ Factors helping Bismarck

Key dates

1849		Erfurt plan	1863		Polish revolt
1850		Capitulation of Olmütz	1864		Austria and Prussia fought Denmark
1851		German Confederation restored	1866	June	Start of Seven Weeks' War
1854–6		Crimean War		July	Battle of Sadowa
1859		North Italian War		Aug.	Treaty of Prague
1861		William I became King of Prussia			
1862		Bismarck became Prussia's minister-president	1867		North German Confederation created

The position of Austria after 1848

 How strong was Austria's position in Germany after 1848?

The counter-revolution in Austria after 1848 went further than in any other German state. The constitution of March 1849 was revoked in 1851. Thereafter, the young Emperor Franz Joseph ruled as an absolute monarch. The army acted as a police force and martial law was enforced in regions deemed to be infected with liberalism. As well as enforcing its authority within its own empire, the Austrian government was determined to maintain its power within Germany.

The Prussian Union Plan

Despite his refusal to accept the imperial crown offered by the Frankfurt Parliament, Prussian King Frederick William IV was attracted to the idea of a united Germany with himself at its head, providing he had the consent of the princes. In 1849 General Radowitz, an ardent nationalist, came up with the Prussian Union Plan. His proposal for a *Kleindeutschland*, under Prussian leadership, met with Frederick William's approval.

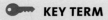 **KEY TERM**

Reich The German word for empire.

According to the plan, there would be a German Federal ***Reich***, which would exclude Austria. It would have a strong central government, based on the constitution drawn up by the Frankfurt Parliament (see page 46), with the King of Prussia as emperor. Although Austria would not be a member of the *Reich*, there would be a special relationship, a permanent 'union', between the *Reich* and the Habsburg Empire.

This complicated plan, which tried to provide a compromise between *Kleindeutschland* and *Grossdeutschland* solutions, was unacceptable to Austria. Austrian Prime Minister Schwarzenberg saw it as a devious scheme to reduce Austrian influence in Germany. He was not, however, immediately able to mount effective opposition to it, as internal Austrian problems, especially a Hungarian uprising, occupied his attention. This allowed Prussia, whose army was the strongest in Germany in 1849, to press on with the plan. A 'Three King's Alliance' between Prussia, Saxony and Hanover was the first step. Then a number of smaller states were persuaded to fall in with the Prussian proposals.

Encouraged by his success, Radowitz called a meeting of representatives of all the German states to Erfurt in March 1850 to launch the new *Reich*. Twenty-eight states agreed to the creation of the Prussian-dominated Erfurt Union. However, several important states, suspicious of Prussian ambitions and fearful of Austria's reaction, declined to join.

Austrian opposition

Schwarzenberg, having suppressed the Hungarian rising, was able to reassert Austria's position in Germany. He put forward a scheme of his own for a *Grossdeutschland* to be governed jointly by delegates from Austria, Prussia and the larger German states. Attracted by the way this proposal seemed to offer them greater political influence, some of the larger states (for example Hanover and Saxony) deserted Prussia and gave their support to Austria.

Schwarzenberg now summoned the *Bundesrat* of the old German Confederation, thought to have been dead and buried, to meet in Frankfurt in May 1850. The response was good and he was able to announce that the *Bundesrat* and Confederation were both alive and well. Thus, by the summer of 1850 there were two assemblies claiming to speak for Germany: the Prussian-led Erfurt Parliament and the Austrian-led Frankfurt *Bundesrat*.

Prussia versus the Confederation

A showdown soon occurred. A revolution in Hesse-Cassel, a member state of the Erfurt Union, prompted its ruler to request help from the Frankfurt *Bundesrat*. But the Erfurt Parliament also claimed the right to decide the dispute. Hesse-Cassel was of strategic importance because it separated the main part of Prussia from the Rhineland, and therefore controlled communications between the two. The Prussian army mobilised. Austria replied with an ultimatum that only the troops of the old Confederation had the right to intervene.

Small-scale fighting broke out between Prussian and Confederation troops. Frederick William, who had no wish for war, dismissed Radowitz. Edwin Manteuffel, the new Prussian minister-president (prime minister), was also anxious to avoid an all-out war.

The capitulation (or humiliation) of Olmütz

A meeting between Manteuffel and Schwarzenberg was arranged at Olmütz and on 29 November 1850 Prussia, under pressure from Russia and fearful of antagonising Austria, agreed to abandon the Prussian Union Plan. The two men also agreed to a conference of states being held at Dresden in 1851 to discuss the future of Germany. Schwarzenberg had won a major diplomatic victory and Prussia had suffered a huge humiliation.

The revival of Austria did not go as far as Schwarzenberg had hoped, however. His proposal for an Austrian-dominated 'Middle Europe', incorporating the 70 million people of all the German states and the Habsburg Empire, was not acceptable to the smaller German states, as it would have increased the power of the larger states at their expense. There was strong pressure for a return to the situation pre-1848. Prussia supported this. Given that the Prussian Union Plan was lost, anything from Prussia's point of view was better than accepting the Austrian counterplan.

In May 1851, the German Confederation of 1815 was formally re-established and an alliance between Austria and Prussia appeared to signal a return to the policy of close co-operation. However, relations between Prussia and Austria were far from close. Many Prussians blamed Austria for the humiliation of the 'Capitulation of Olmütz'. Most were totally opposed to Austria's ambitions to bring the entire Habsburg Empire into the Confederation. Some were determined that Prussia should one day dominate a united Germany. Austria clearly stood in the way.

> **?** Why, according to Source A, did Bismarck believe that Prussia would have to fight Austria?

SOURCE A

Otto von Bismarck, a Prussian statesman, writing in 1856 to Minister Manteuffel, quoted in J.H. Robinson, editor, *Readings in European History*, Ginn & Co., 1904.

Because of the policy of Vienna, Germany is clearly too small for us both; as long as an honourable arrangement concerning the influence of each in Germany cannot be concluded and carried out, we will both plough the same disputed acre, and Austria will remain the only state to whom we can permanently lose or from whom we can permanently gain. I wish only to express my conviction that, in the not too distant future, we will have to fight for our existence against Austria and that it is not within our power to avoid that, since the course of events in Germany has no other solution.

Austrian political, economic and financial problems

In the 1850s the Austrian government made efforts to centralise the state. Centralisation meant control from Vienna by Germans. All civil servants, judges and army officers had to speak German. This led to unrest among the many non-Germans within the Austrian Empire.

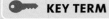

KEY TERM

Concordat An agreement between the Vatican and a government.

The 1855 **concordat** with the Catholic Church, which strengthened the Church's hand in matters such as education, made Catholicism to all intents and purposes the state religion in Austria. As well as adding to the disaffection among the non-Catholic nationalities, the concordat alienated German Protestants and anti-clerical liberals. This dashed the hopes of those who still dreamed of creating a greater Germany.

In 1849 Schwarzenberg, realising the political implications of Prussia's economic success, proposed establishing a *Zollunion*, an extended customs union, between Austria and the *Zollverein* (see pages 20–1). This move failed. So too did Schwarzenberg's efforts in 1851 to establish an alternative customs union to include Austria and those German states still outside the *Zollverein*. Thus, while Austria clung to its political leadership of the Confederation, it was effectively isolated from the Prussian-dominated economic coalition of the German states. Not all was doom and gloom on the Austrian economic front: during the 1850s there was both industrial expansion and rising exports, and peasants were freed from feudal dues. Nevertheless, Austrian government finances remained a serious problem. While taxes were increased and government expenditure reduced, this was not sufficient to reduce the huge deficit left over from the Metternich era. Military operations against the 1848 revolutionaries had only increased the deficit. Although Austria did not join the **Crimean War**, its finances were damaged by the cost of keeping its army mobilised and ready for action. Austria's financial difficulties meant that it lacked the means to reform its army.

KEY TERM

Crimean War A war fought by Britain, France and Turkey against Russia between 1854 and 1856. Most of the fighting was in the Crimea – a southern part of Russia. The war ended with Russia's defeat.

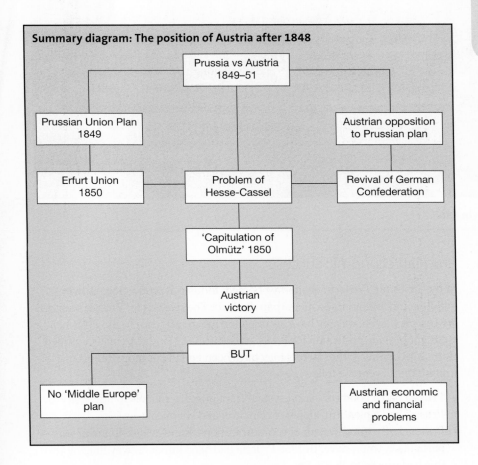

Summary diagram: The position of Austria after 1848

2 The position of Prussia after 1848

▶ *How strong was Prussia's position in Germany after 1848?*

Despite the serious political setback in 1850–1, Prussian power within Germany grew considerably in the 1850s. Prussia was a curious mixture: politically reactionary and repressive, socially reforming and economically prosperous.

SOURCE B

The Krupp works in Essen in 1866.

? Why was the industrial activity shown in Source B so important for Prussia?

Prussian economic success

In the 1850s the Prussian economy boomed. Industrial production, railway building and foreign trade more than doubled. The reasons for Prussia's success are complex. Scholars may have ascribed too much influence to the *Zollverein*. It did not provide protection for Prussian industries. Nor did it create a unified German economy. Other factors may have been equally or more important. Among these were the following:

- Prussia had a good education system from primary schools to university level.
- Prussia had a plentiful supply of coal, iron and chemicals.
- Prussia had a good system of communications. Railway development was particularly impressive. In 1850 Prussia had 5865 km of railway line; by 1870 this had grown to 18,876 km.
- Railway development encouraged a host of other industries, for example, coal and iron and steel.
- A number of key individuals played vital roles in ensuring that Prussian industrialisation forged ahead. Alfred Krupp was particularly important. In 1846 he employed just 140 workers. By the 1860s his iron and steel works at Essen found work for thousands of Prussians (see Source B). Krupps became the main manufacturer of weapons for the Prussian army.

Historians disagree about the role played by the Prussian state in the country's industrial development. The Prussian government subsidised railway building, used the Prussian state bank to finance industrial pilot projects and set up technical schools. Some think that this state investment helped economic development. Others are convinced that it hindered:

- The Prussian government did not follow a consistent or clear policy with regard to investment.
- Prussian entrepreneurial activity in some areas, for example, mining, banking and textiles, may have held back potentially more valuable private investment.

For whatever reason, or more likely combination of reasons, by the mid-1850s Prussia was industrially expanding. Economic and financial power gave Prussia a considerable advantage in its rivalry with Austria.

The political situation

After 1848 Prussia had a constitution with universal suffrage. However, since voters were divided into three classes according to the amount of taxes they paid, the system was hardly democratic. In 1849, 4.7 per cent of voters chose one-third of the electors. Another third were elected by 12.6 per cent of those eligible to vote and the remaining third by 82.7 per cent. The upper house was the preserve of Prussia's landowning aristocracy. The Prussian king, who still controlled the army, had the power of veto and the right to rule by decree, and thus retained considerable power.

The growth of liberalism

Despite repressive and reactionary policies after 1848–9, Prussian liberalism grew in strength. It was supported by an increasingly self-confident middle class. Professors, teachers, civil servants, Protestant pastors, businessmen and lawyers joined the great national liberal associations and subscribed to liberal journals. Liberals formed a coherent and influential force not just in Prussia but across Germany. Wherever there were elected assemblies, the liberals formed a majority. Prussia was no exception. Its three-class electoral system actually gave a great advantage to the middle-class liberal elite. Liberal strength was a force that no politician could afford to ignore.

Nevertheless, for much of the 1850s there was general political apathy in Prussia: few people bothered to make use of their franchise and politics was the concern of a small elite – for the most part lawyers and civil servants. Right-wing liberal politicians, traumatised by the experience of 1848, which showed how easily mass involvement in politics could descend into revolution, remained suspicious of full democracy. They were less concerned with strengthening parliament than with ending the dominant influence of the aristocracy and the army over the government. However, left-wing liberals still argued in favour of universal suffrage and insisted that the masses could be trusted to vote for men of substance and culture. There was one thing on which both liberal wings could agree: national unity was the absolute priority.

Conservative reform

Manteuffel had no time for democracy and governed without parliament for the whole of his time as minister-president (1850–8). He imposed strict censorship and did his best to restrict the freedom of political parties to hold meetings. Nevertheless, he believed that ministers had a duty to govern well, and that this meant governing in the interests of all the people. He also believed that the best way to reduce the chance of revolution was to improve the living conditions of peasants and workers.

Reform in the countryside

Manteuffel was concerned to help the peasantry, whom he regarded as the basis of popular support for the monarchy. Consequently:

- All peasants were freed from their feudal obligations to their landlords.
- Special low-interest government loans were available to enable peasants to buy their land; 600,000 did so.
- Where there was overpopulation and great pressure on land, the government gave peasants financial help to move to less populated areas of Prussia.

Reform in the towns

Given Prussia's economic growth, there was a general improvement in urban living standards in the 1850s. There were also government efforts to improve factory workers' conditions:

- Payment of a standard minimum wage was encouraged.
- Inspectors were appointed to improve working conditions in factories.
- Children under twelve years of age were forbidden to work in factories.
- Industrial courts were set up to help in the settlement of disputes.

The international situation

Prussia, despite being a growing economic power, seemed to be a second-rate player in the 1850s. Having avoided military conflict with Austria in 1850, it played no role in the Crimean War. However, by remaining strictly neutral, Prussia managed to keep on good terms with the other European powers, especially Russia.

Austria also remained neutral, but gained little respect because of its wavering diplomacy. While generally siding against Russia, it did commit itself fully to Britain and France. By 1856 Austria had thus lost the friendship of Russia without obtaining that of Britain and France.

Prussia might have profited from the **North Italian War** in 1859 if it had supported Piedmont and France against Austria. However, popular feeling in Prussia, as in most German states, was anti-French. Prussia tried to benefit by offering Austria help in exchange for conceding Prussian primacy in Germany. Austria's speedy defeat – its underfinanced and ineptly led army was defeated at

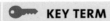

KEY TERM

North Italian War In 1859 French Emperor Napoleon III supported Piedmont against Austria. Piedmont was seeking to increase its influence in northern Italy at Austria's expense. Austria was defeated.

the battles of Magenta and Solferino by French troops – and willingness to make peace with Napoleon III prevented Prussia's aims being realised. But, at least the war had been a severe blow to Austrian prestige. Austria lost Lombardy (in northern Italy) to Piedmont. Moreover, the cost of the war had a terrible effect on Austria's already strained finances.

King William I

Frederick William, whose mental balance had always been precarious, became increasingly unstable, until, in 1858, he was declared insane. His brother William became regent, and when Frederick William died in 1861, William succeeded to the Prussian throne.

William I, already 63 when he became king, was to reign for another 27 years. A soldier by training and a conservative by instinct, William was practical, hard-headed and inflexible – the complete contrast to Frederick William. Only Bismarck, his chief minister for nearly the whole of his reign, was ever able to make him change his mind. A devout Protestant, he believed that he was answerable only to God, which made it difficult to argue with him. He was prepared to listen to advice from ministers, but not necessarily to act on it. At heart he was an absolutist.

On becoming regent, he dismissed Manteuffel, replacing him with a ministry containing both liberals and conservatives. The atmosphere of comparative freedom led people to talk of a 'new era'. The 1858 elections gave the moderate liberals a small majority in parliament. They hoped to play a significant role in government. William had no intention of allowing them to do so.

Reform of the army

The strengthening of the army was one of William's main concerns. He believed that it was the key to Prussia's future greatness. Little had been done to reform or increase the size of the Prussian army since 1815. The mobilisation of the army during the North Italian War had been a disaster. The war was over before it could be organised into readiness. The delay meant that William lost the opportunity to achieve some political advantage.

In 1860 William's new conservative minister of war, **General von Roon**, introduced a bill to reform the army. Roon aimed to:

- double the regular army's size
- increase the period of military service from two to three years
- reduce the role played by the inefficient *Landwehr*
- re-equip the troops.

Roon's bill touched a number of sensitive points as far as the liberal majority in Prussia's Parliament was concerned. Liberals feared that the government might use the expanded army, not for defence from foreign attack, but against

 **KEY FIGURE**

Albrecht von Roon (1803–79)

As minister of war from 1859 to 1873 Roon played a vital role in German unification. A conservative supporter of the Prussian monarchy, he worked hard to improve the efficiency of the Prussian army. His efforts helped to ensure Prussian success in the wars against Denmark, Austria and France.

its own people as had happened in 1848–9 (see pages 50–2). Moreover, the civilian *Landwehr*, despite its military shortcomings, was popular with liberals. They regarded it as a citizens' army, the guarantor of liberal freedoms against the reactionary and aristocratic regular army. Others were more concerned about the three-year service, which they saw as a dangerous step towards the militarisation of society. While there was some room for compromise on detail, both sides believed that important principles were at stake:

- William was determined that army matters should be kept beyond parliamentary control.
- Liberals believed that Parliament should have financial control over army expenditure. Without such a right it had very little power.

Constitutional crisis 1860–2

The army bill led to a constitutional crisis. In 1860 Parliament would agree only to approve the increased military budget for a year and would not agree to extend the term of military service to three years.

In June 1861, radical liberals formed the Progressive Party. The Progressives were committed to a popular rather than a royal army. In the newly elected Parliament in December 1861 the Progressives became the largest party, with 109 seats. Parliament would not pass the money bill for the army and William would not accept two years' military service.

William again dissolved Parliament and replaced his liberal ministers with conservatives. The May 1862 elections were a disaster for the king and a triumph for the Progressives who, in alliance with the other opposition groups, now had an overall majority in the lower house.

In September, Parliament again refused to pass the army bill. Some Prussian conservatives hoped that this would lead to a royal coup and the overthrow of the constitution. Instead, William, fearing civil war, contemplated abdication. However, on 22 September, on the advice of Roon, he appointed Otto von Bismarck as chief minister. Bismarck, who accepted the post only on condition that he could do as he saw fit, was thus able, as he himself put it, 'to make his own music'. His appointment was one of the most momentous occasions in Prussian, German and European history.

The constitutional crisis solved

Bismarck's appointment as minister-president was seen as a deliberate affront to the liberals. They regarded him as a bigoted reactionary. Given that Bismarck had no ministerial experience, he was not expected to last long in power.

SOURCE C

Bismarck's first speech to the Prussian Parliament, 30 September 1862, from http://germanhistorydocs.ghi-dc.org/sub_document.cfm?document_id=250.

Germany is not looking to Prussia's liberalism, but to its power; Bavaria, Württemberg, Baden may indulge liberalism, and yet no one will assign them Prussia's role; Prussia has to coalesce and concentrate its power for the opportune moment, which has already been missed several times; Prussia's borders according to the Vienna Treaties [of 1814–15] are not favorable for a healthy, vital state; it is not by speeches and majority resolutions that the great questions of the time are decided – that was the big mistake of 1848 and 1849 – but by iron and blood.

Bismarck's first speech to the Prussian Parliament (see Source C above) was not his greatest effort. What he had meant to say was that if Prussia was to fulfil its role in leading Germany towards greater unity, it could not do so without an efficient army, which the king's government was seeking to build. His speech, aimed at winning liberal support, badly misfired. He failed to build any bridges to his political opponents.

In the end, Bismarck solved the problem of the military budget by withdrawing it, declaring that Parliament's support for the army bill was unnecessary as the army reforms could be financed from taxation. To liberal suggestions that the people refuse to pay taxes, Bismarck replied that he had 200,000 soldiers ready to persuade them.

Parliament declared Bismarck's actions illegal, but he ignored it. The taxes were collected and the army was reorganised as if Parliament did not exist. Civil servants who objected to Bismarck's actions were dismissed. For four years (and through two wars), he directed Prussian affairs without constitutionally approved budgets and in the face of fierce parliamentary opposition. New elections in 1863 gave the liberals 70 per cent of the parliamentary seats. 'Men spat on the place where I trod in the streets', Bismarck wrote later. But he rightly judged that his opponents would avoid an appeal to force: few wanted a repeat of 1848.

Look at Source C. What did Bismarck mean by the phrase 'iron and blood'?

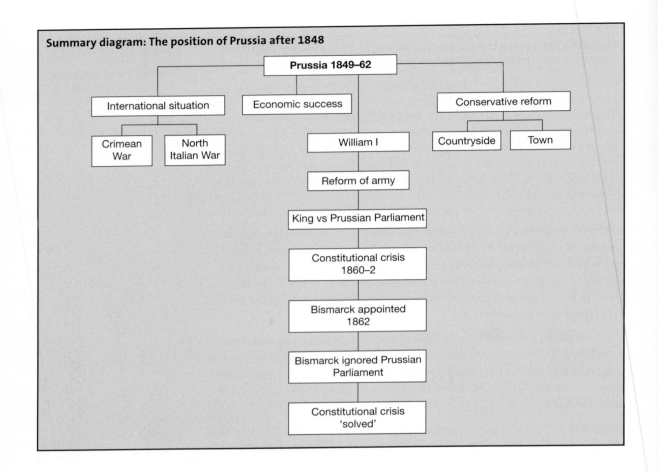

Summary diagram: The position of Prussia after 1848

Prussia 1849–62

- International situation
  - Crimean War
  - North Italian War
- Economic success
  - William I
  - Reform of army
  - King vs Prussian Parliament
  - Constitutional crisis 1860–2
  - Bismarck appointed 1862
  - Bismarck ignored Prussian Parliament
  - Constitutional crisis 'solved'
- Conservative reform
  - Countryside
  - Town

③ Bismarck: the man and his aims

▶ *What were Bismarck's main aims?*

Bismarck's early life

Bismarck's father was a moderately wealthy *Junker*. The *Junkers* were the landowning nobility, with their own rules of conduct based on an elaborate code of honour, devotion to the military life, a strong sense of service to the Prussian state and an even stronger sense of their own importance. Most were deeply conservative. Bismarck was proud of his *Junker* descent and all his life liked to present himself as a *Junker* squire. However, he was too clever, too enterprising and too non-conformist to be a typical *Junker*.

Bismarck's mother came from a middle-class family of Hamburg merchants. Many of her relatives were civil servants, university professors or lawyers. Most were politically liberal. Bismarck seems to have been ashamed of this side of his family, often speaking of them in a disparaging way. He did not get on well with his mother, but from her he inherited his intelligence and determination.

Sent to school in Berlin, he proved resistant to education, although he later became a good linguist, fluent in French, English and Russian. He went on to university, where he wasted a good deal of time and money, drank too much and got into debt, but proved himself a crack shot and an expert fencer. He developed a reputation as a duellist (in one year fighting 25 duels). Passing his law examinations, he won entry to the Prussian civil service and spent four years as a less than committed civil servant. A year of military service followed, enjoyed neither by Bismarck nor by the army.

On his mother's death in 1839, he helped to run the family estates. Country life soon bored him, and he found entertainment chasing after peasant girls and playing wild practical jokes on his neighbours. By the time he was 30, Bismarck had achieved little. Then in 1847 two events occurred to change the direction of his life. First, he married and secondly, he became involved in Prussian politics. His wife, Johanna von Puttkamer, was deeply religious. Providing a stable background to his life, she brought up their numerous children and overlooked his continued infidelities.

Otto von Bismarck

1815	Born, the son of a *Junker*
1836	Entered the civil service
1839	Returned to manage the family estates
1847	Became an ultra-conservative deputy in the Prussian United *Diet*
1851–9	Served as Prussia's delegate at the *Bundestag*
1859	Appointed Prussian ambassador to Russia
1862	Became minister-president
1864	Initiated war against Denmark
1866	Initiated war against Austria
1870–1	Initiated Franco-Prussian War
1871–90	Served as chancellor of the new German Empire
1898	Died

After 1862 Bismarck became a man of imperious and dominating temperament with an unquenchable thirst for power. He saw himself as a man of destiny, convinced that he would have a great impact on the world. Nevertheless, he once admitted: 'I am all nerves; so much so that self-control has always been the greatest task of my life and still is.' He smoked heavily, consumed huge amounts of alcohol and ate enormous meals. In 1883 his weight reached 114 kilograms.

Given to melancholy, he suffered from periods of laziness. He was also an inveterate womaniser and gambler. Aggressive and emotional, his relations with William I were stormy; their meetings sometimes degenerated into slanging matches. Ruthless, unpredictable, vindictive and unscrupulous, Bismarck could also be charming and witty, a delightful companion and entertaining conversationalist.

Bismarck declared late in his life: 'I have always had one compass only, one lodestar by which I have steered: the welfare of the state … When I have had time to think I have always acted according to the question, "What is useful, advantageous and right for my Fatherland and – as long as this was only Prussia – for my dynasty, and today for the German nation".'

Bismarck's political career 1847–62

In 1847 Bismarck was elected to the Prussian United *Diet*. It marked his entry into public life. During the March days of the Berlin riots in 1848 (see pages 36–7), he involved himself in counter-revolutionary plots. He was excessively anti-liberal. 'Only two things matter for Prussia', he said, 'to avoid an alliance with democracy and to secure equality with Austria.'

In December 1850 he spoke in the Erfurt Parliament in defence of Frederick William's 'surrender' to Austria at Olmütz. He argued that a state should fight only in its own interest – what he called 'state egoism'. He opposed a war for Hesse-Casse: 'Gentlemen, show me an objective worth a war and I will go along with you … woe to any statesman who fails to find a cause of war which will stand up to scrutiny once the fighting is over.' This speech led to Bismarck becoming Prussian envoy to the revived *Bundestag* at Frankfurt, where, apart from a short time in Vienna as Prussian ambassador, he remained until 1859. During his years at Frankfurt, it became his overriding concern to oppose Austria. He therefore moved away from the views of his conservative Prussian associates who had supported his appointment to Frankfurt. They thought that the fight against revolution was still the priority and that it required the solidarity of the conservative powers of Russia, Austria and Prussia.

As he became increasingly anti-Austrian, Bismarck became convinced that war between Prussia and Austria was unavoidable. He believed that such a conflict would eventually lead to a divided Germany, with a Protestant north and a Catholic south. By 1858 he was arguing that Prussia should seek support among German nationalists and a year later that Austria should be driven out of the Confederation and a *Kleindeutschland* established under Prussian control. In 1859 Bismarck was moved from the *Bundestag* to become Prussian ambassador in Russia.

By the early 1860s Bismarck had a reputation as a tough, ambitious and ruthless politician. Although viewed (mistakenly by contemporaries) as a conservative reactionary and (correctly) as a loyal supporter of the monarchy, he was also seen (with far more justification) as an unpredictable maverick. However, he was also a realist.

Bismarck's aims

Initially, Bismarck's main aim was Prussian domination of north Germany rather than full national unity. He was essentially a Prussian patriot rather than a German nationalist: his loyalty was to the Prussian king – not to the German people. Liberal nationalists viewed him with disfavour in the early 1860s, seeing him not as a potential unifier but as an anti-liberal reactionary. In the late 1840s and early 1850s Bismarck had shown little but contempt for nationalism. However, by the late 1850s, his views began to change. Aware of the popular appeal of German nationalism, he realised that the movement might be manipulated in the interests of enhancing Prussian power. Indeed, he tended to see Prussian and German interests as one and the same. He said in 1858 that there was 'nothing more German than the development of Prussia's particular interests'.

Convinced that great issues are decided by might not right, Bismarck was determined to make Prussia as mighty as possible. Prussian leadership in Germany would ensure Prussian might. While he was determined to end Austrian primacy in the Confederation, he was not necessarily committed to war. A diplomatic solution, in his view, was a preferable option.

Realpolitik characterised Bismarck's political career from first to last. He had contempt for idealism and idealists. While he was a sincere Protestant, he was able to divorce personal from political morality. In his view, the end justified the means. He recognised that a conservative regime could no longer operate without popular support, not least that of the liberal bourgeoisie whose power was growing. He hoped to achieve conservative ends by means that were far from conservative. His unscrupulous methods occasionally brought him into conflict with William I and the Prussian military and political elites. But while many distrusted his tactics, most respected his judgement. Indispensable to the Prussian monarchy for nearly 30 years, he made the difficult unification process appear, with hindsight and at the time, easy.

SOURCE D

Words (allegedly) spoken by Bismarck to Benjamin Disraeli, a leading British politician in 1862. (This quote was written down many years later by someone who was not present at the meeting!) From J. Steinberg, *Bismarck: A Life*, Oxford University Press, 2011.

As soon as the army shall have been brought into such a condition to command respect, then I will take the first opportunity to declare war with Austria, to burst asunder the German Confederation, bring the middle and smaller states into subjection and give Germany a national union under the leadership of Prussia.

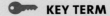

KEY TERM

Realpolitik The term is used to describe the ruthless and cynical policies of politicians, like Bismarck, whose main aim was to increase the power of a state.

Given that Source D was written down many years later, how reliable a source is it for Bismarck's aims in 1862?

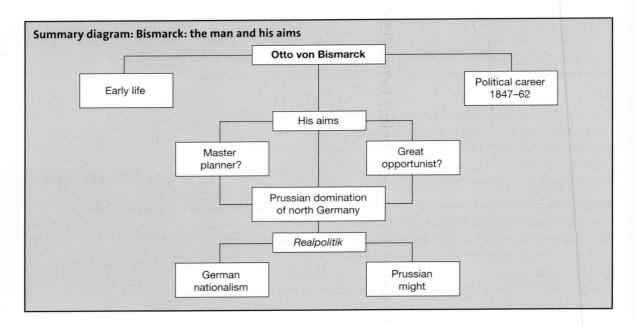

Summary diagram: Bismarck: the man and his aims

4 Austro-Prussian conflict

▶ *Why did Austria and Prussia go to war in 1866 and why did Prussia win?*

Relations between Austria and Prussia, cool before 1862, became icy after Bismarck's appointment. In December 1862 he warned Austria that it was inviting catastrophe unless it recognised Prussia as an equal in Germany. By 1863 it was clear that Bismarck and Austria were at odds over the future German development. In 1863 the prospect of Bismarck defeating Austria and bringing about a Prussian-dominated Germany seemed highly unlikely. Bismarck's own position in Prussia seemed vulnerable. Prussian (and German) liberals regarded him with hostility and contempt. Prussia's position in Germany seemed similarly vulnerable. Its territories straddled across central Europe. Austria had a larger army and a population almost twice that of Prussia. Most German states had no wish to be dominated by Prussia.

The Polish revolt

In the late eighteenth century Prussia, Russia and Austria collectively had divided Poland among them. Relations between Prussia and its Polish citizens had been uneasy and Poles had been blamed, without much evidence, for some of the disturbances of 1848. Bismarck thought they were troublemakers.

In 1863, when the inhabitants of Russian Poland rose in revolt against Russian rule, Bismarck viewed the situation with concern. The revolt might escalate into a general Polish uprising. Tsar Alexander II ordered the revolt to be suppressed.

France, Austria and Britain protested and offered mediation. Bismarck took the opportunity to gain Russian friendship by offering military assistance. The tsar, confident that he could defeat the Poles unaided, rejected the offer, but agreed to a convention by which Prussia would hand over to the Russians any Polish rebels who crossed the border.

Prussian – and German – liberals, who hated autocratic Russia, protested at Bismarck's action. So, too, did France, Britain and Austria. Bismarck found himself isolated. In an attempt to improve his diplomatic position, he claimed that the convention did not exist because it had never been ratified. This angered the tsar and Prussia was left seemingly friendless.

The Polish rising was finally suppressed in 1864. Prussia emerged from the affair less disastrously than Bismarck expected. Given that the tsar had been deeply offended by Austrian and French criticism, it was likely that Russia would remain neutral in the event of Prussia going to war with Austria or France.

The problem of Schleswig and Holstein

In November 1863 the childless King Frederick VII of Denmark died. Frederick had also ruled the duchies of Schleswig and Holstein that had been under Danish rule for 400 years. The population of Schleswig was mixed Danish and German, while that of Holstein was almost entirely German. Holstein was a member of the German Confederation; Schleswig was not. There had been trouble over the duchies in 1848. Holsteiners had rebelled against Denmark and Prussian troops had marched to their aid in support of the Frankfurt Parliament, until Russian intervention had forced the Prussian army to make peace.

A treaty signed in London by the Great Powers in 1852 had agreed that Frederick would be succeeded as ruler of Denmark and of the duchies by Christian of Glucksburg, heir to the Danish throne through marriage to the king's first cousin. Schleswig and Holstein contested his claim on the grounds that inheritance through the female line was forbidden in the duchies. Schleswig-Holsteiners put forward their own claimant, the Prince of Augustenburg. The Prince, however, did not object to being passed over in the treaty, having been well paid to agree, although he never formally renounced his rights.

When Christian became King of Denmark in November 1863, government officials in Holstein refused to swear allegiance to him, and the son of the Prince of Augustenburg now claimed both duchies on the grounds that his father had not signed away his rights to them. This move was passionately supported by German nationalists. King Christian immediately put himself in the wrong by incorporating Schleswig into Denmark, thereby violating the 1852 Treaty of London. In December 1863 the smaller states of the German Confederation, condemning Christian's action as tyrannical, sent an army into Holstein on behalf of the Duke of Augustenburg, the Prince of Augustenburg's son. The Duke became the most popular figure in Germany, a symbol of German nationalism.

Bismarck's aims

Bismarck was not influenced by German public opinion. However, he did see that the crisis offered splendid opportunities. He hoped to annex the two duchies, strengthening Prussian power in north Germany and winning credit for himself into the bargain. He had no wish to see the Duke of Augustenburg in control of another independent state in north Germany. Nor did he care at all about the rights of the Germans within the duchies. 'It is not a concern of ours', he said privately, 'whether the Germans of Holstein are happy.'

Austrian–Prussian co-operation

Bismarck first won Austrian help. Austrian ministers had very different aims from Bismarck. Austria, while supporting the Augustenburg claim, was suspicious of rampant German nationalism. Anxious to prevent Bismarck from allying Prussia with the forces of nationalism, Austria was happy to pursue what appeared to be the traditional policy of co-operating with Prussia. Bismarck, implying that he too supported Augustenburg, kept secret his own expansionist agenda. Agreeing to an alliance, Austria and Prussia now issued an ultimatum to Denmark threatening to occupy Schleswig unless it withdrew the new constitution within 48 hours. Denmark refused. Thus, in January 1864 a combined Prussian and Austrian army advanced through Holstein and into Schleswig. In April, Prussian troops stormed the Danish fortifications at Duppel in a widely publicised action which won the grudging admiration of most German nationalists.

Denmark agreed that the Schleswig-Holstein matter should be resolved by a European conference. However, the London Conference (April–June 1864) failed to reach agreement. Counting on Britain's support, Denmark refused to make concessions and fighting recommenced. Despite British Prime Minister Palmerston's boast that 'if Denmark had to fight, she would not fight alone', there was little Britain could actually do. Denmark thus had little choice but to surrender in July 1864.

The results of the Danish War

By the Treaty of Vienna in October 1864, the King of Denmark gave up his rights over Schleswig and Holstein, which were to be jointly administered by Austria and Prussia.

As Bismarck probably intended, the question of the long-term fate of the duchies now became a source of severe tension between the two German powers. Public opinion in Germany and the duchies expected that Augustenburg would become duke. However, Bismarck proposed that he be installed only on conditions that would have left him under Prussia's power. This was totally unacceptable to Austria and to the duke, who refused to become a Prussian puppet. Austria turned to the *Bundesrat*. A motion calling for the recognition of the Duke of Augustenburg easily passed. But Prussia ensured that nothing was done. Thus, by the summer of 1865 the future of the duchies was still not settled, and relations between Austria and Prussia had deteriorated. Austria continued to support Augustenburg's claim while Prussia worked for annexation.

The Convention of Gastein

Neither Austria nor Bismarck wanted war at this stage. Austria, almost financially bankrupt, regarded war as too expensive a luxury. Bismarck was aware that William I was reluctant to fight a fellow German state. Nor was he convinced that the Prussian army was yet ready to fight and win. While Bismarck and William I were visiting the fashionable Austrian spa town of Bad Gastein, an Austrian envoy arrived to open negotiations. As a result of this meeting it was agreed in August l865, by the Convention of Gastein, that:

- Holstein (the duchy nearer to Prussia) would be administered by Austria.
- Schleswig would be administered by Prussia.
- The two powers would retain joint sovereignty over both duchies.

Bismarck knew that he could now pick a quarrel with Austria over Holstein at any time he wanted.

Bismarck's motives

Bismarck's motives in dealing with the Schleswig-Holstein affair remain a subject of debate. Had he used the duchies, as he later claimed, as a means of manoeuvring Austria into open confrontation with Prussia? Or did he (whatever he said later) have no clear policy at the time except to 'allow events to ripen'? Historian A.J.P. Taylor thought that he 'may well have hoped to manoeuvre Austria out of the Duchies, perhaps even out of the headship of Germany, by diplomatic strokes … . His diplomacy in this period seems rather calculated to frighten Austria than to prepare for war.'

Whatever his precise aims, there seems little doubt that he exploited the Schleswig-Holstein situation to the full, displaying considerable diplomatic skill.

The meeting at Biarritz

The particular problem of the duchies was solved, albeit it temporarily, but the more general problem of rivalry between Prussia and Austria remained. While Bismarck may not have wanted war at this stage, he realised that it was a distinct possibility. He therefore did all he could to strengthen Prussia's international position. Confident that Britain and Russia would not support Austria, he still feared France.

In October 1865 Bismarck met the French Emperor Napoleon III at Biarritz in the south of France. Historians continue to debate what occurred. Almost certainly nothing specific was agreed, if only because neither man wanted a specific agreement. Bismarck was not prepared to offer German territory in the Rhineland in return for France's neutrality. Napoleon, calculating that a war between the two German powers would be exhausting and inconclusive, intended to remain neutral and then to turn this to advantage by mediating between the two combatants, gaining a much greater reward in the process than anything Bismarck could currently offer. Given Napoleon's anti-Austrian stance, it took little skill on Bismarck's part to secure the emperor's good wishes.

War with Austria

Over the winter of 1865–6 Prussian–Austrian relations worsened. Prussia found every possible excuse to denounce Austria for violating the terms of the Convention of Gastein. Austria, convinced that war was inevitable, determined on a policy of confrontation with Prussia. It did so from a weak position:

- Austria had no allies.
- Austria was on the verge of bankruptcy.
- Holstein was sandwiched between Prussian territory.

In February 1866, at a meeting of the Prussian Crown Council, Bismarck declared that war with Austria was only a matter of time. It would be fought not just to settle the final fate of the duchies, but over the wider issue of who should control Germany. Bismarck carefully laid the groundwork for war. A secret alliance was made with Italy in April 1866, by which Italy agreed to follow Prussia if it declared war on Austria within three months. In return, Italy would acquire Venetia from Austria when the war ended.

Table 3.1 Prussian, German and Austrian population and trade

	Population (millions)		Relative share of world manufacturing output (%)		Key outputs in 1870	
	1840	1870	1830	1860	Coal	Steel
Prussia	14.9	19.4	3.5	4.9	–	–
Germany	32.6	40.8	–	–	23.3	0.13
Austria-Hungary	30 (est.)	34.8	3.2	4.2	6.3	0.02

Table 3.2 Prussian, French and Austrian troop numbers

Year	Prussia	France	Austria
1850	131,000	439,000	434,000
1860	201,000	608,000	306,000
1866	214,000*	458,000	275,000
1870	319,000†	452,000	252,000

Table 3.3 Railways (kilometres in operation) in Prussia, France and Austria

Year	Prussia	France	Austria
1850	5,856‡	2,915	1,579
1860	11,089	9,167	4,543
1870	18,876	15,544	9,589

*In 1866 Italy, Prussia's ally, had an army of 233,000.

†By 1871 the German states under Prussia's leadership could mobilise 850,000 men.

‡The figures are for the territory of the 1871 *Reich*.

Immediately after the treaty with Italy had been signed, Bismarck stoked up tension with Austria over Holstein and over proposals to reform the Confederation. Bismarck knew that these proposals, which included setting up a representative assembly elected by universal male suffrage and expelling Austria from the Confederation, would be unacceptable to Austria. The Austrians, afraid of a surprise attack, were forced to take what appeared to be the aggressive step of mobilising in April 1866. Prussia mobilised in May, seemingly as a response to Austrian threats.

Britain, France and Russia proposed a congress to discuss the situation. Bismarck felt compelled to agree: to do otherwise would put him in a weak position. But he was very relieved when Austria refused, making the congress unworkable. The situation deteriorated further when, in early June, Austria broke off talks with Prussia and, in breach of previous promises, referred the problem of the duchies to the *Bundestag*. Bismarck's response was to send a Prussian army into Austrian-controlled Holstein on 9 June. Austrian troops were permitted to withdraw peacefully.

To Bismarck's surprise and disappointment this did not immediately lead to war. To stir things up, he presented to the *Bundestag* an extended version of his proposals for a reform of the federal constitution:

- Austria was to be excluded from the Confederation.
- There should be a national parliament elected by universal suffrage.
- All troops in north Germany should be under Prussian command.

The next day Austria asked the *Bundestag* to reject Prussia's proposals and to mobilise for war. Censured by the *Bundestag*, the Prussians withdrew from the Confederation, declared it dissolved and invited all the other German states to ally themselves with them against Austria. However, most began mobilising against Prussia.

Bismarck now issued an ultimatum to three northern states, Hanover, Hesse-Cassel and Saxony, to side with Prussia or else to be regarded as enemies. When the ultimatums were rejected, Prussian troops invaded the three states on 15 June. Hesse-Cassel and Saxony offered no resistance; Hanoverian forces were quickly defeated.

The Seven Weeks' War

The future of Bismarck, Prussia and Germany lay with the Prussian army. Since the shambles of 1859 (see page 69), reforms had been successfully carried out and the army was now under the command of **General Moltke**, a gifted military leader. Advance planning and preparation, particularly in the use of railways for moving troops, meant that mobilisation was much more efficient than that of the Austrian army. Moreover, Prussia had a large core of troops who were far better trained, disciplined and equipped than their Austrian counterparts.

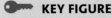

KEY FIGURE

Helmuth von Moltke (1800–91)

Moltke, who rose to the rank of German field marshal, was chief of staff of the Prussian army for 30 years. He planned and led the successful military operations during the Austro-Prussian war of 1866 and the Franco-Prussian War of 1870–1.

Austria's position was far from hopeless:

- It had more soldiers: 400,000 to the Prussians' 300,000.
- Most of the other German states supported Austria.
- Austria had the advantage of a central position.
- Initially many Prussians were lukewarm about the war.
- Prussia's industrial power would make little difference if the war was short.

The Italians fulfilled their part of the secret treaty by following Prussia into the war. This meant that Austria was forced to fight on two fronts, in the north against Prussia and in the south against Italy.

The Italian army, weak and inefficient, was defeated by the Austrians at the Battle of Custoza on 24 June. To prevent the victorious Austrians in the south from linking up with their troops in the north, Moltke determined to invade Bohemia. One single-track railway ran from Vienna to Bohemia. By contrast, Prussia used five lines to bring its troops southwards. Moltke adopted the risky strategy of dividing his forces for faster movement, only concentrating them on the eve of battle. Fortunately for Prussia, the Austrian high command missed several opportunities to annihilate the separate Prussian armies.

The Battle of Sadowa

On 3 July 1866 the major battle of the war was fought at Sadowa (called Königgrätz by the Prussians). Nearly half a million men were involved, with the two sides almost equally balanced. The Austrians were well equipped with

> ? What does Source E appear to be showing? Was the drawing likely to have been produced by the Austrians or the Prussians?

SOURCE E

A contemporary illustration of the Battle of Sadowa 1866.

artillery, and used it effectively at the start of the battle, but they were soon caught in a Prussian pincer movement. The Prussians brought into use their new **breech-loading needle gun**. Its rate of fire was five times greater than anything the Austrians possessed, and it proved decisive. The Austrian army fled in disorder. Austria suffered 45,000 casualties, Prussia 9000. The Prussians had won the battle and with it the war.

The Austrian government recognised that further fighting would almost certainly lead to further defeats and might even result in a break-up of the Austrian Empire. For Austria the priority was a rapid end to the fighting, at any reasonable cost. Prussia was now in a position to dictate terms as the victor. It was a personal victory for Bismarck, and put him in a position to dominate not only Prussia, but also the whole of Germany for the next quarter of a century.

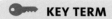

KEY TERM

Breech-loading needle gun This gun, which loaded at the breech rather than the barrel, could fire seven shots a minute. It could also be fired lying down rather than standing up.

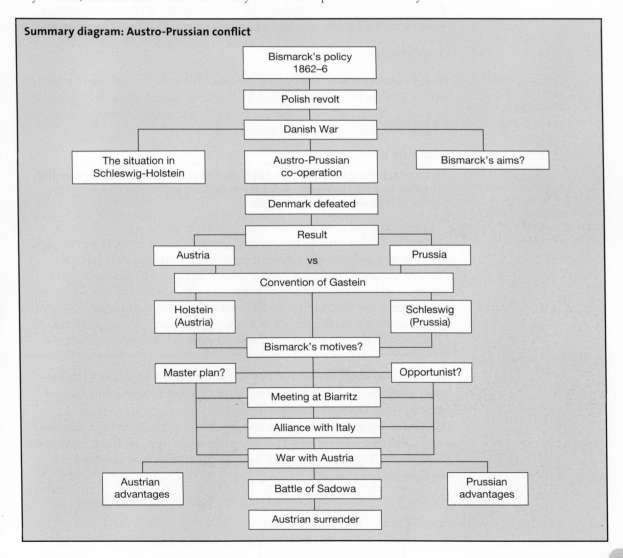

Summary diagram: Austro-Prussian conflict

⑤ Prussian ascendancy

▶ *What were the main results of the Seven Weeks' War?*

Bismarck returned to Berlin with the king and Moltke to a hero's welcome. A grateful Prussia presented him with a reward of £60,000, with which he bought an estate in Pomerania. He was promoted to major general in honour of the victory. It had been noticeable that at meetings of the war cabinet he had been the only one present wearing civilian clothes. Any uniform he was then entitled to would have marked him as an officer of lower rank than anyone else there, and he could not have borne that. Now he was a high-ranking officer he could flaunt his uniform on an equal footing, and he never again appeared in public except in full dress uniform. He had earned his spurs and intended to wear them in a Prussia, and later a Germany, dominated by military power.

The aftermath of victory

Austria was at Prussia's mercy after Sadowa. William I, once reluctant to wage war on a fellow monarch, now proposed an advance on Vienna and a takeover of Austria. Bismarck, fearful that France and Russia might intervene, counselled caution. He wrote to William as described in Source F.

SOURCE F

Bismarck, writing to William I in 1866, quoted in Otto von Bismarck, *Bismarck, the Man and the Statesman: Being the Reflections and Reminiscences of Otto, Prince Von Bismarck*, volume 2, 1899.

We have to avoid wounding Austria too severely; we have to avoid leaving behind in her unnecessary bitterness or feeling or desire for revenge. We ought to keep the possibility of becoming friends again. If Austria were severely injured, she would become the ally of France and of every opponent of ours … German Austria we could neither wholly nor partly make use. The acquisition of provinces like Austrian Silesia and part of Bohemia could not strengthen the Prussian state; it would not lead to an amalgamation of German Austria with Prussia, and Vienna could not be governed by Berlin as a mere dependency.

?• Why, according to Source F, did Bismarck oppose imposing a harsh peace on Austria?

At a noisy and angry meeting of the war cabinet on 23 July, William I and his senior generals raged against Bismarck's policy of not annexing any Austrian territory, while Bismarck threatened suicide if his advice was not taken. In the end Bismarck got his way. The war was brought to a speedy end and a moderate peace concluded with Austria. The only territory lost by Austria as a result of the Seven Weeks' War (Holstein apart) was Venetia in Italy. Austria agreed to pay war reparations to Prussia.

The Treaty of Prague

An armistice was signed between Prussia and Austria in July. This was followed by the Treaty of Prague in August. The terms of the treaty were mainly concerned with the remodelling of northern Germany:

- Prussia annexed a good deal of territory, including Schleswig and Holstein, Hesse-Cassel, Hanover, Nassau and Frankfurt.
- All other German states north of the River Main, including Saxony, were to be formed into a North German Confederation under Prussian leadership (see Figure 3.1 on page 86).

Bismarck opposed pressing for the unification of all Germany in 1866. As well as the threat of French intervention, he feared that if Prussia absorbed too much too soon, this might be more trouble than it was worth. The four Catholic states south of the River Main – Bavaria, Württemberg, Baden and Hesse-Darmstadt – thus retained their independence. Nevertheless, all four states agreed to sign a secret military alliance with Prussia, whereby, in the event of war, they would not only fight alongside Prussia, but also put their armies under the command of the King of Prussia.

The Treaty of Prague is usually seen as a milestone on the way to German unity. Ironically, the destruction of the German Confederation could be seen as dividing rather than uniting Germany. After 1866 Germans were separated into three distinct units:

- the North German Confederation
- the four South German states
- the Austrian Empire.

North Germany

If Bismarck had shown a calculated moderation in his treatment of Austria, he showed little in the way of clemency to some of his fellow north Germans. Hesse-Cassel, Nassau, Hanover, Frankfurt and Schleswig-Holstein were not consulted about uniting with Prussia; they were just annexed. The King of Hanover was driven out and his personal fortune confiscated. (It came in useful to Bismarck later when it was used to bribe the King of Bavaria.)

Those north German states, such as Saxony, not annexed by Prussia were left with some independence within the North German Confederation. Perhaps Bismarck acted in this way in order to show those Germans south of the Main how advantageous membership of a Prussian-controlled federation could be. More likely, he saw no advantage to Prussia in annexing all the north German states. Such action would only lead to a dilution of Prussian culture and traditions. Instead of Prussia absorbing Germany, Germany would end up absorbing Prussia.

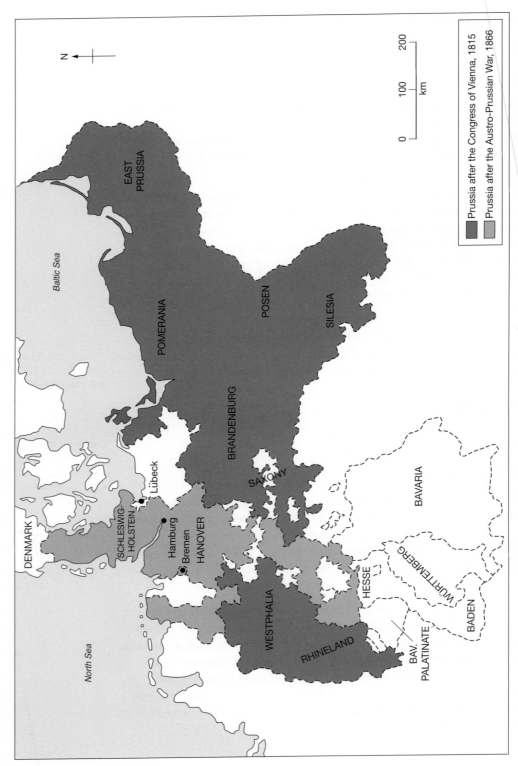

Figure 3.1 Prussia before and after the Austro-Prussian war.

The North German Confederation

At the end of 1866 Bismarck began drafting the constitution for the North German Confederation. This was accepted by April 1867 and came into effect in July. The Confederation lasted only four years, but its constitution was to continue, largely unaltered, as the constitution of the German Empire. It was designed to fit the requirements of Prussian power and Bismarck's own political position.

Bismarck was always opposed to the idea of parliamentary government on the British model, which reduced the crown to symbolic status and put power in the hands of a parliament. His declared view of the political abilities of his fellow Germans was low: 'Considering the political incapacity of the average German, the parliamentary system would lead to conditions such as had prevailed in 1848, that is to say weakness and incompetence at the top and ever new demands from below.'

The Structure of the North German Confederation

- The King of Prussia was president of the North German Confederation and also the commander-in-chief, and had the power of declaring war and making peace. He appointed and could dismiss the federal chancellor.
- The states, including Prussia, had substantial rights, keeping their own rulers and being governed by their own laws and constitutions with their own parliamentary assemblies. They had their own legal and administrative systems, and local taxation met the cost of government services.
- The *Bundesrat* was the upper house of the Confederation's Parliament. Here the various states were represented by delegates who acted on the instructions of their governments. The number of delegates was fixed in relation to the size of the state: out of 43 votes, Prussia had seventeen, Saxony four and most of the others one each. Decisions were made by a simple majority vote.
- The *Reichstag* was the lower house of the Confederacy's Parliament. It was elected by universal male suffrage – a seemingly giant step towards democracy. However, its powers were limited.
- The federal chancellor (the chief minister) was the main driving force in the Confederation. He represented the Prussian king in the *Bundesrat*. He was not responsible to the *Reichstag* nor did he need majority support in it. He was responsible only to the president of the Confederation.
- All laws needed approval of the *Reichstag*, the *Bundesrat* and the King of Prussia as president of the Confederation. They also needed the signature of the chancellor.

Given his views, Bismarck's insistence on universal male suffrage in the election of the *Reichstag* is surprising. However, he believed that the traditional loyalties of peasants would preserve the conservative order in Germany. Nor did Bismarck intend the *Reichstag* to play a significant part in public life, essentially it was little more than an organ of public opinion. Speaking in confidence to a Saxon minister, Bismarck declared that he was trying 'to destroy parliamentarianism by parliamentarianism'. In effect, he hoped that the activities of a weak *Reichstag* would help to discredit parliamentary institutions in German eyes. Certainly, the democratic election process did not compensate for the great weakness of the *Reichstag*, which was that ministers, including the chancellor, were not members of it and were not responsible to it.

Popular support for Bismarck

On the same day as the Battle of Sadowa, elections were held in Prussia. Patriotic war fever resulted in a big increase in the number of conservatives elected to the Prussian Parliament. The numbers jumped from 34 to 142, while the liberal parties were reduced from 253 to 148. Moreover, after Prussia's victory, many liberals changed their attitude to Bismarck. He was now acclaimed rather than maligned. This ensured an era of harmony between Bismarck and the Prussian Parliament. At the beginning of the new session Bismarck spoke of the need for the government to work jointly with Parliament to build a new Germany. He cleverly requested Parliament to grant indemnity for any actions taken by the government during the previous four years without Parliament's consent. Most conservatives were delighted that he made no apology for what he had done. But most liberals saw Bismarck's action as conciliatory and were comforted by the fact that Bismarck had acknowledged that he had long ignored parliamentary rights. Only seven votes were cast against the indemnity bill.

Prussia's military and political triumph left most Germans dazed and confused. German liberals had long loathed Bismarck for trampling on the Prussian constitution. But he had succeeded in creating a united Germany. Moreover, he had begun the war with a call for a national parliament based on universal suffrage. A large section of the old Liberal Party formed itself into the National Liberal Party, pledged to support Bismarck in his nationalist policy, but equally pledged to maintain liberal constitutional principles against any government attempt to undermine them. Progressive Liberals, by contrast, remained deeply suspicious of Bismarck, fearing that a Germany formed under his leadership could never become an acceptable constitutional state.

On the right, the Prussian *Junker* Party opposed Bismarck as a traitor to his class, whittling away at the royal prerogative, supporting constitutionalism and democracy, and losing Prussia's identity in the new unified North Germany. Moderate conservatives formed a new party, the Free Conservatives. They, together with the National Liberals, were to provide the support that Bismarck needed to carry out his policies.

? Look at Source G. To what extent – and why – was Miquel pledging support for Bismarck?

SOURCE G

National Liberal leader Johannes Miquel in 1866, quoted in Andrina Stiles and Alan Farmer, *The Unification of Germany 1815–90*, Hodder & Stoughton, 2001, p. 74.

The time for idealism is over. German unification has descended from the realm of speculation to the prosaic world of reality. Today politicians should be much less concerned than ever before with what is desirable in politics as opposed to what is attainable.

The first *Reichstag*

The first North German *Reichstag* was elected in February 1867. The National Liberals were the largest single party in it and held the balance of power between Bismarck's conservative supporters and his various opponents. They were able to win a number of concessions from Bismarck, now the federal chancellor. These included the right to pass an annual budget. This financial control was very limited because it did not include control over the military budget, which accounted for about 90 per cent of the Confederation's spending. The Liberals and Bismarck struggled over the question of the military budget and eventually reached a compromise. It would remain outside the *Reichstag*'s control for five years, until 1872. Then the amount of money to be spent on the army would be fixed by law and for this the *Reichstag*'s consent would be required. Generally prepared to support Bismarck's policies, the *Reichstag* carried through an ambitious legislative programme including a range of unifying measures.

Bismarck and Germany

The Treaty of Prague brought huge gains to Prussia. Austria was now forced to withdraw from German affairs, leaving the field clear for Prussian influence to dominate. Two-thirds of all Germans, excluding German Austrians, were now part of the Prussian-dominated North German Confederation. Most north Germans (Hanoverians and Saxons apart) quickly accepted the situation. For many liberal-nationalists there were no irreconcilable differences between Bismarck's Prussian policy and *Kleindeutschland* nationalism. Unification was happening, even if it was being carried out by force, and some liberals believed that the end justified the means. Indeed, after 1866, Bismarck found himself under nationalist pressure, north and south, to complete the process of unification. Recognising that union with the southern states would strengthen Prussia against both France and Austria, Bismarck was not averse to the idea and was prepared to use the rhetoric and emotion of German nationalism to help to bring it about.

In 1866 the tide in south Germany in favour of union with the north seemed to be flowing strongly. Political parties were established in the southern states to work for unity. In 1867 the four southern states were incorporated into the new *Zollparlament*: a parliament elected to discuss the policy of the *Zollverein*. This was intended to encourage closer co-operation between north and south. However, by 1867 local loyalties in the south re-emerged. Many southern Catholics regarded Prussia with suspicion. The foreign minister of Baden described the North German Confederation as a 'union of a dog with its fleas'. In 1868 the southern states elected a majority of delegates (49 to 35) to the *Zollparlament* opposed to union with the north. National Liberals, who had hoped that the *Zollparlament* would be the motor for national unification, were bitterly disappointed. Bismarck was not too concerned. He believed that in good time, whether by war or simply as a result of evolution, the southern states would fall like ripe fruit into Prussia's basket.

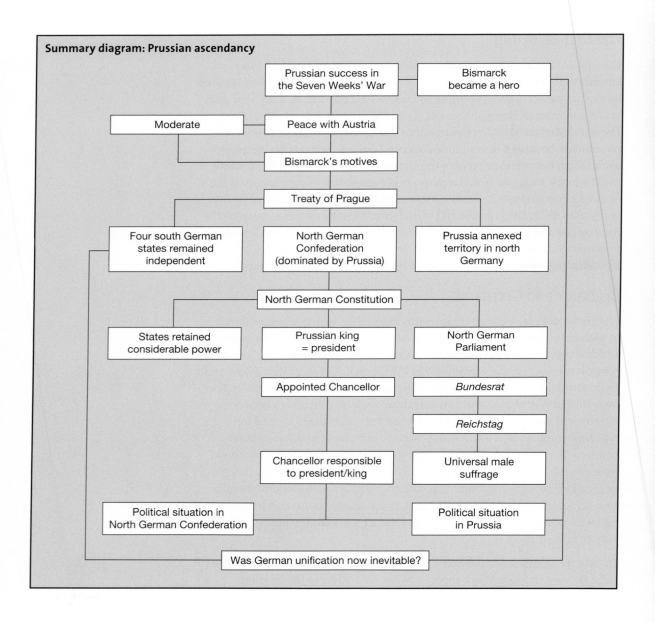

Summary diagram: Prussian ascendancy

6 Factors helping Bismarck

▶ *What factors helped Bismarck to achieve success pre-1870?*

In 1869 Bismarck wrote: 'I am not so arrogant as to assume that the likes of us are able to make history. My task is to keep an eye on the currents of the latter and steer my ship in them as best I can.' He steered brilliantly. Nevertheless, a variety of factors enabled him to bring about German unification.

The Prussian army

German unification was the immediate result of three short wars: against Denmark (1864), Austria (1866) and France (1870–1). The Prussian army thus made Germany a reality. The fighting capacity of the Prussian army improved immensely in the early 1860s thanks to the efforts and ability of War Minister Roon and General Moltke, chief of the general staff. Roon ensured that Prussian forces were increased, better trained and well armed. Moltke was Europe's greatest military genius since Napoleon. Under Moltke, the general staff became the brains of the Prussian army, laying plans for mobilisation and military operations. In particular, Prussian military chiefs were quick to see the potential of railways (for rapid movement of troops) and the telegraph (for controlling dispersed forces).

Prussian economic success

Prussian economic growth in the 1850s and 1860s outstripped that of Austria and France. By the mid-1860s Prussia produced more coal and steel than France or Austria and had a more extensive railway network. In 1865 it possessed 15,000 steam engines with a total horsepower of 800,000. Austria, by contrast, had 3400 steam engines with a total horsepower of 100,000. The economic and financial strength of Prussia gave the military resources it needed to challenge first Austria and then France. A key industrialist was Alfred Krupp, whose iron foundries in the Ruhr produced high-quality armaments.

Economic unity and the *Zollverein*

The continued spread of the railway and the growth of an increasingly complex financial and commercial network helped to draw all parts of Germany into closer economic unity. So did the Prussian-dominated *Zollverein*, which by 1864 included virtually every German state except Austria. However, while the *Zollverein* ensured that Prussia had considerable economic influence in Germany, this was not translated into political domination. Many German states supported Austria politically to counterbalance economic subordination to Prussia. In 1866 most *Zollverein* states allied with Austria against Prussia.

German nationalism

The failure of the 1848 revolution was a serious blow to German nationalism. However, the idea of a unified state persisted in the hearts and minds of liberal-nationalists. In September 1859 the **German National Association** was formed. Stimulated by the success of Italian nationalism, it promoted the idea that Prussia should lead the German cause (as the state of Piedmont had led the cause of North Italian nationalism) and become more liberal in outlook. But gone was the romantic idealism of 1848. Many nationalists now accepted that nothing could be achieved without power. Only Prussia seemed to have that power. At its peak the National Association had only 25,000 members. However,

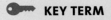

KEY TERM

German National Association (*Deutscher Nationalverein*) A political organisation in the German Confederation from 1859 to 1867. It was formed by moderate democrats who wanted a liberal, parliamentary *Kleindeutsch* Prussian-led national state.

it included many influential men and had close links with a range of other organisations, especially with liberal parties that won growing support in many states, including Prussia, in the early 1860s.

There is no doubt that nationalist sentiment was strong among middle-class Germans who, as a result of industrialisation, were growing in economic and social power. The middle classes tended to lead public opinion. Books and newspapers supported the idea of national unity. Moreover, fears of French expansion were still prevalent. Popular nationalism, strongest in the Protestant north, was a force that could not be ignored by Bismarck. However, there is plenty of evidence to suggest that many Germans had little interest in national unity. There was certainly no massive sentiment in favour of a Prussian-dominated Germany.

The weakness of Austria

Austria was a power in decline after 1848–9:

- The Austrian economy was largely agricultural, with pockets of industry confined largely to the western regions.
- Austria faced the growing problem of minority nationalism (especially in Italy).
- Austria had mounting financial problems.
- The Crimean War weakened Austria's diplomatic position.
- Defeat in the North Italian War (1859) was a serious blow to Austrian prestige.
- Austrian leaders displayed a lack of political and diplomatic skill.

The international situation

The fact that Prussia was regarded as a second-rate power in 1862 helped Bismarck. He was able to achieve supremacy in Germany without arousing the hostility of Prussia's neighbours:

- The prevailing view in Britain was that it had nothing to fear from Protestant Prussia and that a strong Germany would be a useful bulwark against France or Russia.
- Russia, concerned with reform at home, showed little interest in central Europe. Its sympathies lay with Prussia. Russia had still not forgiven Austria for its policy during the Crimean War.

Summary diagram: Factors helping Bismarck

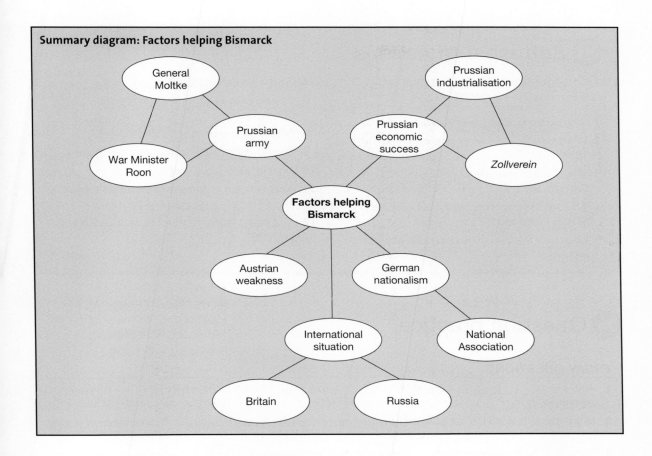

Chapter summary

After 1849 Austria and Prussia jockeyed for position within the German Confederation. While Austria appeared to be Germany's strongest power in the 1850s, Prussia was growing in economic and military strength. Bismarck, appointed minister-president of Prussia in 1862, was determined to expand Prussian power at Austria's expense and was prepared to use 'blood and iron' policies to achieve his aims. A successful war with Denmark (1864) over Schleswig-Holstein helped Bismarck's cause. The results of this war enabled him to pick a quarrel with Austria. Prussia defeated Austria in the Seven Weeks' War (1866). Prussian victory enabled Prussia to take control of north Germany. However, the position of the four south German states – Bavaria, Wurttemburg, Baden and Hesse-Darmstadt – remained to be resolved.

Refresher questions

Use these questions to remind yourself of the key material covered in this chapter.

1 Why did the Prussian Union Plan fail?

2 What were the main developments in Austria after 1848?

3 What were the main developments in Prussia in the years 1850–62?

4 Why was there a constitutional crisis in Prussia between 1860 and 1862?

5 What were the main influences on the young Bismarck?

6 What were Bismarck's aims in 1862?

7 Why did Prussia and Austria go to war with Denmark?

8 What were the results of the Danish War?

9 Why did Austria and Prussia go to war in 1866?

10 Why did the Prussians win?

11 What were the main results of the Seven Weeks' War?

12 What factors helped Bismarck to achieve success pre-1870?

 Question practice

ESSAY QUESTIONS

1 How accurate is it to say that the political consequences of the 1848–9 revolutions in the German states were limited?

2 To what extent was Prussian economic progress responsible for Prussia's political and diplomatic success in the 1860s?

3 'There was no massive sentiment in favour of a Prussian-dominated Germany.' How far do you agree with this statement?

INTERPRETATION QUESTION

1 Evaluate the interpretations in both the passages and explain which you think is a more convincing explanation of the situation as it developed in 1864 with regard to Prussia and Austria.

PASSAGE A

From A.J.P. Taylor, *Bismarck: The Man and the Statesman*, Hamish Hamilton, 1955, p. 73.

The alliance [between Austria and Prussia] signed on 16 January 1864, provided only for joint action against the Danish constitution and that the two allies should settle the fate of the duchies together. The alliance has always been regarded as Bismarck's masterstroke. Certainly it prevented Austria or William I from going over to German liberalism. But in international affairs it increased Bismarck's difficulties rather than lessening them. Even he could not yet appreciate how completely the concert of Europe had been disrupted by the Crimean war. He still went on fearing a united European front against Prussia, when in fact her alliance with Austria was the only thing that offended the three non-German Powers. All three were friendly to Prussia, though for different reasons; all three were hostile to Austria and wanted to see her isolated. Russia favoured Prussian aggrandisement, which she thought would make her more secure; Napoleon favoured the national principle; Great Britain wanted a liberal Germany under Prussia. Prussia's stock went down when she made an alliance with Austria; it mounted again only as it became clear that the alliance would not last. If Prussia had acted alone, she could have acquired the duchies and defeated Austria without the diplomatic alarms of the following years. Bismarck was certainly a political genius. But he often displayed the genius of a pavement-artist who first ties himself up with knots and then brilliantly escapes from them. Nor was the alliance designed as a trap for Austria. There was no reason to suppose that joint control of the duchies would necessarily lead to a quarrel.

PASSAGE B

From M. Kitchen, *A History of Modern Germany 1800–2000*, Blackwell, 2006, p. 108.

Bismarck had no sympathy for the baying hordes of Augustenburgers. He did not want to see a new state formed on Prussia's borders. He was fearful that the powers would intervene as they had done in 1848, and that the Russians and French would patch up their differences. He therefore insisted that Christian IX be recognised as the legitimate King of Denmark and Duke of Schleswig-Holstein, although the duchies should remain united. In taking this position he was denounced by the German nationalists as a vile traitor, but he could afford to ignore their emotional protests. The new Austrian foreign minister, Rechberg, was anxious to cooperate with Prussia and agreed that international treaties had to be respected. Bismarck exploited this situation to the full and dragged Austria into blindly supporting his policy in Schleswig-Holstein … This was truly a bravura piece of diplomatic wizardry. The smaller German states wanted the Confederation to go to war with Denmark, but Austria and Prussia threatened to dissolve the Confederation if their policy was not accepted. The Bundestag agreed by a majority of only one vote to an 'Execution' against Charles IX's illegal annexation of Schleswig which was formally confirmed in the new Danish constitution. Federal troops now marched into Holstein, and in February 1864 Austrian and Prussian forces occupied Schleswig. They were soon in Jutland, and on April 8 Prussian troops stormed the Danish fortifications at Duppel in a dramatic and widely publicised action which won the grudging admiration of many a German nationalist.

SOURCE ANALYSIS QUESTION

1 How far could the historian make use of Sources 1 and 2 together to investigate the reasons for Prussian success against Austria? Explain your answer using both sources, the information given about them and your own knowledge of the historical context.

SOURCE I

From the memoirs of General Helmuth von Moltke, published 1893. Von Moltke was the Chief of the Prussian General Staff from 1857 to 1888. He wrote extensively about the military campaigns that he was involved in and is here recalling the background to the 1866 Austro-Prussian War.

The war of 1866 between Prussia and Austria did not begin because the existence of Prussia was threatened, nor was it caused by public opinion and the voice of the people. It was a struggle long foreseen and calmly prepared for. It was recognised as a necessity by the Cabinet, not for territorial expansion, nor for the extension of our influence, nor for material advantage, but for an ideal end – the establishment of power. Not a foot of land was taken from Austria, but she had to renounce all part in the leadership of Germany. Austria had exhausted her strength in conquests south of the Alps, and left the western German provinces unprotected. Austria's centre of gravity lay out of Germany; Prussia's lay within it. Prussia felt itself called upon and strong enough to assume the leadership of the German races.

SOURCE 2

From Alexander Malet, *The Overthrow of the Germanic Confederation by Prussia in 1866*, published 1870. Malet was a British diplomat who was based in Germany in the years 1849–66. He was a friend of Bismarck.

The principles on which the chief alterations in the army organisation were based are sound and practical, as was abundantly proved in the campaign of 1866.

The superiority of the armament of Prussia's infantry, and the diversion of a large part of the strength of Austria against Italy, placed Prussia in the campaign of 1866, in a position of advantage.

The skill of her commanders was admirably seconded by the courage and endurance of the soldiery. A great social and political revolution was accomplished. The transformation of a whole nation into one vast machine – for such is the Prussian army – is no slight triumph of intelligence, and is worthy of all admiration. It works with perfection.

Much has been said of the Prussian needle-gun. It is the first breech-loading arm with which a European army has yet taken the field, and the advantages of this system have been quite sufficiently shown by the Prussian weapon. The advantages which the new method of loading gives to the troops armed with them over their enemies who are armed only with muzzle-loaders are clear.

CHAPTER 4

Prussia and France 1866–71

In 1870 Emperor Napoleon III declared war on Prussia. The Franco-Prussian War was to have huge results for Prussia, Germany, France and Europe. According to British statesman Benjamin Disraeli, it was 'a greater political event than the French Revolution of last century. The balance of power has been entirely destroyed.' Who or what was responsible for the war? Why did the Prussians win? These and other questions will be addressed by examining the following issues:

★ Franco-Prussian relations 1866–70

★ The road to war

★ The Franco-Prussian War 1870–1

★ The results of the war

Key dates

1867		Luxemburg crisis	**1870**	**Oct.**	Surrender of the French army at Metz
1868–70		Hohenzollern candidature crisis			
1870	**July**	Ems telegram	**1871**	**Jan.**	German Second Empire proclaimed at Versailles
	July	Start of Franco-Prussian War			France accepted an armistice
	Sept.	Napoleon III surrendered at Sedan		**May**	Treaty of Frankfurt

1 Franco-Prussian relations 1866–70

▶ *What was the state of relations between Bismarck and Napoleon pre-1870?*

The international situation in 1866 was far better than Bismarck might have expected:

● Britain welcomed Prussia's dominant position in central Europe, regarding it as a welcome counterweight to both France and Russia.
● Russia was pleased that it had a reliable partner against Austria.

- Austria, absorbed with the problem of dealing with its various subject nationalities, especially the Hungarians, was not in a position to mount a war of revenge.

The only real threat was France, led by Emperor Napoleon III. Bismarck knew that Napoleon and many Frenchmen regarded the establishment of a powerful German state as a threat to French security. 'It was France, not Austria, who was defeated at Sadowa', said French politician Adolphe Thiers in 1869.

Napoleon III

The motives behind Napoleon III's foreign policy are difficult to determine. He seems to have wanted simply to restore France to a position of influence in Europe, through peaceful means if possible. In line with his policy of undoing the decisions reached at Vienna in 1815, he showed great sympathy for nationalist movements in Italy and Poland. This sympathy did not extend to Germany.

Napoleon III had difficulty in making a decision and sticking to it. Unlike his uncle, Napoleon I, he lacked the ruthlessness and the will to carry things through to their logical conclusion. This put him at a marked disadvantage when dealing with a man as devious and determined as Bismarck, who was likely to outplay him at his own game.

Relations between Bismarck and Napoleon III pre-1866

Bismarck and Napoleon had first met in Paris in 1855. The meeting was a successful one on a personal level, and the two men parted on friendly terms. They met again at Biarritz in October 1865 (see page 79). Historians have speculated ever since on what passed between them. (There were no records of their meeting.) Perhaps Bismarck made a deal with Napoleon by agreeing on territorial or other rewards for French neutrality in the event of an Austrian–Prussian war. More likely, he suggested that an opportunity might arise for French expansion, perhaps in the Rhineland, after a Prussian victory over Austria. Almost certainly there was no commitment on either side, but there probably were protestations of goodwill and general support.

The situation in 1866

Napoleon III remained neutral in the Austro-Prussian War. He had hoped to turn his neutrality to good advantage by mediating between the combatants and by threatening to join in the war to persuade them to make peace on his terms, which would include territorial gains for France. The speed and scale of Prussia's victory dashed Napoleon's hopes. When he attempted to mediate after the Battle of Sadowa, the offer was declined by Bismarck, who instead sent the Prussian ambassador in Paris to inform Napoleon that Prussian expansion would be limited to north Germany, and that the south German states would remain independent. The division of Germany was thus presented to Napoleon

Louis Napoleon

1808   Born, son of Louis Bonaparte, King of Holland and brother of Napoleon Bonaparte

After 1815   Lived in south Germany and Switzerland

1836   His attempt to provoke a **Bonapartist** rebellion in Strasbourg ended in farce: he was arrested and forced into exile

1840   After an unsuccessful attempt to raise a rebellion at Boulogne, he was sentenced to life imprisonment

1846   Escaped from prison and fled to Britain

1848   Elected president of the new French Republic, following the overthrow of King Louis-Philippe

1852   Became Emperor Napoleon III

1859   Defeated Austria in northern Italy

1870   Led France into the Franco-Prussian War in July. Forced to surrender at Sedan in September.

1873   Died in exile in England

Many scholars who have written about Napoleon III have been less than flattering. He can be seen as promising much but achieving little. He can be criticised for replacing a democratic republic with an authoritarian regime. Arguably, he sought to overcome chronic domestic political tensions by pursuing an adventurous – and highly risky – foreign policy. Some see the disastrous Franco-Prussian War as the fitting finale to a corrupt, incompetent and unstable regime.

But Napoleon III has his admirers. Arguably, the catastrophe of 1870–1 obscured many of his achievements. He can be seen as a far-sighted and pragmatic leader, keen to reconcile the desire for liberty and democracy with the principle of order. As a champion of the principle of nationality, he had a significant impact on the reshaping of mid-nineteenth-century Europe. It was ironic that the forces of German nationalism destroyed him in 1870.

as a reward for his neutrality. Bismarck had some fears that Napoleon might still march to Austria's assistance.

The threat of German unity

After 1866 Napoleon was concerned by the situation in Germany. Prussia now controlled more than two-thirds of Germany and it was unlikely that the remaining third could or would continue an independent existence indefinitely. After the Treaty of Prague, Bismarck extended the *Zollverein* to include the four south German states and involved them in the new *Zollparlament* (see page 000). Although it was nominally concerned only with economic affairs, it seemed that the *Zollparlament* would be a step towards full German unity.

The south German states

The four south German states – Bavaria, Württemberg, Baden and Hesse-Darmstadt – did not present a united front, for they distrusted each other as much as they distrusted Bismarck. In addition, they distrusted Napoleon – with good reason. They believed – correctly – that he had had designs on part of their territory as his reward for French neutrality during the Seven Weeks' War. In July 1866, the French ambassador in Berlin had presented detailed plans to Bismarck for France to acquire part of the Rhineland belonging to Bavaria and

🔑 **KEY TERM**

Bonapartist Supportive of the Bonaparte family. Although Napoleon Bonaparte had been defeated in 1815, many French people regarded his rule with great nostalgia.

Hesse. This idea was firmly rejected by Bismarck, who did not want to give away any German territory to France. But neither, in mid-1866, did he want to alienate Napoleon. He therefore suggested that France should look for expansion, not in the Rhineland, but further north in the French-speaking areas of Belgium and Luxemburg.

The Luxemburg crisis

Having missed the chance to check Prussia's growth of power in 1866, Napoleon needed a diplomatic and territorial success to prove that France remained Europe's greatest power. Luxemburg seemed to provide an opportunity.

Bismarck's policy on the Luxemburg question is difficult to unravel. He began by helping Napoleon to 'persuade' the King of the Netherlands, who was also Duke of Luxemburg, to relinquish the duchy. The king, short of money and with no real interest in Luxemburg, readily agreed. However, Prussia also had certain rights in Luxemburg, in particular to garrison the fortress. This right dated from the Vienna peace settlement of 1815, which had made the fortress part of the German Confederation.

By the end of 1866 Bismarck no longer felt the need to be friendly towards Napoleon, who was stirring up demonstrations in Luxemburg against Prussia. Partly in response to this and partly to encourage nationalist sentiment, Bismarck began to refer to Luxemburg as German, and announced that its surrender to France would be 'a humiliating injury to German national feelings'. He went on to declare: 'If a nation feels its honour has been violated, it has in fact been violated and appropriate action must ensue. We must in my opinion risk war rather than yield.' Anti-French sentiment increased throughout Germany.

Why did Bismarck encourage this nationalist hysteria? It seems unlikely that he wished to start a war with France at this stage. The Prussian army needed time to recover from the Austrian War and the North German Confederation was still fragile. Perhaps his intention was to start a campaign of provocation to drive Napoleon into war in due course. Perhaps, rather than leading, he was himself partly led by German nationalists whom he knew he could not afford to alienate.

Napoleon vs Bismarck

In March 1867 Bismarck released texts of the secret military alliances he had made with the south German states. These showed that the North German Confederation and the four southern states were not as independent of each other as had been assumed.

Napoleon and Bismarck now met head on in a series of diplomatic battles. Napoleon began new negotiations with the King of the Netherlands, playing on the king's fears that Prussia was after a slice of Dutch territory, and offering to protect the Netherlands in return for Luxemburg. From Napoleon's point of view the king wrecked the scheme by agreeing to sell Luxemburg for 5 million guilders, subject to approval by the King of Prussia. This, he must have known, was not likely to be given. Indeed, Bismarck used the patriotic German fervour he had encouraged as an excuse to threaten the Netherlands' king not to give up Luxemburg. Bismarck now appealed to the Great Powers to settle the Luxemburg question. At a conference in London the following was agreed:

- The Prussian garrison should be withdrawn.
- Luxemburg's independence and neutrality would be guaranteed by the Great Powers.

While the outcome of the London conference seemed like a compromise, the fact that there was no territorial gain for France was a heavy blow for Napoleon.

The results of the Luxemburg crisis

The Luxemburg crisis seriously damaged Franco-German relations. Nevertheless, the years 1867–70 were peaceful. Bismarck was still keen to avert war. Fearful of French military strength, he was also concerned that Napoleon might find allies. Austrian Emperor Franz Joseph, hankering after regaining influence in Germany, twice met Napoleon in 1867 to see whether it was possible to reach agreement. Fortunately for Bismarck, these efforts came to nothing. There was no real basis for agreement. Franz Joseph was aware that most German Austrians opposed a pro-French and anti-Prussian policy.

The Luxemburg crisis has been seen as the point at which Bismarck stopped being a Prussian patriot and became a German one. However, there is no evidence that Bismarck himself thought this. He stirred up and used German national feelings quite cynically as a means to increase Prussian influence over the rest of the German states, as well as a weapon against France.

Bismarck's intentions

In a long interview with a British journalist in 1867, Bismarck presented himself as a man of peace (see Source A). Almost certainly, he wanted to allay British fears about Prussian warlike intentions and to reduce the chance of a British alliance with France. Understanding the value of a good public relations system, he did his utmost to present his policies in a favourable light. This makes it difficult to judge his true intentions from his public utterances. He did not always believe what he said, or say what he believed.

It seems likely that after 1866 Bismarck hoped to unite the south German states with the rest of Germany at some stage in the future. But he seems to have been in no hurry to do so. Nor does he seem to have had a master plan to bring about unification. He knew that he had to move cautiously and not neglect Prussian –

? To what extent does Source A suggest that Bismarck favoured peace with France?

SOURCE A

Bismarck, interviewed by a British journalist, in September 1867, quoted in 'Bismarck's Secret Revealed', *Northern Advocate*, **24 April 1915, p. 3 (http://paperspast.natlib.govt.nz/cgi-bin/paperspast?a=d&d=NA19150424).**

What do I think might bring about war? Of course, an excuse would not be wanting if the French really needed one – but I think the greatest damage of all proceeds from Napoleon's vacillating state of mind … He is not the man he used to be – and Europe will never be safe while his present state of intellect continues … There is nothing in our attitude to annoy or alarm France … there is nothing to prevent the maintenance of peace for 10 or 15 years, by which time the French will have become accustomed to German unity, and will consequently have ceased to care about it.

and also north and south German – opinion. All he could do was wait on events and be ready to seize whatever opportunities came along. But he was also aware that a war with France, which raised national consciousness and brought all Germans together, was likely to speed up the unification process. He knew that such a war was likely to be popular in Germany only if France appeared to be the aggressor.

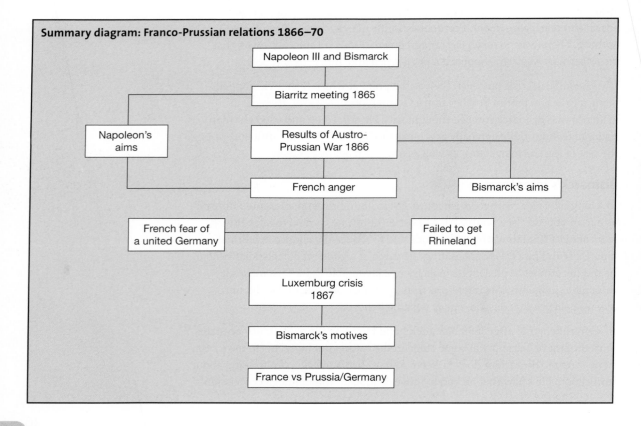

Summary diagram: Franco-Prussian relations 1866–70

The road to war

▶ *Why did France and Prussia go to war in 1870?*

In 1870 Bismarck found opportunities, first in the Hohenzollern candidature issue and then with the Ems telegram, to provoke France and bring about war.

The Hohenzollern candidature

In 1868, the Queen of Spain, Isabella, was driven out of the country by a revolution. The Spanish government made efforts to find a new monarch among the royal houses of Europe. In February 1870 an official offer was made to Prince Leopold of Hohenzollern. Leopold's father referred the request to William I, who as King of Prussia, was head of the Hohenzollern family. William left to himself would have refused consent. He knew that to proceed would provoke French hostility. Napoleon would inevitably see it as a threat to 'encircle' France, with Hohenzollern monarchs in Berlin and Madrid pursuing anti-French policies simultaneously.

William was persuaded to change his mind by Bismarck, who sent him a strongly worded memorandum: 'It is in Germany's political interest that the house of Hohenzollern should gain in esteem and an exalted position in the world.' In the end the king gave his consent, provided that Leopold himself wished to accept the throne. As Leopold did not want to do so, the affair appeared to be at an end. However, Bismarck had secretly sent envoys to Spain, with large sums of money as bribes, to push Leopold's candidacy. He also put pressure on the Hohenzollern family, as a result of which Leopold decided to accept after all. In June, William gave his unconditional consent.

The crisis

Bismarck had planned that the document giving Leopold's acceptance would arrive in Spain and be immediately presented to the **Cortes** for ratification. The news of the ratification would then be announced, amid general rejoicing. However, the message, relayed in code through the Prussian embassy in Madrid, suffered an unforeseen mix-up of dates due to a cipher clerk's error. As a result the *Cortes* was not in session when the document arrived and before it could be recalled the secret of Leopold's acceptance leaked out.

The news reached Paris on 3 July 1870. As anticipated, Napoleon and his new aggressive Foreign Minister Antoine Gramont regarded Leopold's candidature as totally unacceptable. Moreover, Gramont hoped to strengthen Napoleon's position at home by a resounding victory, diplomatically or otherwise, over Prussia. An angry telegram was sent to Berlin asking whether the Prussian government had known of Leopold's candidacy and declaring that 'the interests and honour of France are now in peril'. Count Benedetti, the French ambassador

 KEY TERM

Cortes The Spanish Parliament.

in Berlin, was instructed to go to the spa town at Ems, where William I was 'taking the waters', to put the French case that Leopold's candidacy was a danger to France and to the European balance of power, and to advise William to stop Leopold leaving for Spain if he wanted to avoid war.

William, who had no wish for war, assured the ambassador of Prussia's friendship for France, and on 12 July Leopold's father withdrew his son's candidacy. The affair appeared to have been settled, with the diplomatic honours going to France. Bismarck, in Berlin, spoke of humiliation and threatened resignation. He was saved from having to make good his threat by Gramont and Napoleon.

Goaded by Gramont (who was disappointed that Prussia had backed down), the French emperor overplayed his hand. Leopold's renunciation had been announced in a telegram from his father to the Spanish government. France now demanded an official renunciation from William I, on behalf of Leopold, for all time, and the French ambassador was ordered to see the king again and obtain his personal assurance. They met on 13 July. William found this deeply insulting and refused to give the assurances demanded since he had already given his word. Even so, his reply was conciliatory. As a matter of course he instructed one of his aides to notify Bismarck, in Berlin, of the day's events in a telegram. He also gave Bismarck permission to communicate details to the press.

The Ems telegram

That evening, in Berlin, Bismarck, dining with Generals Moltke and Roon, received the telegram from Ems. Having read it, Bismarck, 'in the presence of my two guests, reduced the telegram by striking out words, but without adding or altering anything'. The shortening of the text had the effect of making the king's message to the French ambassador appear to be an uncompromising response

SOURCE B

From Bismarck's *Memoirs*, written in the 1890s, quoted in J.H. Robinson, editor, *Readings in European History: A Collection of Extracts from the Sources*, Ginn & Co., 1906, pp. 589–90.

After I had read out the concentrated edition to my two guests, Moltke remarked: 'Now it has a different ring; in its original form it sounded like a parley; now it is like a flourish in answer to a challenge.' I went on to explain: 'If, in execution of his Majesty's order, I at once communicate this text ... not only to the newspapers, but also by telegraph to all our embassies, it will be known in Paris before midnight, and ... will have the effect of a red rag upon the Gallic [French] bull.' Fight we must if we do not want to act the part of the vanquished without a battle. Success, however, depends essentially upon the impression which the origination of the war makes upon us and others; it is important that we should be the ones attacked ... .

to the French demand to renounce support for the Hohenzollern candidature for all time. As well as giving the French the impression that King William had insulted Count Benedetti, the changes to the telegram were designed to give Prussians/Germans the impression that Benedetti had insulted William. It succeeded in both its aims.

Bismarck ensured that his amended text of the Ems telegram was published in newspapers in Berlin. Prussian embassies received copies of the text by telegraph with instructions to communicate the contents to foreign governments. When William saw the published version he is said to have remarked with a shudder, 'This is war'.

Historians once believed that Bismarck's alteration of the Ems telegram provoked France into declaring war. However, recently scholars have claimed that the French government was already committed to war before the Ems telegram was published.

The outbreak of war

As Bismarck had anticipated, the publication of the amended Ems telegram did cause eruptions in France. French newspapers, convinced that French honour was at stake, demanded war. Napoleon, urged on by his wife, his ministers, the chamber of deputies and public opinion, declared war on Prussia on 19 July.

It seems likely that Bismarck had been prepared to fight a war against France since 1866, as long as it could appear to be a defensive war, brought about by French aggression. Such a war would almost certainly bring the south German states into the Prussian fold. All that he needed was a suitable opportunity. This occurred with the Hohenzollern candidature crisis, and Bismarck took full advantage of it. However, there is little evidence that he was set on war from 1866 or even that he prepared for it in 1870. He certainly did not control the whole Hohenzollern affair. Nor was it simply opportunism on his part that led to war. Equally important was a series of French diplomatic blunders. Moreover, the French emperor and people in 1870 were ready to fight before the Ems telegram was published. If Bismarck set a trap for France, it was largely one of France's own making.

Bismarck, claiming that France was the aggressor who had 'committed a grievous sin against humanity', called on the south German states to support Prussia in accordance with the terms of their 1866 military alliances. All agreed to do so.

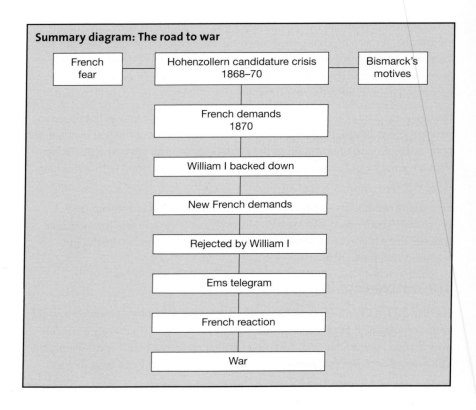

Summary diagram: The road to war

French fear — Hohenzollern candidature crisis 1868–70 — Bismarck's motives

French demands 1870

William I backed down

New French demands

Rejected by William I

Ems telegram

French reaction

War

The Franco-Prussian War 1870–1

▶ *Why did Prussia defeat France?*

Historians are not in agreement about what to call the war. Should it be Franco-Prussian (the usually accepted name) or Franco-German? In different ways it was both. The war was so dominated by Prussian expertise that, in many ways, it was little more than an extended Prussian military enterprise. Bismarck and General Moltke organised the German war effort and Prussian troops outnumbered all other troops in the army. Nevertheless, the war was also the first genuinely German war, in which all the German states fought. At the beginning some support, particularly in the south German states, was less than enthusiastic. But by the end of the war this had changed. All Germans were proud of, and wished to be associated with, Germany's triumph. Moreover, by 1871 all Germany was united by a blind hatred of France and all things French. This was brought about by government propaganda, not least by Bismarck's speeches, letters and newspaper articles.

The diplomatic situation in 1870

- While some Austrians longed for vengeance against Prussia, the Hungarian government was vigorously opposed to war.
- Russia had promised to fight alongside Prussia if Austria joined France: this was enough to keep Austria neutral.
- Denmark toyed with the idea of supporting France in the hope of recovering Schleswig but in the end did nothing.
- Italy made such outrageous demands on France as the price of support, that Napoleon would not accept them.
- Long mistrustful of Napoleon's ambitions, Britain was unwilling to come to France's assistance, particularly after Bismarck made it appear as if the French emperor was about to invade Belgium in defiance of the longstanding British guarantee of Belgian independence. He did this by publishing in *The Times* draft documents given to him by the French ambassador in 1867, when they were discussing possible 'compensation' for French neutrality during the Seven Weeks' War. Bismarck appears to have kept these documents carefully for use in just such circumstances as arose in July 1870.

Early German success

Most Europeans expected a French victory:

- France's population was 38 million, that of Germany 32 million.
- The French army had been successful in both the Crimean War (1854–6) and the North Italian War (1859).

However, the Prussian army, with troops from the other German states, was quickly mobilised. Mobilisation had been well planned, and some 470,000 troops had been moved by train to the borders of Alsace (see Figure 4.1 on page 108) by the beginning of August. Six German railway lines ran to the French–German frontier: France had only two. The German soldiers were under the command of the brilliant General Moltke. French mobilisation was slower and not complete by the time Napoleon III arrived at Metz to take supreme command at the end of July. The French army was less than 300,000 strong and it had no plan of campaign.

Moltke's grand strategy was initially bungled by the mistakes of his field commanders. French troops, armed with the ***chassepot* rifle** and with elementary machine guns (the *mitrailleuses*), fought well. However, the firepower of Germany's Krupp breech-loading artillery proved decisive and German forces were victorious at Spicheren (5 August) and Worth (6 August).

Metz

Traumatised by defeat, Napoleon and his chief commander Marshall Bazaine went on the defensive, withdrawing 180,000 men into the fortress of Metz. On 14 August, German armies crossed the Moselle river at several points and

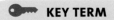

KEY TERM

***Chassepot* rifle** A breech-loading rifle, named after the man who invented it.

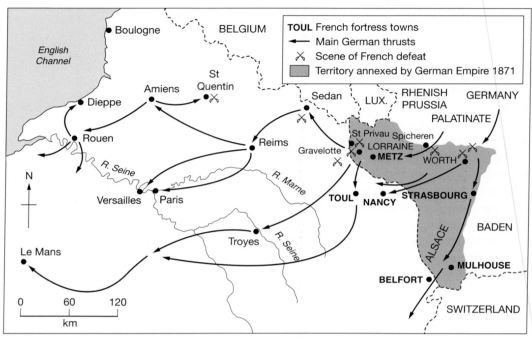

Figure 4.1 The Franco-Prussian War.

advanced beyond Metz to cut off the French escape route to Paris. Two days later the French army in Metz attempted to escape northwards but was defeated, first at Mars la Tour (16 August) and then at Gravelotte (18 August), and forced to retreat back into the fortress. This meant that the bulk of Napoleon's finest troops were out of action.

Sedan

Napoleon had left Metz when the fighting began, and reached the Marne River where a new French army was hurriedly collected under the command of General MacMahon. MacMahon set off with 130,000 men to rescue the Metz army. German troops intercepted MacMahon's forces at Beaumont (30 August) and drove them back towards Sedan, near the Belgian border. The French army was then encircled by the Germans.

On 1 September, the most important battle of the war began, watched from a hilltop by William I, Moltke, Bismarck and a selection of German princes. French efforts to break out of Sedan failed. Blasted by German artillery, which had a longer range and a higher rate of fire, they suffered nearly 40,000 casualties. Prussian losses were 9000. That night Bismarck, Moltke and MacMahon met to discuss surrender terms. Napoleon agreed to these terms on 2 September.

SOURCE C

A letter from Bismarck to his wife, written on 3 September 1870, quoted in C.D. Warner, editor, *Library of the World's Best Literature: Ancient and Modern*, Connoisseur Edition, 1896 (www.gutenberg.org/files/13520/13520-8txt).

Yesterday morning at five o'clock, after I had been negotiating until one o'clock A.M. with Moltke and the French generals about the capitulation [surrender] to be concluded, I was awakened by General Reille, with whom I am acquainted, to tell me that Napoleon wished to speak with me. Unwashed and unbreakfasted, I rode towards Sedan, found the Emperor in an open carriage, with three aides-de-camp and three in attendance on horseback, halted on the road before Sedan. I dismounted, saluted him just as politely as at the Tuileries [Palace in Paris] … We then sent one of the [officers] to reconnoitre, and discovered two and one-half miles off, in Fresnois, a small château situated in a park. Thither I accompanied him with an escort … and there we concluded with the French general-in-chief, Wimpffen, the capitulation by virtue of which forty to sixty thousand Frenchmen, – I do not know it accurately at present, – with all they possess, became our prisoners. Yesterday and the day before cost France one hundred thousand men and an Emperor. … It is an event of great weight in the world's history … .

Why might Source C be useful for historians? ?

Under the terms of surrender, the Germans took prisoner 84,000 men, 2700 officers, 39 generals and one emperor. Later additions brought the total number of prisoners to over 104,000. Napoleon remained a prisoner until 1872 before going into exile in England. When news of the defeat and the emperor's capture reached Paris on 4 September, Napoleon was deposed by a revolutionary government. The Second Empire was abolished and the Third French Republic was proclaimed in its place.

The end of the war

The war should have finished at this point. There were few French troops available to continue the fighting; most of them either had surrendered at Sedan or were still besieged in Metz. The new French Government of National Defence wanted peace but was not prepared to surrender an inch of its territory. Bismarck was not prepared to accept this: he made it clear he intended to annex the provinces of Alsace and Lorraine. Thus, the war continued. By 20 September German forces had completed the encirclement of Paris. Bazaine's army of 140,000 men in Metz surrendered in October. German forces comprehensively defeated several newly raised French armies sent to relieve France's capital. By January 1871 Parisians, desperately short of food, were also subject to bombardment by German guns. On 28 January 1871 the French government finally agreed to accept an armistice.

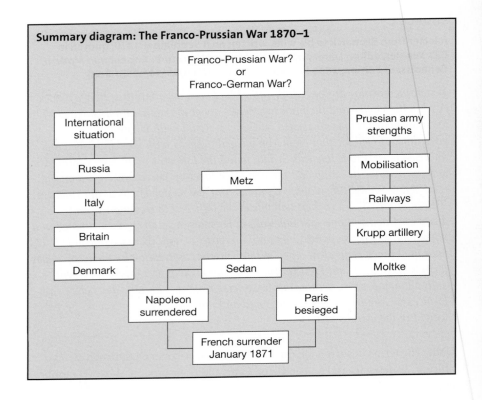

Summary diagram: The Franco-Prussian War 1870–1

The results of the war

► *What were the main results of the Franco-Prussian War?*

From the start of the war Bismarck was determined that King William I of Prussia should become Emperor of Germany. This proved no easy matter. The four south German states had to accept him. Moreover, William himself was reluctant to accept a 'German' title, which would take precedence over his Prussian one. He was also determined that the offer of the imperial crown should come from the German princes, not from the people, as in 1849 (see page 46).

The south German states

Bismarck was helped by the fact that the successful war against France created a tidal wave of German patriotism. Germans – north and south, Protestant and Catholic, rich and poor – supported the war and revelled in German–Prussian success. Popular pressure in the southern states for turning the wartime alliance into a permanent union grew. This strengthened Bismarck's negotiating hand with the south German rulers. Seeking to preserve Prussian influence at the same time as creating a united Germany, he was determined that the new *Reich* would have a constitution similar to that of the North German Confederation (see page 87). South German rulers, by contrast, wanted a looser system in which they retained more rights.

Bismarck had to use all his diplomatic skill to get his way. His trump card was the threat to call on the German people to remove those rulers who stood in the way of unity. He also made some symbolic concessions, most of which meant little in practice. (Bavaria, for example, was allowed to retain its own peacetime army and a separate postal service.) King Ludwig II of Bavaria, who was particularly reluctant to co-operate, was finally won over by a secret bribe. Bismarck, using money confiscated from the King of Hanover in 1866 (see page 85), agreed to pay Ludwig a huge pension to pay off his debts.

In November 1870, separate treaties were signed with each of the four southern states by which they agreed to join the German Empire. The new *Reich* was to be a **federal** state: constituent states retained their monarchies and had extensive power over internal matters. But real power was to rest in the hands of the emperor, his army officers and his handpicked ministers, of whom Bismarck, the new imperial chancellor, would be chief.

The German Empire

Ludwig II, well rewarded by Bismarck for his pains, agreed to put his name to a letter asking William to accept the title of emperor. The other princes were then persuaded to add their names, and the document was sent to William.

SOURCE D

William proclaimed emperor in the Hall of Mirrors at Versailles. Anton von Werner's famous painting was completed in 1885.

 **KEY TERM**

Federal A government in which several states, while independent in domestic affairs, combine together under a central authority.

Is Source D likely to be an accurate depiction of the event?

The appeal was seconded in December 1870, by a deputation to William from the North German *Reichstag*.

On 18 January 1871 King William I of Prussia was proclaimed Kaiser, or German emperor, not in Berlin, but in the French palace of Versailles just outside Paris (see Source D). There was some difficulty about William's precise title. He had set his heart on 'Kaiser of Germany', but as part of a deal made with Ludwig II, Bismarck had agreed that the title should be 'German Kaiser'. The situation was saved by the Grand Duke of Baden, who neatly got round the problem by shouting out 'Long live his Imperial and Royal Majesty, Kaiser William'. William, gravely displeased, pointedly ignored Bismarck as the royal party left the platform. Bismarck, given his overall success, could afford to disregard William's displeasure.

The fact that William had been proclaimed German emperor at Versailles was a bitter pill for the French to swallow, and added to the humiliation of the surrender which came ten days later.

The Treaty of Frankfurt

The peace treaty between France and Germany was signed at Frankfurt in May 1871:

- German troops were to remain in northern and eastern France until a heavy fine of £200 million had been paid. The indemnity was the equivalent of that imposed on Prussia in 1807 by Napoleon Bonaparte (see page 5).
- Alsace and the eastern half of Lorraine were annexed to Germany.

These harsh terms caused consternation in France and were to lead to long-lasting enmity between France and Germany. 'What we have gained by arms in half a year, we must protect by arms for half a century', said Moltke. Why did Bismarck impose such a humiliating treaty on France, so different from the one which ended the war with Austria?

- Alsace was largely German-speaking and so were many people in Lorraine. Strasbourg had been an imperial city in the days of the Holy Roman Empire.
- Although Alsace and Lorraine were rich in iron ore, Bismarck's interest in them was not essentially economic.
- There were good strategic reasons for taking both provinces. Bismarck believed that the French defeat, irrespective of the peace terms, turned France into an irreconcilable enemy. He thus wished to ensure that France was so weakened that it could pose no future threat to Germany. The fortresses of Metz and Strasbourg were crucial. Metz, in Moltke's view, was worth the equivalent of an army of 120,000 men.
- During the war, the German press had portrayed France as the guilty party. Most Germans thus believed it needed to be punished. One way of doing this was to annex Alsace and Lorraine.

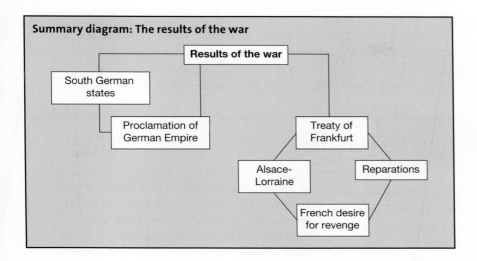

Summary diagram: The results of the war

Results of the war

South German states

Proclamation of German Empire

Treaty of Frankfurt

Alsace-Lorraine

Reparations

French desire for revenge

5 Conclusion

▶ *How skilful was Bismarck in the period 1862–71?*

Bismarck was the chief architect of the German Empire. In his memoirs, written in the 1890s, he depicted himself as a statesman who foresaw events and brilliantly achieved his goals. He left readers in no doubt that he was a veritable superman, working from the start of his political career for German unification. Some historians credit him with having a long-term strategy to wage war on Austria and France in order to create a united Germany under Prussian control.

Other historians are not convinced. A.J.P. Taylor, for example, claimed that Bismarck was merely an opportunist, cleverly exploiting his enemies' mistakes and taking calculated risks which happened to be successful. Bismarck himself said: 'one must always have two irons in the fire'. He often had many more than two. In consequence, it is difficult to disentangle with any certainty his motives or the extent to which he planned ahead. Most historians think it unlikely that an unskilled statesman could have had so much luck. Nor is it likely that a skilled statesman had no plans. The consensus is that Bismarck, at the very least, had an outline view of what he wished to achieve from 1862. However, it is likely that he did not plan in any sense of mapping out a specific set of moves. He sought instead to reach his usually limited and clearly defined goals by taking advantage of situations which he had either helped to create or that simply presented themselves to him. The exact means of achieving his aims were left to short-term decisions based on the situation at the time.

It is possible to argue that Bismarck did not make Germany; rather, Germany made Bismarck. A variety of factors – German nationalism, Prussian economic growth, the international situation, the Prussian army – were such that Bismarck was able to gain the credit for bringing about a unification which may well have developed naturally, whoever had been in power. However, whatever view is taken about the 'inevitability' of German unification, it is clear that it happened as it did and when it did largely as a result of Bismarck's actions. Perhaps his main skill as a diplomat lay in his ability to isolate his enemy.

Chapter summary

Relations between Bismarck and French Emperor Napoleon III deteriorated after 1866. Napoleon, threatened by the growth of Prussian power, was further alienated by Bismarck's actions. French overreaction to the Hohenzollern candidature crisis and the Ems telegram led to the outbreak of the Franco-Prussian (or Franco-German) War in July 1870. France, diplomatically isolated, proved no military match for Prussia/Germany. French forces were quickly defeated and Napoleon III was forced to abdicate. War dragged on for a few more months but the new French government surrendered in January 1871. France was forced to pay a heavy indemnity and to surrender Alsace-Lorraine. The south German states, which had fought alongside Prussia, agreed to join a new German Empire. This was proclaimed at Versailles in January 1871.

Refresher questions

Use these questions to remind yourself of the key material covered in this chapter.

1 What had been the state of relations between Bismarck and Napoleon pre-1866?

2 Why did Franco-Prussian relations deteriorate after 1866?

3 Did Bismarck plan war against France from 1866?

4 How did Bismarck use the Hohenzollern candidature issue?

5 Did the Ems telegram cause war?

6 Why was Bismarck in a strong diplomatic position in 1870?

7 Why did Prussia win the war?

8 What were the main results of the war?

9 Was Bismarck right to impose a harsh treaty on France?

10 How skilful was Bismarck in 1870–1?

Question practice

ESSAY QUESTIONS

1 How accurate is it to say that Bismarck's political skills were primarily responsible for the success of German unification in the years 1862–71?

2 'The Prussian army, rather than Bismarck's diplomatic skills, brought about German unification.' How far do you agree with this statement?

3 How far was Bismarck's diplomacy responsible for the unification of Germany in the years 1862–71?

INTERPRETATION QUESTION

1 Evaluate the interpretations in both of the two passages and explain which you think is a more convincing explanation of Bismarck's actions prior to the Franco-Prussian War.

PASSAGE A

From A.J.P. Taylor, *Bismarck: The Man and the Statesman,* **Hamish Hamilton, 1955, pp. 121–2.**

Bismarck had neither planned the war nor even foreseen it. But he claimed it as his own once it became inevitable. He wished to present himself as the creator of Germany, not as a man who had been mastered by events. Moreover, attention had to be diverted from his carelessness in giving France an opportunity to humiliate Prussia and from his discreditable manoeuvres to shift the responsibility from this on to the king. Therefore, against all the previous statements, the war with France had to appear necessary and inevitable, long-planned by the master-statesman. Bucher, his closest associate, was soon calling Leopold's candidature 'a trap for France'; and Bismarck himself claimed to have provoked the war by the Ems telegram. Probably he came to believe his own story and spoke in all sincerity on 30 July 1892 when he declared: 'We could not have set up the German Reich in the middle of Europe without having defeated France … the war with France was a necessary conclusion.' Yet Germany had no reason for a war against France; and its gains proved a perpetual embarrassment. In truth, the French blundered into a war which was not unwelcome to them; and Bismarck, though taken by surprise, turned their blunder to his advantage.

PASSAGE B

From M. Kitchen, *A History of Modern Germany,* **Blackwell, 2006, pp. 115–17.**

For Bismarck, 1866 had only brought a temporary solution to the German problem. Having once conjured up the support of liberal nationalists, nothing short of the creation of a nation-state would suffice to integrate them in a monarchical and conservative system dominated by Prussia. Bismarck had no idea how or when this national policy could be realised, and he was secure enough to wait upon events. He was ready to seize any opportunity to secure this ultimate goal. Above all he was determined to maintain firm control and not allow liberal nationalists or public opinion undue influence. His was a revolutionary policy designed to overthrow the power-political balance of Europe, but it was to be a revolution from above that could not be allowed to slip out of his hands … .

The gridlock over German unification was broken by events outside its borders. In 1868 the Spanish army deposed the absolutist queen and sought to establish a constitutional monarchy. The French supported a Bourbon candidate, but the military preferred the German Prince Leopold of Hohenzollern-Sigmaringen, the south German and Catholic branch of the Prussian ruling house. At first Bismarck paid little attention to the Hohenzollern candidature but by the winter of 1869, when it was clear that the Spanish were anxious to go ahead, he lent it his full support … Bismarck hoped to gain support in the south for his German policy by backing the prince and to mobilise German national sentiment by confronting France.

SOURCE ANALYSIS QUESTIONS

1 Why is Source 1 valuable to the historian for an enquiry about the causes of the Franco-Prussian War? Explain your answer using the source, the information given about it and your own knowledge of the historical context.

2 How much weight do you give the evidence of Source 2 for an enquiry into the outbreak of the Franco-Prussian War? Explain your answer using the source, the information given about it and your own knowledge of the historical context.

3 How far could the historian make use of Sources 1 and 2 together to investigate the reasons for the start of the Franco-Prussian War? Explain your answer using both sources, the information given about them and your own knowledge of the historical context.

SOURCE 1

A telegraph message sent by a secretary of King William I from Ems to Bismarck on 13 July 1870, quoted in Otto von Bismarck, *Bismarck, the Man and the Statesman: Being the Reflections and Reminiscences of Otto, Prince Von Bismarck*, volume 2, 1899.

His Majesty writes to me: 'Count Benedetti [the French ambassador] spoke to me on the promenade to demand from me, finally in a very importune manner, that I should authorise him to telegraph at once that I am bound myself for all future time never again to give my consent if the Hohenzollerns should renew their candidature. I refused at last somewhat sternly, as it is neither right nor proper to undertake engagements of this kind for all time. I told him that I had as yet received no news, and as he was earlier informed from Paris and Madrid than myself, he could see clearly that my government had no more interest in the matter'. His Majesty has since received a letter from Prince Charles Anthony [Leopold's father]. His Majesty, having told Count Benedetti that he is awaiting news from the Prince, has decided not to receive Count Benedetti again, but only to let him be informed through an aide-de-camp: 'That his Majesty has now received from the Prince confirmation of the news which Benedetti has already received from Paris, and had nothing further to say to the ambassador'. His Majesty leaves it to your Excellency to decide whether Benedetti's fresh demand and its rejection should be at once communicated to our ambassadors, to foreign nations and to the press'.

SOURCE 2

From Otto von Bismarck, *Bismarck, the Man and the Statesman: Being the Reflections and Reminiscences of Otto, Prince Von Bismarck*, volume 2, 1899.

In view of the attitude of France, our national sense of honour compelled us, in my view, to go to war: and if we did not act according to the demands of this feeling, we should lose the entire impetus towards our national development won in 1866 … Under this conviction I made use of the royal authorisation to publish the contents of the telegram: and in the presence of my two guests reduced the telegram by striking out words, but without adding or altering, to the following form: 'After the news of the renunciation of the Hereditary Prince of Hohenzollern has been officially communicated to the Imperial government of France by the Royal Government of Spain, the French ambassador further demanded of His Majesty the King, at Ems, that he would authorise him to telegraph to Paris that His Majesty the King bound himself for all time never again to give his consent, should the Hohenzollerns renew their candidacy. His Majesty the King, thereupon decided not to receive the French ambassador again, and sent the aide-de-camp on duty to tell him that His Majesty had nothing further to communicate to the ambassador.

CHAPTER 5

Bismarck's Germany 1871–90

Otto von Bismarck dominated Germany for the two decades after 1870. His prestige as the creator of the new Empire was enormous. What were Bismarck's aims after 1871 in both domestic and foreign policies and how successful was he in achieving them? To what extent was he 'the Iron Chancellor' – a man who was determined and ruthless in pursuit of his goals? This chapter will examine these questions through the following themes:

★ The German Empire in 1871

★ Bismarck's domestic policy 1871–90

★ Bismarck's foreign policy 1871–90

★ Bismarck's fall

The key debate on *page 151* of this chapter asks the question: How successful was Bismarck from 1871 to 1890?

Key dates

1871		German Empire proclaimed	1882		Triple Alliance
1872–3		May Laws	1883		Sickness Insurance Act
1873		Three Emperors' League	1884		Accident Insurance Act
1878	June–July	Congress of Berlin	1887		Reinsurance Treaty between Germany and Russia
	Oct.	Anti-Socialist Law passed	1888		Death of William I
1879	July	German Tariff Act			William II became Kaiser
	Oct.	Dual Alliance between Germany and Austria-Hungary	1889		Old-age pensions introduced
1881		Three Emperors' Alliance	1890		Kaiser Wilhelm II dismissed Bismarck

The German Empire in 1871

► *Who held control in the* Reich?

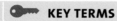 **KEY TERMS**

Second German Empire
The first empire was the Holy
Roman Empire, established
by Charlemagne. The
second empire was the one
established by Bismarck.

Reichstag The National
Parliament, elected by all
males over 25 years of age.

Bundesrat The Federal
Council, comprising 58
members nominated by state
assemblies. Its consent was
required in the passing of
new laws.

The **Second German Empire** was proclaimed on 18 January 1871 in the palace of Versailles. King William I of Prussia became the new German Emperor (Kaiser) with Bismarck as his imperial chancellor. What was the new German Empire like?

The German Constitution

The constitution of the empire incorporated the main provisions of the constitution of the North German Confederation, drawn up by Bismarck in 1867 (see page 87):

- Germany was to be a federal state.
- Powers and functions were divided between the central government and 25 state governments (see Figure 5.1 on page 119).
- While no longer sovereign or free to secede, the states preserved their own constitutions, rulers, parliaments and administrative systems.

The German political system defies classification. Historians have variously described it as a military monarchy, a Prussian autocracy, a semi-autocracy or a constitutional monarchy. The complex system can be seen (positively) as creating a delicate equilibrium with the key institutions keeping each other in check. It can also be seen (negatively) as creating major tensions, not least between monarchical and parliamentary claims to power, and between federal and state power.

Prussia had huge influence:

- As German emperor, the Prussian king was head of the imperial executive and civil service and supreme warlord of the *Reich*'s armed forces.
- Prussia possessed 60 per cent of Germany's population and two-thirds of its territory. Prussia returned 235 deputies out of a total of 397 in the ***Reichstag***. The fact that it had seventeen seats in the ***Bundesrat*** meant it could block any unwelcome constitutional amendments.
- Except from 1872 to 1873 and from 1892 to 1896, the imperial chancellor was always simultaneously prime minister of Prussia.
- Prussian and imperial institutions were so intertwined that they could hardly be distinguished. The Prussian minister of war was also the imperial minister of war. Imperial secretaries of state worked closely with Prussian ministers.
- Prussia, with its house of peers and a parliament elected by a three-class system, was dominated by the aristocracy, the rich, the military and a conservative civil service. This hindered the development of parliamentary democracy in Germany as a whole.
- Not surprisingly, Prussia's aristocracy enjoyed a dominant position in the political, military and administrative structure of the Empire.

Emperor

- Always the King of Prussia
- Could appoint and dismiss the Chancellor
- Could dissolve the *Reichstag*
- Controlled foreign policy
- Could make treaties and alliances
- Commanded the army
- Could declare war and make peace
- Supervised the execution of all federal laws
- Possessed the right to interpret the constitution

Chancellor

- Chief Minister of the *Reich*
- Not responsible to *Reichstag*, only to the Emperor
- Decided upon *Reich* policy outlines
- Chaired sessions of the *Bundesrat*
- Could 'hire and fire' state secretaries responsible for the various government ministries
- Could ignore resolutions passed by the *Reichstag*
- Office was normally combined with the Minister-Presidency of Prussia

Federal
Centralised government with specific responsibilities for the *Reich* as a whole, e.g. foreign affairs, defence, civil and criminal law, customs, railways, postal service

Reich **government**

State
Regional government with specific responsibilities for individual states, e.g. education, transport, direct taxation, police, local justice, health

Bundesrat

- The Federal Council
- Comprised 58 members nominated by state assemblies
- Consent was required in the passing of new laws
- Theoretically able to change the constitution
- A vote of 14 against a proposal constituted a veto
- Prussia had 17 of the 58 seats
- Bavaria had six seats and the smaller states one each
- In theory, it had extensive powers. In practice, it usually rubber stamped the Chancellor's policies

Reichstag

- The national parliament
- Elected by all males over 25 years of age
- Could accept or reject legislation, but its power to initiate new laws was negligible
- State secretaries were excluded from membership of the *Reichstag* and not responsible to it
- Members were not paid
- Could approve or reject the budget
- Elected every 5 years (unless dissolved)

Figure 5.1 The German constitution.

For all the complaints about a 'Prussianisation' of Germany, the identity of 'old Prussia' was significantly diluted by its integration into the *Reich*. Prussia could no longer be governed without consideration of the wider interests of Germany. Prussian influence was slowly undermined by the need to make concessions to the states. Non-Prussians soon held important posts in government both in the *Reich* as a whole and in Prussia.

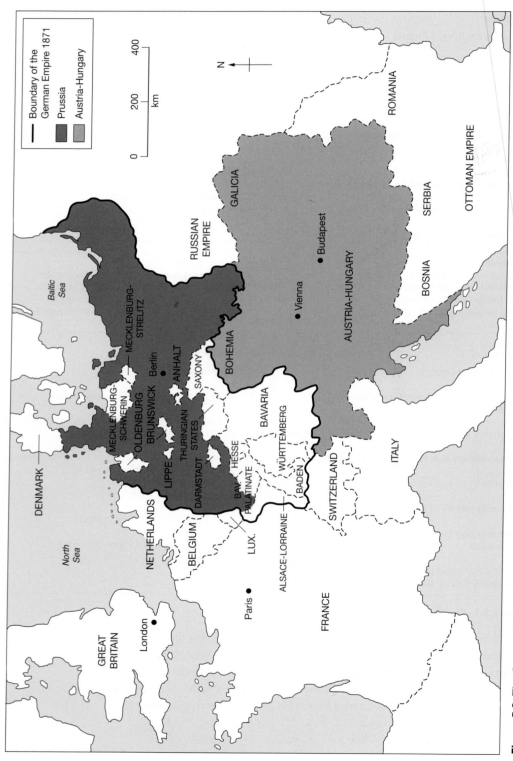

Figure 5.2 The German Empire in 1871.

Bismarck as imperial chancellor

After 1871 Bismarck was Prussian prime minister and foreign minister and imperial chancellor. As such, he exercised most of the powers ascribed to the crown in the constitution. His influence over William I gave him an immensely strong position, which he exploited.

Loathing the existence of any rival authority, Bismarck ensured that other ministers were little more than senior clerks, carrying out his orders. There was nothing that resembled an imperial cabinet. Bismarck dominated the secretaries of state and made sure that they did not confer with the kaiser without his permission. His mistrust of potential rivals encouraged him to rely increasingly on his son Herbert, who was secretary of state of the foreign office from 1886.

While Bismarck exerted a tight grip over all aspects of policy, foreign and domestic, in the *Reich* and in Prussia, there were practical and theoretical limitations to his power, especially in domestic affairs:

- The fact that Germany was a federal state reduced his influence.
- The *Reichstag* was a major constraint (see below).
- Bismarck's long absences from Berlin (he liked to spend time on his country estates) and his poor health (often stomach troubles arising from overeating and excessive drinking) reduced his control of day-to-day decision-making.

Many contemporaries viewed Bismarck with awe: a legend in his own lifetime. Recent historians have often been less impressed. They have represented him as more a lucky opportunist than a master-planner. They have also drawn attention to his less desirable attributes: his vindictiveness, his intolerance of criticism and his frequent use of bullying to get his way. It should be said that these methods did not always succeed. After 1871 he was persistently thwarted in his efforts to shape the domestic developments of the *Reich*.

The weakness of the *Reichstag*

Bismarck was anxious for political power in Germany to remain in traditional hands – in those of the emperor, his army officers, his ministers – and particularly in his own. Arguably, the constitution gave little opportunity for the exercise of democracy. The *Reichstag*, for example, could censor the chancellor but not secure his dismissal. It could itself be dismissed at any time and new elections called. Bismarck regarded the *Reichstag* with some disdain: a collection of squabbling politicians who did not reflect popular opinion.

Characteristically, Bismarck was ready to work with the *Reichstag* only on condition that it adopted his proposals or some compromise acceptable to him. If agreement could not be reached, he usually dissolved the *Reichstag* and called for fresh elections. He was prepared to use all the means at his disposal, not least the exploitation of international crises, to swing public opinion in elections to secure the passage of contentious legislation.

Reichstag politicians have often been criticised by historians for failing to do more to exploit their potential power. However, they faced a difficult task. The balance of power was tilted sharply in favour of the monarchy and most Germans remained deeply respectful of authority, believing that it was right and proper that the emperor, or his chancellor, should rule. There was no widespread conviction that power should be in the hands of the political party which happened to have a majority of seats in the *Reichstag*.

Even members of left-wing parties did not expect the *Reichstag* to exercise much control over government. The most that they hoped for was that it would have some influence on government decisions.

The (potential) strength of the *Reichstag*

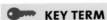

KEY TERM

Fig-leaf of despotism
Something intended to cover the fact that Germany was ruled by an authoritarian government.

Socialist leader August Bebel claimed that the *Reichstag* was the '**fig-leaf of despotism**'. However, in reality, the *Reichstag* had more power than Bebel suggested and Bismarck had envisaged:

- The Second German Empire needed a vast number of new laws and no bill could become a law until it passed the *Reichstag*. The government also needed more money, which only the *Reichstag* could provide. Bismarck, therefore, was forced to negotiate deals and grant concessions.
- The *Reichstag* was an open forum of debate whose members enjoyed parliamentary immunity. Debates were widely reported in the press. The chancellor and the ministers of state could be questioned and embarrassed.
- For many Germans, the *Reichstag* – not the kaiser – was the focus of national attention.
- No parliament in the world in the 1870s was elected on a broader franchise.
- Universal male suffrage promoted the development of mass political parties with popular appeal (see Table 5.2 on page 126). While these parties were in no position to form governments, Bismarck could not afford to ignore them. Although under no constitutional obligation to adopt policies approved by the *Reichstag*, he did need to secure support for his own legislative proposals.
- What is striking is how troublesome the *Reichstag* was for Bismarck, criticising and often thwarting his plans. Indeed, historians may have overemphasised the way that the *Reichstag* bowed to Bismarck and not emphasised enough the way that he bowed to *Reichstag* pressure. On several occasions in the 1880s he explored the possibility of changing the constitution – proof of the *Reichstag*'s influence.

The *Reichstag* was thus neither an all-powerful parliament nor simply a pliant instrument under Bismarck's control. It was something in between. It certainly acquired a genuine popular legitimacy and became a focal point for those whom Bismarck saw as 'enemies of the state': Poles, Catholics and socialists.

The role of the army

The army played an important role in the *Reich*, as it had done in Prussia. It was essentially Prussian. The Prussian army was by far the largest of the four armies that comprised the German armies. The three other contingents, from Bavaria, Saxony and Württemberg, all came under the emperor's command in time of war and followed the Prussian lead in organisation, instruction and weaponry.

Prussian-German officers owed personal loyalty to the king/emperor, not the state. The system of conscription ensured that all German men served for two to three years in the army. This gave officers ample opportunity to build on the values already inculcated at school: discipline, pride in military institutions and love of the fatherland.

As the creator of the *Reich*, the army had a special place in the minds of most Germans. After 1871 it was taken for granted that the army's needs must always come first and that the highest virtues were military ones. Uniforms encouraged respect and obedience, and both Bismarck (see page 84) and the kaiser always wore military uniform in public.

Given that the military budget was not subject to annual approval, the army was virtually independent of *Reichstag* control. It was not bound to consult any civilian authority before acting. Many army officers were hard-line conservatives. They had little time for the *Reichstag* and even less for liberals and socialists. Indeed, some army officers were as much concerned with the 'enemy' within as they were with Germany's enemies beyond the *Reich's* borders. If called upon, they were ready to disperse demonstrations, break strikes and crush any attempt at revolution.

German disunity

The new *Reich* was far from united:

- Each state had its own traditions. Each also had powers over education, justice, agriculture, religious matters and local government.
- Over 60 per cent of the population were Protestant, but Catholicism was strong in Alsace-Lorraine, in southwest Germany, in the Rhineland and among the Poles.
- Ten per cent of the *Reich's* population were non-German minorities.
- There were economic and social divisions: between rich and poor, and between the industrialising north and west and the predominantly rural south and east.

Thus, a major problem was how to unite Germany in fact as well as in theory. Pre-1871 nationalism had been generally seen as a progressive force which aimed to sweep away the old regime and introduce liberal and representative government. After 1871 German nationalism became more conservative. The German nation was now identified with the new *Reich*, any criticism of which was denounced as unpatriotic. A distinct national identity developed that transcended that of the member states. Arguably, non-Prussian Germans became more Prussian while Prussians became more German.

German economic development

The results of the war against France stimulated the German economy. Alsace-Lorraine, for example, contained Europe's largest deposits of iron ore and production increased rapidly after 1871. The injection of the French indemnity payments into the German economy (see page 112) helped to cause a spectacular, if short-lived, boom. The boom assisted German banks, which, in turn, provided capital for new railways and new industries such as electricity and chemicals. Between 1871 and 1890 coal production soared, steel production increased by some 700 per cent and the railway network doubled.

Table 5.1 Germany in 1870 and 1890 compared to Britain and France

	Germany		Britain		France	
	1870	1890	1870	1890	1870	1890
Population (millions)	41	49	32	38	36	38
Coal (millions of tonnes)	38	89	118	184	13	26
Steel (millions of tonnes)	0.3	2.2	0.6	3.6	0.08	0.6
Iron ore (millions of tonnes)	2.9	8.0	14	14	2.6	3.5

Growing industry swelled the ranks of the German industrial working class. In 1871 only five per cent of Germans lived in urban areas. By 1900 nearly twenty per cent did so. This had political as well as economic consequences. Many of the proletariat were attracted to socialism. The peasantry, declining in numbers, tended to be more conservative.

German society

German society, despite all the economic changes, remained divided along traditional class lines. What mobility there was tended to be within a class rather than movements between different classes. The higher levels of the civil service and the army remained predominantly the preserve of the nobility. The most direct threat to the nobility's supremacy came from wealthy industrialists who tried to emulate, rather than supersede, the nobles.

While the middle classes were expanding, most Germans were agricultural or industrial workers. For many farm labourers life was hard and industrial employment seemed an attractive option. Thus, there was a drift to the cities, even though the living and working conditions of the proletariat remained poor.

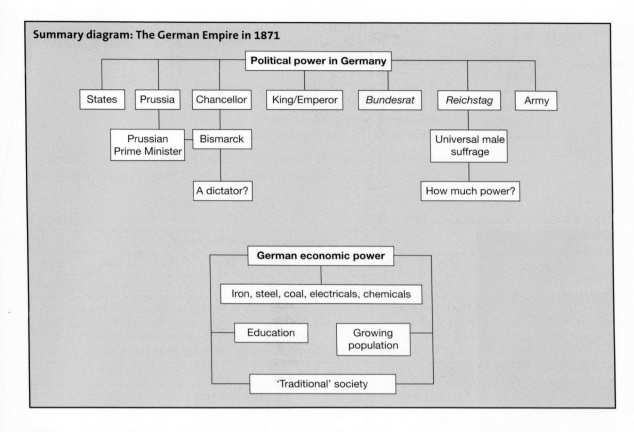

Summary diagram: The German Empire in 1871

Bismarck's domestic policy 1871–90

▶ *How effectively did Bismarck handle domestic matters from 1871 to 1890?*

Bismarck dominated most aspects of German policy – foreign and domestic – from 1871 to 1890. In foreign policy he acted alone. German diplomacy was very much a one-man affair, even if at times he had to fight tooth and nail with William I in order to get his way. But in domestic affairs, Bismarck took advice, listened to suggestions and seized on the ideas of others.

The liberal era 1871–9

After 1871, Bismarck, who claimed to stand above party or sectional interest, needed a parliamentary majority. Although he was by no means a true liberal, he had little alternative but to work with the National Liberals, who were the strongest party in the *Reichstag* for most of the 1870s (see Table 5.2 on page 126). In some respects the National Liberals were ideal allies. Most of them applauded

Bismarck's success in creating a united Germany and were eager to help him consolidate national unity. In the early 1870s a great deal of useful legislation was passed:

- A national system of currency was introduced.
- A **Reichsbank** was created.
- All internal tariffs were abolished.
- There was much legal standardisation.

The National Liberals and Bismarck also united against the Catholic Church. Nevertheless, relations between Bismarck and the National Liberals were always

Table 5.2 Germany's political parties 1871–90

Party	Number of seats in *Reichstag*							
	1871	1874	1877	1878	1881	1884	1887	1890
The National Liberals	125	155	128	99	47	51	99	42
The main support for this party came from the Protestant middle class. The party had two principal aims: (a) the creation of a strong nation-state and (b) the encouragement of a liberal constitutional state; the former in practice being the priority. Until 1878 the National Liberals were Bismarck's most reliable *Reichstag* allies.								
The Centre Party	58	91	93	94	100	99	98	106
This party defended the interests of the Catholic Church.								
The Social Democratic Party (SPD)	2	9	12	9	12	24	11	35
Having close links with the trade unions, this was predominantly a working-class party. It fought for social reforms.								
The German Conservative Party	57	22	40	59	50	78	80	73
This party was mainly composed of Prussian landowners. Sceptical about the unification of Germany, it came to support Bismarck after 1878.								
The Free Conservatives	37	33	38	57	28	28	41	20
Drawn from a wider geographical and social base than the German Conservatives, the party contained not just landowners, but also industrialists and professional and commercial interests. It offered Bismarck steady support.								
The Progressives	47	50	52	39	115	74	32	76
A liberal party but one which, unlike the National Liberals, remained opposed to Bismarck's pursuit of a powerful nation-state at the expense of liberal constitutional principles.								
National Groups	14	30	30	30	35	32	29	27
Reichstag members representing Alsatians, Poles and Danes.								
Guelphs	9	4	10	4	10	11	4	11
Hanoverians who were supporters of the deposed King George.								

uneasy. Politically, Bismarck did not agree with their hopes for the extension of parliamentary government. He became increasingly irritated as they opposed a number of his proposals.

The army budget

The army budget was a particular bone of contention. In 1867 Bismarck and the National Liberals agreed that the military budget should remain at a fixed level outside *Reichstag* control until 1872. During the Franco-Prussian War the fixed budget was extended until 1874. In 1874, Bismarck presented a law proposing that an army of over 400,000 men should be automatically financed by federal expenditure.

Given that 80 per cent of all federal expenditure was on the army, this threatened seriously to reduce the *Reichstag*'s monetary powers. The measure – the 'Eternal Law' – was thus opposed by the National Liberals. Accusing them of trying to undermine German military strength, Bismarck threatened to call new elections. The National Liberals shrank from a constitutional conflict similar to that which had brought Bismarck to power in 1862 (see pages 70–1). A compromise was eventually reached. The military budget was fixed for seven years at a time, rather than voted for annually or fixed permanently.

The *Kulturkampf*

Much of the 1870s was dominated by Bismarck's clash with the Catholic Church: the **Kulturkampf**. There were a number of reasons for this clash:

- Two-thirds of Germans, mainly those in Prussia and the north, were Protestant. One-third were Catholic.
- In the late nineteenth century the Catholic Church and the state came into conflict in several countries. In 1864 Pope Pius IX's *Syllabus of Errors* had condemned as erroneous every major principle for which liberals stood. In 1870 the Vatican Council laid down the doctrine of papal infallibility. This ruled that papal pronouncements on matters of faith and morals could not be questioned.
- These papal measures aroused great alarm in liberal circles. Many of Germany's most enlightened men believed – amazingly – that the future of mankind was at stake. It seemed certain that militant Catholicism would interfere in the *Reich*'s domestic affairs and support reactionary causes. The National Liberals, in particular, were determined to do battle with the Catholic Church in what they saw as a life and death struggle for freedom and progress against the forces of backwardness.

The Centre Party

German Catholics formed their own party, the Centre Party, in north Germany in 1870 to defend their interests. After the creation of the empire, it joined forces with south Germans, Poles and the people of Alsace-Lorraine, becoming the second largest party in the *Reichstag* in 1871. It was unique among German

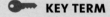

KEY TERM

Kulturkampf A struggle for culture or a struggle for civilisation. In Germany, the struggle was between the state and the Catholic Church.

parties in drawing its support from all social strata. It favoured greater self-rule for the component states of the *Reich*. It also objected to state interference in the Church's traditional sphere of influence: the education system.

Bismarck and Catholicism

Bismarck, a sincere Protestant, viewed the Catholic minority with suspicion. His greatest concern in domestic policy was to unify and consolidate the new *Reich*. Suspicious of those who opposed his creation, he saw plots and subversive activities everywhere. Many of the national minorities – the French in the west and the Poles in the east – who had no wish to be within the *Reich* were Catholic. So were Germans in the southern states, many of whom still tended to identify with Austria rather than with Prussia. So too were the Rhinelanders, some of whom still resented being 'Prussian' (despite being part of Prussia since 1815).

Bismarck saw the success of the Centre Party in 1871 as a grave danger to the empire's unity. He thought that Centre politicians would encourage **civil disobedience** among Catholics whenever the policies of the state conflicted with those of the Church. His suspicions deepened when he observed how rapidly the party became a rallying point for opponents of the empire.

Whether he really believed that the anti-Prussian political alignment in the *Reichstag* was a papal-inspired conspiracy of malcontents bent on destroying the *Reich* is debatable. But the *Kulturkampf* was widely understood at the time to be a war against internal opponents of unification.

It may be that the *Kulturkampf* was also a calculated political ploy on Bismarck's part: to put himself at the head of a popular, Protestant crusade. It certainly enabled him to work closely with the National Liberals in the 1870s.

The 'Old Catholics'

Some 5000 Catholics, known as 'Old Catholics', refused to accept the decree on papal infallibility and broke with the Church. When Old Catholic teachers and professors were dismissed by Catholic bishops, Bismarck had an excellent excuse to attack the Catholic Church. Maintaining that the Prussian government was committed to the principle of religious toleration, he condemned the Catholic Church's actions in a series of newspaper articles in 1872. This marked the start of the *Kulturkampf*.

Actions against the Catholic Church

While the *Kulturkampf* was centred on Prussia and directed against the Catholics of the Rhineland and Poland, its effects were felt throughout the *Reich*, and legislation against the Church was passed by Prussia, by other state governments and by the *Reichstag*.

KEY TERM

Civil disobedience Refusal to obey state laws and regulation.

In 1872 Catholic schools were brought directly under the supervision of the state. In 1872 the *Reichstag* forbade the **Jesuit order**, whose members had always been supporters of papal authority, to set up establishments in Germany and empowered state governments to expel individual Jesuits. In May 1873, Dr Adalbert Falk, the Prussian minister of religion and education, introduced a package of measures known as the May Laws. These aimed to bring the Catholic Church under state control:

- All candidates for the priesthood now had to attend a **secular** university before commencing training.
- All religious appointments became subject to state approval.
- In 1874 obligatory civil marriage was introduced in Prussia.

In 1875, the *Kulturkampf* reached a climax:

- Laws empowered Prussia to suspend subsidies to the Church in parishes where the clergy resisted the new legislation.
- All religious orders, except nursing orders, were dissolved.

Clergy could be fined, imprisoned and expelled if they failed to comply with the legislation, which was vigorously enforced in Prussia by Falk. By 1876 all but two of the twelve Prussian Catholic bishops were in exile or under house arrest and more than 1000 priests had been suspended from their posts.

The results of the *Kulturkampf*

The results of the *Kulturkampf* were not what Bismarck had hoped. Attempts to repress Catholicism met with considerable opposition. Pope Pius IX counterattacked, threatening to excommunicate those who obeyed the oppressive laws. Only 30 out of 10,000 Prussian Catholic priests submitted to the new legislation. Catholic communities sheltered defiant priests and fiercely maintained their religious culture and identity.

Bismarck's hope of destroying the Centre Party backfired: the *Kulturkampf* strengthened rather than weakened his political opponents. In 1871 the Centre won 58 seats; in 1874 it won 91 seats. Bismarck's hope of leading a popular Protestant crusade also failed to materialise. Protestants opposed some of the *Kulturkampf* legislation because it limited the influence of the Protestant – as well as the Catholic – Church in education. Many on the left disliked the violation of fundamental civil rights, not least freedom of conscience.

The end of the *Kulturkampf*

By 1878 Bismarck accepted that the *Kulturkampf* had failed:

- He had underestimated the enemy: the Catholic Church had more popular support than he had expected.
- By opening up a rift between the *Reich* and its Catholic subjects, the *Kulturkampf* had increased disunity, not removed it.

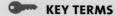

KEY TERMS

Jesuit order A Catholic order of militant priests founded in 1534 by Ignatius Loyola.

Secular Non-religious and non-spiritual: civil, not ecclesiastical.

Anxious to have the Centre Party on his side against a potentially worse enemy – socialism – Bismarck was ready to cut his losses and end the *Kulturkampf*. His opportunity came with the death of Pope Pius IX in 1878. His successor Leo XIII was conciliatory and direct negotiations led to improved relations between Bismarck and the Church. Falk was dismissed in 1879 and some of the anti-Catholic measures were repealed: exiled clergy, for example, were allowed to return. However, the Catholic Church did not win a complete victory. Many of the May Laws remained in force; for example, civil marriage remained compulsory, Jesuits were forbidden to enter Germany and the state continued to oversee all permanent Church appointments.

Bismarck withdrew from a dangerous battlefield. Typically, he sought to turn failure to advantage, by henceforward harnessing Catholic political power in the *Reichstag* to the support of conservative, protectionist and anti-socialist measures.

Economic protectionism

In the early 1870s Bismarck left economic matters in the hands of Rudolf von Delbrück, a capable administrator who continued the free-trade policies of the *Zollverein* (see pages 20–1). Support for free trade was an essential principle of most National Liberals. In 1879, however, Bismarck ditched both free trade and the National Liberals. Aligning himself with the Conservative and Centre parties, he supported the introduction of tariffs to protect German industry and farming. What were his motives?

Economic and financial factors

There were strong economic and financial reasons for introducing protective tariffs. In the late 1870s German agriculture suffered from the effects of a series of bad harvests and from the importation of cheap wheat from the USA and Russia. As the price of wheat fell, German farmers suffered. As a landowner himself, Bismarck understood the dangers of a prolonged agrarian depression. He also feared that if Germany was reliant on foreign grain, it would be seriously weakened in time of war. Protectionism would aid German self-sufficiency.

A slow-down in industrial growth after 1873 helped to produce a crisis of confidence in free trade. Industrialists and workers looked to the government to protect their interests and alleviate their distress. The adoption of protective tariffs by France, Russia and Austria in the late 1870s seemed to make it all the more desirable to follow suit.

Another consideration influencing Bismarck was the fact that the federal government's revenue, raised from customs duties and indirect taxation, was proving woefully inadequate to cover the growing costs of armaments and administration. In order to make up the deficit, supplementary payments were made by individual states, a situation that Bismarck found distasteful. He hoped that new tariffs would give the federal government a valuable extra source of income, ensuring that it was financially independent of both the states and the *Reichstag*.

Political factors

Bismarck realised there were political advantages in abandoning free trade. By the late 1870s landowners and industrialists were clamouring for protective tariffs. By espousing protectionist policies, Bismarck could win influential support.

Although he had worked with the National Liberals, he had never been particularly friendly with them. Their insistence on parliamentary rights and refusal to pass anti-socialist legislation irritated him. Moreover, in the 1878 elections, the National Liberals lost some 30 seats. The combined strength of the two Conservative parties was now sufficient to outvote them in the *Reichstag*. In pursuing the protectionist case, popular with the Conservatives, Bismarck saw his chance to break with the National Liberals and broaden his political support.

The 1879 Tariff Act

By 1879 protectionists, made up mostly of Conservatives and Centre Party members, had a majority in the *Reichstag*. Bismarck now introduced a general tariff bill.

SOURCE A

Part of Bismarck's address to the *Reichstag* in May 1879, quoted in Andrina Stiles and Alan Farmer, *The Unification of Germany 1815–90*, Hodder & Stoughton, 2001, p. 111.

The only country [which persists in a policy of free trade] is England, and that will not last long. France and America have departed completely from this line; Austria instead of lowering her tariffs has made them higher; Russia has done the same … . Therefore to be alone the dupe of an honourable conviction cannot be expected from Germany for ever … . Since we have become swamped by the surplus production of foreign nations, our prices have been depressed; and the development of our industries and our entire economic position has suffered in consequence. Let us finally close our doors and erect some barriers … in order to reserve for German industries at least the home market, which because of German good nature, has been exploited by foreigners.

Study Source A. What arguments did Bismarck use in support of the Tariff Act?

In July 1879 a tariff bill passed through the *Reichstag* and duties were imposed on imports. The political results were far-reaching. Bismarck had now firmly committed himself to the Conservative camp. The National Liberal party splintered. Those who still believed in free trade and parliamentary government broke away, eventually uniting with the Progressives to form a new radical party in 1884. Other National Liberals remained loyal to Bismarck but he was no longer dependent on their backing. In that sense, the 'liberal era' was effectively at an end.

Historians continue to debate the economic effects of the abandonment of free trade. Arguably, protective tariffs consolidated the work of unification by drawing north and south Germany closer together and accelerated the growth of a large internal market. Protection might have meant higher bread prices, but this did not mean that workers had lower living standards. Tariffs did serve to protect German jobs.

The Centre Party and the National Liberals determined to frustrate Bismarck's attempt to make the government less dependent on the states and *Reichstag*. A Centre Party deputy, Count George von Frankenstein, put forward a scheme whereby all revenues coming to the federal government in excess of 130 million marks were to be divided up among the states, and would then be returned as part of the state payments. As a result of the 'Frankenstein Clause' the budgetary rights of the *Reichstag* and the state parliaments were preserved. Bismarck thus failed to secure the financial independence he sought.

Bismarck and socialism

In 1875 moderate and revolutionary socialists united to form the Social Democratic Party (or SPD). The party's declared aim was the overthrow of the existing order. But it also declared that it would use only legal means in the struggle for economic and political freedom. The new party called for **nationalisation** of banks, coalmines and industry, and for social equality.

The socialist threat

Bismarck was hostile to socialists, regarding them as dangerous revolutionaries. Rather than underestimating the enemy, as with the *Kulturkampf*, it may be that he overestimated the socialist threat. Socialists were not as strong or as revolutionary as he feared and they liked to appear. However, Bismarck's fears were rational. Socialism was a threat to the kind of society he intended to maintain. Socialists did preach class warfare and did talk of the dictatorship of the proletariat. Moreover, as Germany became more industrialised, swelling the ranks of the proletariat, socialist support increased. In 1877 the SPD won nearly 500,000 votes, giving them twelve seats in the *Reichstag*.

Assassination attempts

In 1876 Bismarck tried to pass a bill preventing the publication of socialist propaganda. It was defeated. Other measures to prosecute the SPD also failed to get through the *Reichstag*. In May 1878 an **anarchist** tried to assassinate Emperor William I. The would-be assassin had no proven association with the SPD, but Bismarck, like many of his contemporaries, drew no clear distinction between anarchism and socialism and saw the murder attempt as part of a 'red' conspiracy. However, his efforts to push through a bill against socialism were defeated by National Liberal members, concerned about civil liberties.

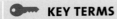

KEY TERMS

Nationalisation
Government ownership.

Anarchist A person whose ideal society is one without government of any kind. Late nineteenth-century anarchists often sought to bring about such a condition by terrorism.

A week later there was a second attempt on William's life that resulted in the emperor being seriously wounded. Again the failed assassin had no direct SPD link. But Bismarck criticised the National Liberals for failing to pass the anti-socialist bill that might have protected the emperor. Scenting political advantage, he dissolved the *Reichstag*.

Bismarck's manoeuvre succeeded. The electorate, deeply shocked by the murder attempts, blamed the SPD and the National Liberals. The SPD vote fell from 493,000 in 1877 to 312,000 while the National Liberals lost 130,000 votes and 29 seats.

Bismarck's actions against socialism

Bismarck now got his way in the new *Reichstag*. An anti-socialist bill, supported by Conservatives and most National Liberals, was passed in October 1878. The following restrictions were imposed:

- Socialist organisations, including trade unions, were banned.
- Socialist meetings were to be broken up.
- Socialist publications were outlawed.

Between 1878 and 1890 some 1500 socialists were imprisoned and a great many emigrated. However, the Anti-Socialist Law, far from eliminating socialism, served to rally the faithful and fortify them in their beliefs. Moreover, the law, which was differently implemented in different German states, did not prevent SPD members from standing for election and speaking freely in both the *Reichstag* and state legislatures. After the dip in 1878, the SPD won increasing support. By 1890 it had over a million voters and 35 seats.

In short, Bismarck's attack on socialism was no more successful than his attack on the Catholic Church. His repressive measures may have helped to increase support for the SPD and ensured that moderate and revolutionary socialist factions remained united.

State socialism

Bismarck not only used repression in his efforts to destroy socialism. He hoped to wean the working classes from socialism by introducing various welfare (state socialism) measures, designed to assist German workers. These measures may not have been as cynical as some of Bismarck's critics have implied. A devout Christian, Bismarck was conscious of a moral obligation to aid those in need. There was a strong tradition in Prussia and other parts of Germany, and a general belief, right and left, that one of the state's most important moral objectives was the promotion of the material well-being of its citizens:

- In 1883 the Sickness Insurance Act provided medical treatment and up to thirteen weeks' sick pay to 3 million low-paid workers. The workers paid two-thirds of the contribution and the employers one-third.

- A worker who was permanently disabled or sick for more than thirteen weeks was given protection by the Accident Insurance Act of 1884. This was financed wholly by the employers.
- Finally, in 1889 came the Old Age and Disability Act, which gave pensions to those over 70, and disablement pensions for those who were younger. This was paid for by workers, employers and the state.

SOURCE B

Bismarck speaking in the *Reichstag* in 1881, quoted in Andrina Stiles, *The Unification of Germany 1815–90*, Hodder & Stoughton, 1986, p. 94.

A beginning must be made with the task of reconciling the labouring classes with the state. A remedy cannot be sought only through the repression of socialist excesses. It is necessary to have a definite advancement in the welfare of the working classes. The matter of first importance is the care of those workers who are incapable of earning a living. Previous provision for guarding workers against the risk of falling into helplessness through incapacity caused by accident or age have not proved adequate and the inadequacy of such provision has been a main contributing cause driving the working classes to seek help by joining the Social Democratic movement.

According to Source B, why did Bismarck support the introduction of welfare measures?

How successful was state socialism?

Bismarck's hopes that the working class could be won over by state socialism were not fully realised. Many workers thought them a 'sham', particularly as the government still opposed the formation of trade unions. The welfare legislation was not particularly generous. Nor did Bismarck grant unemployment insurance. Moreover, many workers continued to labour under harsh conditions and while such conditions persisted, the SPD was assured of a future. Bismarck, believing that employers must control their factories, opposed demands for state intervention to regulate working hours and limit child and female employment.

Nevertheless, Bismarck's measures:

- laid the foundations of the welfare state in Germany
- were the first of their kind in the world and became a model of social provision for other countries.

Treatment of the national minorities

Bismarck regarded the national minorities – the Danes, French and Poles – as potential 'enemies of the state'. He thus sought to reduce their influence:

- The Polish language was outlawed in education and law courts.
- Alsace-Lorraine was not granted full autonomy. Instead, it became a special region under direct imperial rule, with a governor and Prussian civil servants. The German language was imposed in schools and local administration.

However, Bismarck did not rely solely on repression. Those French people who disliked German rule were allowed to leave (400,000 had done so by 1914). The German governors of Alsace-Lorraine made great efforts to conciliate the French-speaking provinces. It does seem that the national minorities' alienation from the *Reich* probably lessened over the years. School, conscription and everyday experience 'Germanised' many minorities.

Political developments in the 1880s

In 1881 Bismarck suffered a setback at the polls. The three liberal parties, the National Liberals, the 'Secession' Liberals (who had split from the National Liberals) and the Progressives, all gained seats from the Conservatives. This resulted in Bismarck no longer being able to depend on *Reichstag* support. But in the 1884 election Bismarck rallied patriotic support with his colonial policy (see pages 144–5) and the Conservative parties won seats from the Liberal parties.

By 1887 Bismarck was at odds with the *Reichstag* over the renewal of the army grant or **Septennates**. The current Septennates were not due to expire until 1888, but the international situation alarmed the generals, who pressed for an early renewal. So, in late 1886 Bismarck asked the *Reichstag* to agree to substantial military increases. The *Reichstag* agreed, but only on condition that in future it was allowed to review military expenditure every three years.

Bismarck was furious: 'The German army is an institution which cannot be dependent on short-lived *Reichstag* majorities', he declared. Dissolving the *Reichstag*, he conjured up a picture of a revenge-seeking France, ready for war at any moment. Germany would remain in danger until the Septennates were passed and only the Conservatives and National Liberals could be relied on to pass them. Bismarck's electoral stratagem worked. The Conservatives and National Liberals won an absolute majority in 1887 and the Septennates were passed.

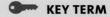 **KEY TERM**

Septennates The arrangement whereby military spending was agreed for seven years.

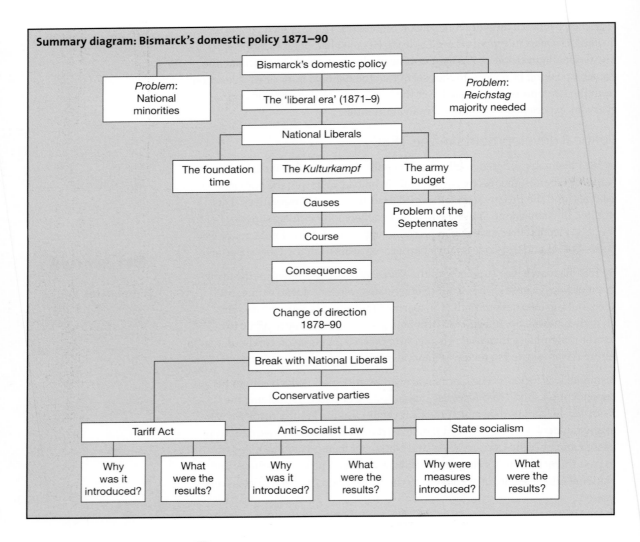

Summary diagram: Bismarck's domestic policy 1871–90

Bismarck's domestic policy

Problem: National minorities

The 'liberal era' (1871–9)

Problem: Reichstag majority needed

National Liberals

The foundation time

The *Kulturkampf*

The army budget

Causes

Problem of the Septennates

Course

Consequences

Change of direction 1878–90

Break with National Liberals

Conservative parties

Tariff Act

Anti-Socialist Law

State socialism

Why was it introduced?

What were the results?

Why was it introduced?

What were the results?

Why were measures introduced?

What were the results?

3 Bismarck's foreign policy 1871–90

▶ *What were Bismarck's main aims in foreign policy after 1871 and how successful was he in achieving them?*

The creation of a united Germany in 1871 caused a revolution in the European balance of power. Overnight Germany became the strongest nation on the continent. It was conceivable that Bismarck might attempt further expansion. In fact, this was far from his intent. Aware that Germany was surrounded by resentful and anxious neighbours, he made it clear that Germany was now a '**satiated power**', with no further territorial ambitions. Consequently, he was not interested in attaching Austrian Germans to the new *Reich*. He believed that any attempt to extend Germany's frontiers further would unite the other powers against it. Convinced that further wars could only threaten the *Reich*'s security, his main aim was to maintain peace.

SOURCE C

"AU REVOIR!"

A cartoon published in Britain in 1871.

> What point is the cartoonist trying to make in Source C?

France seemed the main threat to peace. Many French people, resenting France's defeat in 1870–1 and the loss of Alsace-Lorraine, wanted revenge. However, France without allies did not pose a serious danger: Bismarck was confident that Germany could defeat France again if necessary.

Bismarck's main fear was that France might ally with either Russia or Austria. Germany might then have to fight a war on two fronts. He was determined to avoid this possibility by isolating France and remaining on good terms with both Russia and Austria. His main problem was that there was always the possibility of friction between Austria and Russia over the Balkans, where their interests were at variance.

The problem of the Balkans

The Balkans was the most troublesome area of Europe:

- The Turkish government's authority in many Balkan areas was only nominal.
- People of various races and religions coexisted in a state of mutual animosity.
- The **Slavs** were becoming fiercely nationalistic.

Russia sought to assist the Slavs to obtain independence from Turkey. As leader of the **Orthodox Church**, the tsar felt a moral obligation to aid Christian Slavs if their Muslim rulers treated them too oppressively. Russia also sought to profit from Turkey's weakness by winning control of **the Straits**.

Austria was opposed to the expansion of Russian power so close to its territories. In addition, Russia's encouragement of Slav nationalism could serve as a dangerous example to national groups within the Habsburg Empire. Austria thus sought to maintain the **Ottoman Empire**. It feared that if the multinational Ottoman Empire collapsed, its own similarly multinational empire might follow.

Bismarck had no territorial ambitions in the Balkans: he once remarked that the area was not worth 'the healthy bones of a single Pomeranian musketeer'. However, if Austria and Russia fell out over the Balkans, Germany might have to choose between them and the rejected suitor might find a willing ally in France.

Although Bismarck faced problems in the Balkans, he had a strong hand:

- He enjoyed far more control of foreign affairs than domestic matters.
- Germany was the greatest military power in Europe.
- His friendship was eagerly sought by Austria and Russia, in part because of their growing antagonism in the Balkans.
- It was unlikely that tsarist Russia would seek alliance with **republican** France.
- Britain was reasonably friendly to Germany.

The Three Emperors' League

Austria, fearing a German–Russian agreement, took the initiative in pressing for a Three Emperors' alliance. Following a meeting in 1872, the emperors of Germany, Russia and Austria reached an agreement known as the Three Emperors' League or *Dreikaiserbund*. The emperors identified republicanism and socialism as common enemies and promised to consult on matters of common interest or if a third power disturbed Europe's peace.

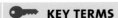

KEY TERMS

Slavs People who regard themselves to be of the same ethnic group and whose language is Slavonic. Slavs include Russians, Czechs, Serbs and Bulgarians.

Orthodox Church The Greek or Eastern Christian Church.

The Straits The Bosphorus and Dardanelles, which link the Black Sea with the Mediterranean Sea.

Ottoman Empire The Turkish Empire, which was ruled by the Ottoman family.

Republican Of, or favouring, a government without a monarch.

The 1875 war scare

After 1871, France made determined efforts to throw off the effects of defeat. Its rapid military reorganisation and the prompt repayment of the war indemnity, ensuring the end of German military occupation by 1873, alarmed Bismarck. In 1875 he reacted to French recovery and rearmament by provoking a diplomatic crisis. He prohibited the export of horses to France and the *Berlin Post* carried an article 'Is War in Sight?' Bismarck expected that the other powers would similarly put pressure on France, discouraging it from further military expansion. He miscalculated. Britain and Russia supported France, forcing Bismarck to offer assurances that Germany was not contemplating another war. The crisis thus ended in a diplomatic victory for France.

The Balkan crisis 1875–8

In 1875 Christian peasants in Bosnia and Herzegovina revolted against Turkish rule. In April 1876 the revolt spread to Bulgaria and in July Montenegro and Serbia declared war on Turkey. Thousands of Russian volunteers joined the Serbian army amidst a wave of popular pro-Slav fervour. There was thus pressure for Russian intervention in the Balkans. It was likely that Austria would oppose anything that smacked of Russian expansionism. Determined to avoid taking sides, Bismarck had somehow to convince both Austria and Russia of Germany's goodwill and prevent them from quarrelling.

The situation in 1876

Bismarck was helped by the fact that Tsar Alexander II and his Foreign Minister Gorchakov had no wish to find themselves in a Crimean situation again, at war with Turkey and isolated. Gorchakov, recognising that Turkey's fate concerned all the great powers, preferred international discussion to unilateral action. Austrian Foreign Minister Andrassy, aware that German support was unlikely in the event of a clash with Russia, tried to collaborate with Gorchakov in an attempt to limit the effects of the crisis.

The Turkish atrocities in 1876 in Bulgaria (10,000 Bulgarians were allegedly killed), however, changed the situation. The carnage stirred public opinion in both Britain and Russia, with important effects:

- Britain was prevented temporarily from pursuing its traditional policy of supporting Turkey against Russia.
- In Russia, the Bulgarian atrocities and the defeat of Serbian and Montenegrin forces enflamed **Pan-Slavist** sentiment to such an extent that the tsarist government found itself under mounting pressure to intervene in the Balkans.

In November 1876 Alexander II declared that if his 'just demands' for the protection of Balkan Christians were not agreed to by Turkey, and the other great powers would not support him, then he was prepared to act independently.

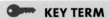 **KEY TERM**

Pan-Slavist Someone who supported the union of all Slav peoples.

Russian and Austrian policy was suddenly out of step and both turned to Germany for support. In December, the tsar asked for an assurance of German neutrality in the event of an Austro-Russian war. Bismarck was evasive. He similarly refused Andrassy's offer of an Austro-German alliance against Russia.

The Russo-Turkish War 1877–8

In January 1877 Russia managed to buy Austrian neutrality in the event of a Russo-Turkish war by agreeing that Austria would receive Bosnia-Herzegovina, and promising that no large state would be set up in the Balkans. In April Russia declared war on Turkey.

Courageous Turkish defence of the fortress of Plevna deprived Russia of a quick victory. It also caused British opinion to swing back in favour of the Turks. Nevertheless, Plevna finally fell in December 1877 and by January 1878 the Russians threatened Constantinople.

The Treaty of San Stefano

In March 1878 Russia imposed the Treaty of San Stefano on the Turks. This treaty significantly improved Russia's position in the Balkans:

- An enlarged Bulgaria (under Russian occupation) was to be created.
- Serbia, Montenegro and Romania were to be fully independent of Turkey.
- There was no mention of Austria taking Bosnia-Herzegovina.

Austria and Britain opposed the creation of an enlarged Bulgaria, which would give Russia enormous influence in the Balkans and also a strategically important Aegean coastline. Austria mobilised its army. Britain dispatched the fleet to Turkish waters. Faced with the threat of a major war, which it was in no economic or military state to fight, Russia agreed to an international conference to revise the peace terms. Bismarck, somewhat reluctantly, offered his services as the 'honest broker'. He realised that he was likely to be blamed by one or the other, or even by both, of his allies for their disappointments.

The Congress of Berlin

The fact that the congress took place in Berlin was a sign of Germany's new power and Bismarck's prestige. Much negotiation had been done before the congress met. Nevertheless, the congress was not all plain sailing. At critical moments, only Bismarck's energetic intervention saved the day. By the Congress of Berlin:

- Enlarged Bulgaria was divided into three.
- Bulgaria proper was granted complete independence under Russian supervision.
- The province of Eastern Roumelia was to have a form of self-government under nominal Turkish rule.
- Macedonia was returned to Turkish rule.

- Russia recovered southern Bessarabia from Romania.
- Austria was to occupy Bosnia-Herzegovina.
- Britain gained Cyprus.

Figure 5.3 The Balkans in 1878.

For Bismarck, the congress was a mixed blessing. His main desire – that of keeping peace – had been achieved. However, Russia felt that it had suffered a humiliating diplomatic defeat. Having done all the fighting, it had then seen Britain and Austria get away with some major spoils. Russia blamed Bismarck. Alexander II described the congress as 'a coalition of the European powers against Russia under the leadership of Prince Bismarck'. Russo-German relations quickly deteriorated. The introduction of German protective tariffs in 1879 (see pages 131–2) did not help matters, given Russia's dependence on wheat exports to Germany.

By 1878–9 the *Dreikaiserbund* was well and truly dead. Bismarck was now in a potentially dangerous position. There was suddenly the real possibility of a Franco-Russian alliance.

The Dual Alliance

In 1878–9 it seemed to Bismarck that Germany was faced with the stark choice of continuing Russian hostility or allying with Russia. An alliance would jeopardise his relationship with Austria and risk enmity with Britain. He had no wish to be isolated. His greatest fear was that somehow (and somewhat improbably) Russia, France and Austria would ally and that this would lead to Germany's destruction.

Bismarck's response to the pressure from Russia was to put out feelers for an alliance with Austria. In October 1879 Bismarck and Andrassy agreed to the Dual Alliance:

- This committed both countries to resist Russian aggression.
- If either Germany or Austria were at war with a third power, the other partner would remain neutral unless Russia intervened.

The alliance was to last for five years. However, the option to renew the arrangement was taken up so that it became the cornerstone of German foreign policy, lasting until 1918. The Dual Alliance was something of a 'landmark'. Previous treaties had usually been concluded on the eve of wars. This was a peacetime engagement. It encouraged other powers to negotiate similar treaties until all Europe was divided into pact and counter-pact.

Emperor William, who regarded good relations with Russia as of vital importance, was reluctant to sign the Dual Alliance. He feared it increased the likelihood of Russia and France allying. In the end Bismarck forced the Emperor's hand by threatening resignation. Grudgingly, William gave way.

Why did Bismarck agree to the Dual Alliance?

Bismarck claimed that the Dual Alliance was the fruition of a grand design cherished since 1866. There is, in fact, no evidence that he had it in mind before 1879. In reality, he acted on the spur of the moment to deal with an emergency situation.

In 1879, the Dual Alliance provided Germany with an ally with whom it could weather the storm of Russian hostility. Bismarck chose to ally with Austria rather than Russia partly because he felt that Austria would be easier to control and partly because an alliance with a fellow German power was certain to be more popular in Germany.

Bismarck seems to have regarded the Dual Alliance as a temporary expedient to preserve the precarious balance of power in the Balkans and to compel a friendlier Russian attitude towards both Austria and Germany. It was not a final choice between Austria and Russia. Bismarck never wavered in his belief that some form of *Dreikaiserbund* was Germany's best hope.

The Three Emperors' Alliance

Russia, alarmed at its isolation and not anxious to ally with France, soon turned back to Germany. However, more than eighteen months elapsed before a new *Dreikaiserbund* was signed. This was partly due to the unsettled situation in Russia following the assassination of Alexander II (in 1881) and the accession of Tsar Alexander III. Austria was also opposed to the entire project. However, Andrassy finally yielded to Bismarck's pressure and in 1881 the Three Emperors' Alliance, a secret treaty of three years' duration, was signed. It aimed at resolving Austro-Russian disputes in the Balkans and at reassuring Russia that it did not need to seek accommodation with France. The three powers agreed the following:

- If Russia, Germany or Austria were at war with another power, the others would remain neutral.
- The Balkans was to be divided into 'spheres of influence'; Russian interests were recognised in the eastern portion, Austrian interests in the western.
- Austria acknowledged Russian ambitions to recreate an enlarged Bulgaria; Russia accepted Austria's right to annex Bosnia-Herzegovina.

Although Russia continued to resent the Dual Alliance, it was pleased with the new *Dreikaiserbund*. Russia's partners had written off half the Balkans and had committed themselves to Russia if it came to blows with Britain. Bismarck was also pleased. His confident assertion to Emperor William that Russia would return to the fold had come to pass and the conservative alliance was restored.

The Triple Alliance

Bismarck, hoping to divert French attention away from Alsace-Lorraine, encouraged France to embark on colonial expansion in Africa and Asia. This had the added advantage of alienating France from Britain. In 1881, with Bismarck's support, France seized Tunis. This angered Italy, who had designs on the same territory.

In 1881 Italy made overtures to Austria aimed at securing an alliance. Austria had little interest in the Italian bid for closer ties but Bismarck, although having a poor opinion of Italy's strength, saw its potential. Bringing Italy closer to the Dual Alliance would secure Austria's vulnerable southern flank and deprive France of a potential ally. Accordingly, in 1882 the Triple Alliance was signed:

- If any of the signatories were attacked by two or more powers, the others promised to lend assistance.
- If France attacked Germany, Italy would provide support to its partner.
- If Italy was attacked by France, both Germany and Austria agreed to back Italy.

Bismarck and colonies

In 1881 Bismarck declared that 'so long as I am chancellor we shall pursue no colonial policy'. He knew that the acquisition of colonies might well alienate Britain, the strongest colonial power. However, in 1884–5 Germany was suddenly to acquire an overseas empire. Why did Bismarck change his mind?

- In the early 1880s colonialism became fashionable. Many European nations were interested in carving up Africa. Enthusiastic pressure groups sprang up agitating for colonies on economic grounds and as a sign of national greatness. The German Colonial Union, founded in 1882 with support from major industrialists, did much to interest German public opinion in overseas expansion.
- Within Germany there was concern about the consequences of protectionist policies. Trading companies were complaining of being squeezed out of parts of Africa by foreign rivals. Bismarck hoped that colonies might benefit the German economy by providing new markets and raw materials.
- Bismarck had a sharp eye for a new opportunity. In the mid-1880s he seriously considered the possibility of a lasting reconciliation with France. Co-operation with France in the colonial field was the first step. By picking quarrels with Britain over German colonial claims, he aligned Germany on France's side.
- Bismarck also had good political reasons to support German colonialism. The 1884 elections were in the offing. He needed an issue that would weaken the liberal parties. Colonialism was a convenient way of rallying patriotic support.

The German overseas empire

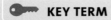

KEY TERM

Entente A friendly understanding rather than a binding agreement.

In 1884 Bismarck deliberately picked quarrels with Britain over colonial claims in South-West Africa and sided with France in opposition to British plans in Egypt. The Franco-German **entente** reached its high water mark at the Berlin Conference of 1884–5, called to regulate the affairs of central Africa. Facing a Russian threat in central Asia, Britain had no wish to antagonise Germany and was not opposed to its acquiring colonies. Thus, between 1884 and 1885 Germany acquired South-West Africa, Togoland, the Cameroons, German East Africa and some Pacific islands – a million square miles of land in total (see Figure 5.4 on page 145 and Figure 6.1 on page 178).

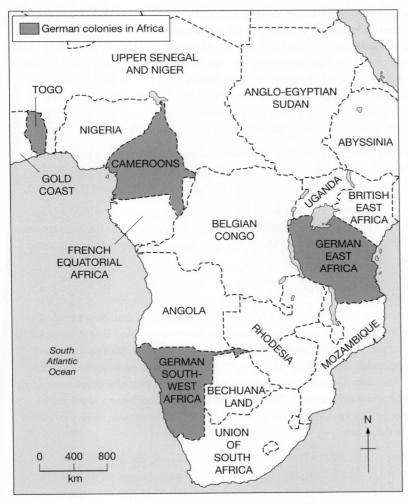

Figure 5.4 German colonies in Africa in 1890.

Bismarck's interest in colonial matters was short-lived. By 1887 he was resisting demands for further colonial expansion on the grounds of Germany's continental security. As German relations with France and Russia deteriorated (see below), he had no wish to alienate Britain. Thus, he made substantial concessions to Britain when East Africa was partitioned in 1889. A German official observed that a 'good understanding with England means much more to Bismarck than the whole of East Africa'.

The Bulgarian crisis

A crisis in Bulgaria in 1885–6 shattered the Three Emperors' Alliance, due for renewal in 1887. Austria and Russia again squared up against each other in the Balkans. Bismarck refused to take sides in the dispute. He warned the Austrians that Germany would not help them. He also warned Russia that he would not abandon Austria.

As Austro-Russian relations worsened, Bismarck's fears of France revived. In 1886 General Boulanger became French war minister and talked of a war to recover Alsace-Lorraine. Franco-German relations quickly deteriorated. To make matters worse, Pan-Slav advisers of the tsar, sympathetic to France and hostile to Germany, seemed to be exerting great influence in Russia. For domestic reasons, Bismarck may well have exaggerated the danger of war. However, he was clearly alarmed by the prospect of a Franco-Russian alliance and felt that diplomatic precautions were needed to safeguard Germany.

In February 1887 the Triple Alliance was renewed on terms more favourable to Italy than those obtained in 1882. Bismarck persuaded Austria to promise to consult Italy on all matters affecting the Balkans, the Adriatic and the Aegean.

In March 1887, with Bismarck's full backing, Britain, Austria and Italy signed the First Mediterranean Agreement, committing themselves to the maintenance of the *status quo* in the eastern Mediterranean: an action that was clearly anti-Russian.

The Reinsurance Treaty

Events now turned in Bismarck's favour. France, suddenly cautious, avoided Russian feelers and conservative Russian ministers convinced Tsar Alexander III that an agreement with Germany was better than nothing. Bismarck jumped at the suggestion and in June 1887 the Reinsurance Treaty was signed. By this, if either Russia or Germany were at war with a third power, the other would remain benevolently neutral. The provision would not apply to a war against Austria or France resulting from an attack on one of these two powers by either Russia or Germany.

The treaty, which did not contravene the Dual Alliance, can be seen as a masterpiece of diplomatic juggling on Bismarck's part. However, its importance should not be exaggerated. If not exactly a desperate stop-gap measure, it was hardly the cornerstone of Bismarck's system; indeed, he seems to have attached little importance to it. It was simply another temporary expedient to remove his fears of a Franco-Russian alliance.

The impact of the Reinsurance Treaty

Russo-German relations did not improve much after 1887. Bismarck was partly to blame for this. In November 1887 he denied Russia access to the Berlin money market for loans to finance industrialisation in order 'to remove the possibility that the Russians wage war against us at our cost'. In consequence, Russia simply turned to Paris, where French financiers were eager to invest money in Russia.

Nor did the Reinsurance Treaty necessarily reduce the danger of a clash over the Balkans. Indeed, the Bulgarian situation continued to cause tension. Bismarck used all his influence to encourage Britain, Italy and Austria to sign the Second

Mediterranean Agreement (December 1887), again guaranteeing the *status quo* in the east Mediterranean. In February 1888 he published the Dual Alliance, partly to warn Russia that Germany would stand by Austria if it came to war and partly to restrain Austria by making it clear that Germany's obligations were limited to a defensive war. The publication, coupled with rumours of the Mediterranean Agreement, persuaded Russia to hold its hand and the Bulgarian crisis fizzled out.

Summary diagram: Bismarck's foreign policy 1871–90

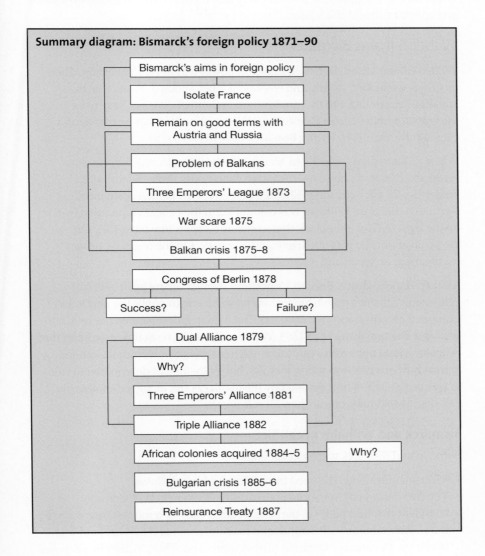

Bismarck's fall

▶ *Why did Bismarck fall from power?*

By the late 1880s Bismarck's position seemed in jeopardy. Emperor William I was in his eighties. If William died, Crown Prince Frederick, a man of liberal views, would ascend the throne. It seemed likely that Frederick would dismiss Bismarck and appoint a liberal chancellor.

Wilhelm II and Bismarck

While William I lived, Bismarck's hold on power was never in question. Their meetings were often stormy and emotional. They shouted, threw things and often quarrelled. But they understood each other. 'It is not easy to be the emperor under such a chancellor', William remarked, but he managed it successfully, mainly by letting Bismarck have his own way.

When William died (aged 90) in March 1888 he was succeeded by his son Frederick. Frederick, however, died from cancer only three months later. Frederick's 29-year-old son Wilhelm then became emperor. A convinced German nationalist, Wilhelm was committed to the belief that he ruled by divine right of God. Wilhelm's character was complex (see page 157). On the positive side, he was intelligent and energetic. On the negative, he was overbearing, arrogant and erratic.

After Frederick's death, Bismarck's position seemed secure again. He had cultivated Wilhelm's friendship for several years and in public the new kaiser expressed his admiration for Bismarck. But a great gulf separated the two, not least age: Bismarck was 73 in 1888, Wilhelm II was 29. Bismarck, assuming that Wilhelm would not involve himself much in matters of government, tended to treat him in a condescending manner. But Wilhelm was determined to rule as well as to reign. 'I'll let the old boy [Bismarck] potter along for another six months', he told his cronies, 'then I'll rule myself'.

Bismarck and Wilhelm in conflict

Wilhelm and Bismarck were soon at odds:

- Wilhelm questioned the need to maintain links with Russia.
- The two disagreed over social policy. Unlike Bismarck, Wilhelm was confident that he could win over the working class by a modest extension of the welfare system, including an end to child labour and Sunday working. Bismarck, by contrast, favoured further repression. Thus, in 1889 he proposed to make the Anti-Socialist Law permanent. Wilhelm was not against renewing the law (he too feared socialism), but he wanted the measure watered down. Bismarck refused. He was then let down by the *Reichstag*, which rejected his entire bill in January 1890. This was a sign that his political power was crumbling.

 NOTE

William (or Wilhelm) II

This book will call the new Kaiser Wilhelm II – rather than William II. This will help to differentiate him from William I.

SOURCE D

'**The Dropping of the Pilot**', a cartoon from *Punch*, **1890.**

What does Source D suggest was the main reason for Bismarck's dismissal?

In February 1890, with new *Reichstag* elections underway, Wilhelm issued a proclamation promising new social legislation. The absence of Bismarck's countersignature from this proclamation caused a sensation. The election was a disaster for Bismarck. His Conservative and National Liberal allies lost 85 seats while the Radicals gained 46 seats and the Socialists won 24 seats.

Bismarck was trapped between an emperor bent on having his own way and a hostile *Reichstag*. In an attempt to recover his position he proposed an extraordinary scheme: the *Reichstag* would be asked to agree to a large increase in the army and a new and extremely repressive anti-socialist law. If, as was probable, they refused, an assembly of German princes would meet, alter the constitution and drastically curtail the *Reichstag*'s powers. Wilhelm refused to support Bismarck's plan and relations between the two men deteriorated further.

Bismarck dismissed

In March 1890 Wilhelm and Bismarck quarrelled about the right of ministers to advise the monarch. Bismarck had revived an old order first issued in 1852, which forbade ministers to approach the Prussian king except through the minister-president. Bismarck interpreted this to mean that all ministers must obtain permission from him as chancellor, before they could discuss any government business with the emperor.

Wilhelm was not prepared for such restrictions and commanded that the 1852 order be withdrawn. At a stormy interview Bismarck nearly threw an inkpot at Wilhelm and then enraged him by letting him see a letter from Tsar Alexander III very disparaging of his talents.

Wilhelm then sent Bismarck an ultimatum: resign or be dismissed. Three days later Bismarck sent a letter of resignation in which he justified his actions, claiming (wrongly) that the real difference between Wilhelm and himself lay in the kaiser's pursuit of an anti-Russian policy. This letter was not made public until after Bismarck's death. The official announcement implied that he had resigned for health reasons and that Wilhelm had made every effort to persuade him to change his mind.

In reality, Bismarck retired with ill grace to write his memoirs and innumerable newspaper articles, invariably critical of Wilhelm. Failing to exert any influence on policy, he was even heard to speak in favour of republicanism: kings, he said, were dangerous if they had real power. He died in July 1898. On his grave were the words, 'Here lies a true servant of the Emperor William I.'

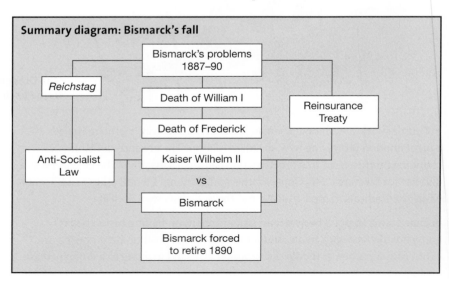

Summary diagram: Bismarck's fall

- Bismarck's problems 1887–90
- Reichstag
- Death of William I
- Death of Frederick
- Reinsurance Treaty
- Anti-Socialist Law
- Kaiser Wilhelm II
- vs
- Bismarck
- Bismarck forced to retire 1890

Key debate

▶ *How successful was Bismarck from 1871 to 1890?*

Historians continue to argue over Bismarck's achievement, his motives and his methods.

EXTRACT I

From M. Kitchen, *A History of Modern Germany 1800–2000*, Blackwell, 2006, p. 175.

Bismarck was a towering genius who left an indelible mark on Germany and on Europe, but his legacy, like that of so many truly great men, was extremely mixed … his power-hungry brutality, his lust for confrontation rather than compromise, and his inability either to delegate authority or to tolerate anyone who even approached being his equal, left a fatal legacy. He was a man of profound and even pathological contradictions, and the ambivalence and inconsistency of his own imperious personality was deeply embedded in the structure of the Reich of which he was the architect.

EXTRACT 2

From W.L. Langer, *European Alliances and Alignments 1871–90*, Vintage Books, 1950, p. 479.

His [Bismarck's] had been a great career, beginning with three wars in eight years and ending with a period of twenty years during which he worked for the peace of Europe, despite countless opportunities to embark on further enterprises with more than even chance of success … No other statesman of his standing had ever before shown the same great moderation and sound political sense of the possible and desirable … Bismarck at least deserves full credit for having steered European politics through this dangerous transitional period without serious conflict between the great powers.

> **?** Which extract do you think provides the fairer summary of Bismarck's career?

Innumerable books have been written about Bismarck. By 1895 there were already 650 biographies available. Twenty years later there were 3500 and the number has gone on increasing ever since.

When it comes to primary evidence the problem is not a lack of material but an excess, much of it conflicting. Bismarck left a wealth of letters, articles, speeches and official reports. There were also his voluminous *Reminiscences*, which are of questionable accuracy: he increased the drama around every event, sometimes embroidering fact with a little fiction, and always presented himself favourably. While in office, Bismarck frequently made totally contradictory statements at the same time about the same events. Historians interpret this differently:

● Some see it as symptomatic of Bismarck's perversity of mind, a desire to confuse or mislead friends and enemies alike.

- Others see it as a lack of settled purpose and an inability to think clearly and coherently in abstract terms.
- Others see it simply as Bismarck's way of 'reasoning out loud', rehearsing a number of different arguments before reaching a decision.

Whatever the reason, it means that Bismarck's own evidence needs to be used with caution. A single letter or speech is not necessarily a true reflection of his policies or intentions at any given time. Therefore it is difficult to disentangle with any certainty Bismarck's motives, or to decide how far he planned ahead. 'Politics', he said, 'is not in itself an exact and logical science but is the capacity to choose in each fleeting moment of the situation that which is least harmful or most opportune.' He was the supreme opportunist, both before and after 1871. Accordingly, his policies can best be described as flexible.

Realpolitik characterised Bismarck's political career from his earliest days. In 1850 he declared that the only sound foundation for a great state is not idealism but 'state egoism' (national self-interest). Thirty years later, his beliefs had not changed. Defending himself against critics in the *Reichstag* who accused him of sudden changes of policy, he said: 'I have always had one compass only, one lodestar by which I have steered: the welfare of the state.'

Bismarck's critics

Bismarck had critics in his own time and has had many since. The main criticisms of his policies post-1871 are as follows:

- He was responsible for France remaining embittered.
- His elaborate alliance system was fragile; little more than a form of crisis management.
- The Dual Alliance, far from being a means by which Germany could control Austria, eventually dragged Germany into war in 1914.
- His acquisition of colonies had negative results. German colonial ambitions alienated Britain in the 1880s and more importantly thereafter when they became the basis for Germany's claim to be a world power. The colonies proved to be an expensive financial burden.
- His influence is often exaggerated. Economic and military strength was the basis of German power – not Bismarck's diplomatic skill.
- The *Kulturkampf* was a major blunder.
- His attack on the socialists was ill advised and unsuccessful.
- His inability either to delegate authority or to tolerate anyone who even approached his equality meant that he effectively ruled as a dictator.
- He left a flawed legacy. Arguably, his strategies and tactics were responsible for **Wilhelmine Germany** and Nazi Germany.

KEY TERM

Wilhelmine Germany The period from 1888 to 1918 when Wilhelm II was kaiser.

Bismarck's admirers

Bismarck's supporters can make the following claims:

- He was not the total reactionary of left-wing myth. His policies helped to promote the consolidation and modernisation of Germany.
- Although his campaigns against 'enemies of the state' – Catholics, socialists and national minorities – were not successful, they were not total failures.
- For most of the 1870s he worked closely with the National Liberals, putting their – liberal – programme into place.
- He pioneered state socialism.
- His policies assisted Germany's economic development.
- The fact that he remained in power for so long is testimony to his political skill.
- He was not a dictator. His powers were far from absolute.
- He brilliantly maintained peace from 1871 to 1890. Historian A.J.P. Taylor wrote: 'Bismarck was an honest broker of peace; and his system of alliances compelled every Power, whatever its will, to follow a peaceful course.'
- Throughout his career he showed sound political sense of the possible and the desirable.
- In foreign policy terms, he possessed long-term vision but also short-term ability to juggle many complex developments simultaneously.

Overall, Bismarck's admirers probably have the best of the argument. Germany did not exist when he became Prussian chief minister in 1862. When he left office in 1890 it was Europe's strongest state. This did not happen by chance. It had much to do with his diplomatic prowess. He manipulated situations even if he did not always create them, and he worked hard and successfully to ensure the outcomes he desired. In so doing he won the trust of few but the respect of virtually everyone he encountered. It was unfortunate that after 1890 Germany was governed by less skilful men.

Chapter summary

The Second German Empire, which came into existence in 1871, had a complex constitution that ensured Prussian dominance over the rest of Germany. Bismarck dominated both Prussia and Germany for nearly two decades after 1871. In terms of domestic policy, the Catholic Church and the perceived socialist threat proved the biggest problems. Bismarck's *Kulturkampf* and his efforts to suppress socialism were far from successful. His welfare measures in the 1880s are often regarded as his greatest domestic achievement.

In foreign affairs, Bismarck believed it was in Germany's best interest to preserve peace. This meant isolating France and maintaining good relations with Austria and Russia, no easy matter given their divergent interests in the Balkans. In 1879 Bismarck signed the Dual Alliance with Austria. In 1887 he signed the Reinsurance Treaty with Russia. He had little interest in colonies (except in 1884–5). By and large, he achieved his diplomatic aims. Following the death of William I, Bismarck's relations with the new king and Parliament deteriorated and he was dismissed by Kaiser Wilhelm II in 1890.

Refresher questions

Use these questions to remind yourself of the key material covered in this chapter.

1 Who held control in the *Reich*?

2 Why was Bismarck so powerful in Germany after 1871?

3 How democratic was Germany?

4 What were the main economic and social developments in Germany between 1871 and 1890?

5 How effectively did Bismarck work with the National Liberals?

6 Why did Bismarck support the *Kulturkampf* and why did it fail?

7 Why did Bismarck come to support protectionist policies?

8 How successful was Bismarck in tackling the socialist 'threat'?

9 What were Bismarck's main aims in foreign policy after 1871?

10 Why did the Balkans pose a serious problem for Bismarck?

11 How important was the Dual Alliance?

12 Why did Bismarck support the acquisition of colonies in 1884–5?

13 Why did Bismarck sign the Reinsurance Treaty?

14 How did Bismarck fall from power?

 Question practice

ESSAY QUESTIONS

1 How accurate is to say that Bismarck had little success in domestic affairs from 1871 to 1890?

2 To what extent was Bismarck responsible for maintaining European peace between 1871 and 1890?

3 To what extent was Bismarck in control of policy in Germany after 1871?

4 'Bismarck's rule in Germany after 1871 was far more successful than is generally admitted.' How far do you agree with this statement?

CHAPTER 6

Germany 1890–1919

Wilhelm II was determined to rule as well as reign. His rule was to culminate in the outbreak of the First World War in 1914. Who exactly exerted decisive influence on policy and events in Wilhelmine Germany? What were the objectives of that leadership? To what extent was Germany responsible for the First World War? This chapter will examine these questions through the following themes:

★ The Wilhelmine political system

★ Economic and social trends

★ Intellectual trends

★ Domestic politics 1890–1914

★ Foreign policy 1890–1914

The key debate on *page 189* of this chapter asks the question: To what extent did Wilhelm II rule Germany from 1890 to 1914?

Key dates

1890	Caprivi appointed chancellor	1909		Appointment of Bethmann-Hollweg as chancellor
1894	Dual Alliance between France and Russia	1914	June	Assassination of Franz Ferdinand
1898	First Navy Law		July	Germany gave Austria the 'blank cheque'
1900	Bülow appointed chancellor			
1904	Entente between Britain and France			
1906	Launch of the *Dreadnought*		Aug.	Start of First World War

1 The Wilhelmine political system

▶ *Who ruled in Wilhelmine Germany?*

At the height of the diplomatic crisis in July 1914, which culminated in the First World War, the Austrian foreign minister asked in frustration: 'Who actually rules in Berlin?' This was a pertinent question, not just in 1914, but throughout Wilhelm's rule.

The kaiser

According to historian Michael Balfour, Wilhelm was 'the copybook condemnation of the hereditary system'. This view may be over-harsh. Wilhelm did have some talents: a quick mind, an excellent memory and a charming manner. Unfortunately, his understanding of issues was often superficial and distorted by his own prejudices. He lacked powers of steady application and his moods and behaviour were liable to wild fluctuations. 'The kaiser is like a balloon', said Bismarck, 'if you do not hold fast to the string, you never know where he will be off to.'

SOURCE A

Count Eulenburg, a close and influential friend of Wilhelm II, gave this note to Berhard von Bülow in July 1897. Bülow, a protégé of Eulenburg, was about to become foreign secretary. From J.C.G. Röhl, *Kaiser Wilhelm II*, Cambridge University Press, 2014, p. 67.

Wilhelm II takes everything personally. Only personal arguments make any impression on him. He likes to give advice to others but is unwilling to take it himself. He cannot stand boredom; ponderous, stiff, excessively thorough people get on his nerves and cannot get anywhere with him. Wilhelm II wants to shine and to do and to decide everything himself. What he wants to do himself unfortunately often goes wrong. He loves glory, he is ambitious and jealous. To get him to accept an idea one has to pretend that the idea came from him … never forget that H.M. needs praise from time to time. He is the sort of person who becomes sullen unless he is given recognition from time to time by someone of importance. You will always accomplish whatever you wish so long as you do not omit to express your appreciation when H.M. deserves it. He is grateful for it like a good, clever child. If one remains silent when he deserves recognition, he eventually sees malevolence in it. We two will always carefully observe the boundaries of flattery.

Arguably, Wilhelm's influence should not be exaggerated. His life was an endless whirl of state occasions, military manoeuvres, cruises and hunting trips. In the first decade of his reign he averaged 200 days a year travelling on official business or private recreation. His social and ceremonial duties meant that he was absent from Berlin for long periods and so he did not have command of the detail of the government's work. Accordingly, it is possible to claim that he did not determine the course of German policy.

The German constitution did grant the kaiser extensive powers, however. He alone had the right to appoint and dismiss the chancellor and his state secretaries completely independent of the *Reichstag*'s wishes. Wilhelm claimed that 'there is only one ruler in the *Reich* and I am he'. He believed that his accountability was to God alone. Given his constitutional powers, no major decision could be taken without his agreement. When he spoke, people, in and out of Germany, listened.

> ? Why, according to Source A, was Wilhelm II ill-suited to ruling Germany?

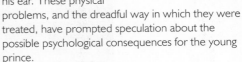

Kaiser Wilhelm II

1859	Born, the eldest child of Crown Prince Frederick and Victoria, eldest daughter of British Queen Victoria
1888	Became kaiser
1890	Dismissed Bismarck; supported the 'new course'
1897	Supported a policy of *Weltpolitik*
1908	Homosexual scandal at Wilhelm's court, involving his close friend Eulenburg
1914	Germany entered the First World War
1918	Abdicated and fled to the Netherlands
1941	Died in Nazi-occupied Netherlands

Most historians are of the view that Wilhelm was arrogant and overtly theatrical: a neurotic braggart, a romantic dreamer, a man who frequently changed his mind. Historian John Röhl, who has devoted his life to studying Wilhelm, calls him a 'boastful autocrat, militarist and racist'. Many scholars, convinced that Wilhelm was, at the very least, deeply disturbed, have spent a great deal of time trying to explain his personality:

- Wilhelm's breech birth delivery resulted in the partial paralysis of his left arm and damage to the balance mechanism in his ear. These physical problems, and the dreadful way in which they were treated, have prompted speculation about the possible psychological consequences for the young prince.
- Close attention has been paid to the strained relationship with his parents. During his adolescent years, he grew apart from them, opposing their liberal sympathies and preferring the company of his grandfather. He particularly enjoyed the regimental life of the military garrison at Potsdam. (His love of military ceremonial verged on the pathological.)
- Some have suggested that Wilhelm's self-assertive and erratic behaviour should be seen as symptoms of insanity, megalomania or sadism.
- More recently, he has been depicted as a repressed homosexual or (more likely) a sufferer from attention deficiency disorder – a mental condition which reveals itself in volatile and irrational behaviour.

The German chancellors

There were four chancellors between 1890 and 1914:

- General Leo Caprivi (1890–4)
- Prince Chlodwig Hohenloe (1894–1900)
- Bernhard Bülow (1900–9)
- Theobold Bethmann-Hollweg (1909–17).

These men were essentially civil servants, not seasoned politician-statesmen like Bismarck. They did not dominate the German political scene as decisively as Bismarck had done. They probably lacked Bismarck's talent. They certainly lacked his prestige and independence. William I had usually deferred to Bismarck, but Wilhelm II was determined to participate in the affairs of state. Political survival for the chancellors was dependent on showing loyalty to Wilhelm and doing his will. This was far from easy when his personal involvement often amounted to little more than whimsical flights of fancy.

The *Bundesrat*

The upper house of the national parliament, which comprised men chosen by the various states, was essentially a conservative body. After 1890 it declined in influence. An increasing number of bills were introduced in the *Reichstag* rather than in the *Bundesrat*.

Table 6.1 *Reichstag* election results 1890–1912

Party	1890	1893	1898	1903	1907	1912
German Conservatives	73	72	56	54	60	43
Free Conservatives	20	28	23	21	24	14
National Liberals	42	53	46	51	54	45
Centre	106	96	102	100	105	91
Left Liberals	76	48	49	36	49	42
Social Democrats	35	44	56	81	43	110
Minorities	38	35	34	32	29	33
Right-wing splinter parties	7	21	31	22	33	19
Total	397	397	397	397	397	397

Table 6.2 Major political parties in the *Reichstag*

SPD	*Sozialdemokratische Partei Deutschlands*. Social Democratic Party. The party of theoretical Marxism. Closely connected with the trade unions and supported by the working classes.
ZP	*Zentrumspartei*. Centre Party. Formed in 1871 specifically to uphold the interests of the Catholic Church. Its appeal was therefore denominational rather than class-based. Despite the *Kulturkampf* it had become an influential political voice in the *Reichstag*.
DKP	*Deustschkonservative Partei*. German Conservative Party. The party of the landowning farming community. Its outlook was ultra-conservative and hostile to the new forces of political and economic liberalism. Especially strong in Prussia.
RP	*Richspartei*. Free Conservative Party. Conservative in outlook, it was backed by both industrialists and landowners.
NLP	*Nationalliberale Partei*. National Liberal Party. Traditionally the party of the economic and political liberalism. A middle-class party, it was increasingly conservative in its policy.
DFP	*Deutsche Freisinnige Partei*. German Free Thought Party (Left Liberals). Formed in 1884 following the secession of the more radical elements from the NLP. In 1893 it split into three factions and was only reunited in 1910 under the new name of the FVP (*Fortschrittleiche Volkpartei*; Progressive People's Party).
National minorities	The independence parties of the ethnic minorities in Germany. Poles, Danes, French in Alsace-Lorraine and Guelphs (Hanoverians).
Right-wing splinter parties	There were a number of ultra-conservative parties, which were nationalistic, anti-socialist and often anti-Semitic.

The *Reichstag*

While the *Reichstag* could discuss, amend, pass or reject government legislation, its power to initiate new laws was negligible. No party or coalition of parties ever formed the government of the day. Even a vote of no confidence in the chancellor had minimal effect. Thus, although Germany had universal male suffrage, the kaiser's authority in many areas was impervious to popular control.

Right-wing parties

On most issues Wilhelm and his governments could rely on the backing of the right-wing parties: the Conservatives, the Free Conservatives and the National Liberals. However, after 1890 the voting strength of these parties was in decline. In 1887 they won 48 per cent of the popular vote; by 1912 their share of the vote was down to 26 per cent. Consequently, the imperial government had to find support from other parties if legislation was to be ratified.

The Centre Party

The Centre Party, which consistently won between 90 and 110 seats, was the largest party in the *Reichstag* until 1912. Representing Catholics, it had a wide spectrum of socio-political views ranging from conservatism to progressive social reform. By 1900 it was the pivotal party, allying with either right or left as the occasion demanded.

The Social Democrat Party

The Wilhelmine era saw the meteoric rise of the Social Democrat Party (SPD). Liberated by the lapse of the Anti-Socialist Law in 1890, the SPD appealed to Germany's growing proletariat. In 1893 it had won 25 per cent of the popular vote. In 1912 it won 35 per cent, becoming the largest party in the *Reichstag*. The SPD was far from united. In 1891 it adopted an uncompromising **Marxist programme** to overthrow the Wilhelmine class system. However, many SPD members, who were committed to democratic socialism, favoured the party's so-called **minimum programme**. Given that most SPD deputies talked in favour of revolution, most of the other political parties regarded the SPD as a force for evil.

Interest groups

In the 1890s professionally led interest groups became powerful. Some were economic **lobby groups** like the Agrarian League and the League of German Industrialists. There were a huge variety of trade unions. There were also nationalist pressure groups. These included the **Pan-German League**, the Navy League and the Colonial Society. These organisations were a symptom of escalating political participation, especially on the part of the middle class.

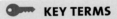

KEY TERMS

Marxist programme
The plan of those who supported the ideas of Karl Marx. Marxists believed that leaders of the proletariat must work to overthrow the capitalist system by (violent) revolution.

Minimum programme
The name given to the plans of moderate socialists who were opposed to violent revolution.

Lobby groups Particular groups who campaign to persuade politicians to pass legislation favouring their interests.

Pan-German League
Formed in 1893, the League was a right-wing nationalist movement. It supported German expansion both in Europe and worldwide.

The states

While the 25 federal states retained control over many domestic matters, imperial authority inexorably gained at the expense of that of the states. This happened not only because of Germany's greater role on the world stage, but because domestically the functions of the *Reich* government expanded, while those of the states remained static. The social insurance schemes (see pages 133–4) were *Reich* measures. Tariffs were *Reich* issues. So were military and naval matters. Urbanisation, better communications, the influence of education and military service eroded provincial isolation and helped by 1914 to bring about a strong sense of German identity. The great issues of the day were German, not state, issues.

Prussia

Prussia was easily the *Reich*'s largest state. Its state parliament, the *Landtag*, elected by a three-class male suffrage system which gave disproportionate political weight to the rich, remained a bastion of conservative interests. German chancellors, with the exception of Caprivi, were also prime ministers of Prussia. (The separation of the two officers proved to be impossible: all chancellors after Caprivi were thus minister-presidents of Prussia.) This dualism meant that, while as imperial chancellors they had often to pursue a liberal policy, as Prussian prime ministers they had to respond to a conservative majority.

The army

Bismarck had fought hard to keep the military under political control. His successors, however, found it hard to stand up to the military chiefs, who frequently had Wilhelm's support. Civilian ministers were not consulted when the general staff drew up its war plans. War, declared Count Schlieffen, head of the general staff from 1891 until 1906, was too serious a business to be left to politicians. Most of Germany's civilian leaders agreed: they did not question the expertise of Schlieffen or his master-plan in the event of war (see page 000).

By 1914 the German army was no longer so Prussian dominated or aristocratically led as it had been under Bismarck. Most officers were now from the middle class. Nevertheless, in 1913 over half the officers of rank of colonel and above were aristocrats. Officers were selected not by competitive examination, but by regimental commanders who tended to pick men of like mind and background. Bourgeois officers aped the ways of their aristocratic brothers-in-arms. The army thus remained a right-wing force whose officers often regarded 'mere' civilians with contempt. Most civilians, by contrast, admired military virtues and had great faith in the army as an institution. The special status of the army was a major stumbling block to a modernisation of the political system.

The structuralist view

From the 1960s the 'structuralist' school of historiography, led by H.U. Wehler, sought to explain history through detailed examination of social, political and economic forces. Wehler and fellow structuralists believed that Wilhelm II lacked the strength of character to determine a coherent and co-ordinated policy. Given the power vacuum, Wehler believed that Prussia's traditional elites – *Junkers*, army officers, leading civil servants and diplomats – exerted a dominating influence over German affairs. According to the structuralists, these elites were determined to maintain their power against the perceived threat of mass democracy. This prompted them to co-operate with the newly emerging leaders of industry and commerce. The structuralists claim that the elites set about imposing anti-democratic and anti-modern values on German society. In Wehler's view, for example, Germany's decision in the 1890s to undertake *Weltpolitik* (see page 177) was 'social imperialism' – an attempt to buttress the position of the elites by diverting the masses away from social and political reform and towards a populist acceptance of the kaiser and the *Reich*.

The anti-structuralist view

While the elites had a considerable influence in the Wilhelmine era, the structuralist interpretation is far too sweeping:

- It exaggerates the unity of purpose within the elites. The conception of the German nobility – or even the Prussian nobility alone – as a single class is nonsense.
- *Junker* influence was in decline, even in the army.
- *Weltpolitik* had little to do with social imperialism.
- Although most members of the German bourgeoisie – academics, clergymen, doctors, lawyers, engineers, bankers, merchants – feared revolution and opposed full democracy, this does not mean they took their cue from the elite.

A reactionary state?

While Wilhelmine Germany can be seen as a reactionary state, in which the old elites exerted huge influence and the kaiser was an authoritarian ruler, Germany was rather more democratic than scholars once believed:

- The German press had considerable freedom and criticisms of the kaiser were commonplace. Wilhelm's expressions of autocratic power, in particular, evoked storms of protest.
- By the early twentieth century, the *Reichstag* had an impressive legislative record and a central place in the popular imagination.
- Given the growth in political activity, Germany's leaders often responded to, rather than manipulated public opinion.

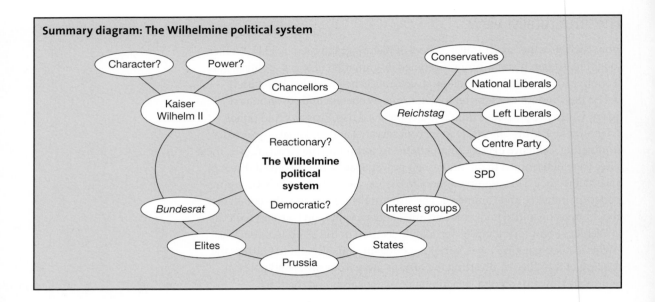

Summary diagram: The Wilhelmine political system

2 Economic and social trends

▶ *Why was Germany so successful economically?*

German industry, strong by the mid-nineteenth century, forged ahead after 1871, profiting from political unity. Between 1870 and 1913, while Britain's productive capacity doubled, that of Germany increased eight-fold. Only the USA showed a faster rate of growth. By 1914 Germany had become Europe's industrial superpower. This was partly the result of continued increases in production in 'old' industries: coal, iron, heavy engineering and textiles. However, what really marked out the German economy was the expansion of newer industries: steel, electrical engineering, chemicals and motor construction:

- German steel production increased nearly nine-fold in this period. By 1914 German output was double that of Britain's (see Table 6.3 on page 164).
- Two German firms, AEG and Siemens, dominated the world electrical industry. By 1914 nearly half the world's electrical products originated from Germany.
- The German chemical industry led the way in the production of fertilisers, dyes and pharmaceutical products.
- Daimler and Benz manufactured the world's first marketable automobile.

Reasons for German economic success

- Germany's population continued to grow rapidly, from just under 50 million in 1890 to almost 68 million in 1914. This provided both the market and the labour force for an expanding economy. Internal migration continued unabated as Germans moved from the countryside into towns. In 1871, 64 per cent lived in the countryside; by 1910 this had fallen to 40 per cent.

- Germany possessed huge natural resources: coal from the Ruhr, Saar and Silesia; iron ore from Alsace-Lorraine and the Ruhr.
- Germany had a splendid railway system.
- Germany had an excellent education system. Its institutes of higher education led the world. As well as offering study in traditional subjects, they made increasing provision for those with technical skills. Between 1890 and 1914 German university enrolments increased from 28,000 to 60,000. A university degree came within the grasp of the lower middle class.
- German industry encouraged scientific research. Many important discoveries, especially in the new industries, resulted from this policy.
- German banks provided generous long-term credit facilities for industrial firms. Representatives of banks were often invited on to the board of directors of firms, thus cementing a close partnership between the banking and commercial sectors of the economy.
- The banks were instrumental in the development of a distinctly German feature of industrialisation: **cartels**. In Britain and the USA the idea of groups of businesses combining together to control prices, production levels and marketing was seen as being against the spirit of free enterprise and against the consumer's interests. In Germany, by contrast, cartels were seen as a sensible means of achieving economic planning, eliminating wasteful competition and promoting efficient large-scale production. In 1875 there were only eight cartels in Germany. By 1905, 366 existed.
- In 1888 agriculture's share of Germany's **gross national product** had been about a half; by 1914 it had shrunk to less than one quarter. Those employed in agriculture dropped from 42 to 34 per cent between 1882 and 1907. Nevertheless, Germany remained largely self-sufficient in terms of food supply.

 KEY TERMS

Cartel An association of manufacturers who come to a contractual agreement about the level of production and the scale of prices and maintain a monopoly.

Gross national product The total value of all goods and services produced within a country.

The standard of living

Not all Germans benefited from the booming economy. The mass of the German population was agricultural and industrial workers. For agricultural labourers, life was particularly difficult. To many on the land, industrial employment seemed an attractive option. But living and working conditions in the industrial towns remained dismally poor for most people. Nevertheless, the standard of living of most Germans was rising. Between 1885 and 1913 real wages rose by over 30 per cent. This was at a time when unemployment rarely exceeded three per cent and when the length of the average working week was falling.

Table 6.3 The development of the German economy

Year	Population (millions)	Percentage of population in towns over 2000
1871	41.1	36.1
1880	42.2	41.4
1890	49.4	42.5
1900	56.4	54.4
1910	64.9	60.0

Output of heavy industry (millions of tonnes)

	Coal			Steel	
Year	Germany	Britain	Year	Germany	Britain
1871	37.7	119.2	1871	0.14	0.41
1880	59.1	149.3	1880	0.69	1.32
1890	89.2	184.5	1890	2.13	3.64
1900	149.5	228.8	1900	6.46	4.98
1910	222.2	268.7	1910	13.10	6.48

Index of industrial production (1913 = 100%)

Year	Per cent
1871	21.1
1880	49.4
1890	57.3
1900	61.0
1910	86.0
1913	100.0

Balance of payments (millions of marks)

Year	Imports	Exports balance	Visible balance	Invisible balance	Overall
1880	2814	2923	+109	+168	+277
1890	4162	3335	−827	+1249	+422
1900	5769	4611	−1158	+1566	+408
1910	8927	7475	−1452	+2211	+759

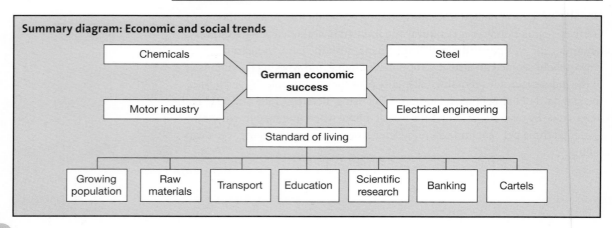

Summary diagram: Economic and social trends

Chemicals — German economic success — Steel

Motor industry — Electrical engineering

Standard of living

Growing population · Raw materials · Transport · Education · Scientific research · Banking · Cartels

3 Intellectual trends

▶ *What were the main right-wing intellectual trends in the period 1890–1914?*

While Marxist ideas were enthusiastically supported by the left, right-wing politicians increasingly espoused nationalism and **anti-Semitism**.

Nationalism

In the mid-nineteenth century German nationalism had been a progressive force that aimed to promote parliamentary government. By the end of the century this had changed. Most nationalists were now conservative, bent on maintaining the *status quo* in a militarised Germany. Many late nineteenth-century European writers, by no means all German, extolled the virtues of the Germanic race. Militant German nationalists were invariably hostile to – and contemptuous of – other races, especially Slavs. This had some impact on the substantial number of non-Germans – Poles, French and Danes – who lived within the *Reich*. Nationalists wanted to create an ethnically and linguistically homogeneous nation-state. They had little respect for minority languages and culture. There was some discrimination against national minorities, particularly the Poles, who comprised five per cent of Germany's population. Prussia's language legislation in Poland gave rise to a political crisis of national proportions, including a mass strike by 40,000 Polish schoolchildren in 1906. Repression fuelled rather than dampened Polish nationalism.

Anti-Semitism

By the late nineteenth century many German nationalists were anti-Semitic. Before this time European anti-Semitism was based to a large extent on religious hostility: Jews were blamed for the death of Christ and for not accepting Christianity. While anti-Semitism did not disappear, hostility towards Jews in Germany was politically insignificant by the mid-nineteenth century. In 1871 the German Empire extended total civil equality to Jews.

Throughout the nineteenth century, thousands of Russian Jews, fleeing from persecution, settled in Germany. Many prospered, becoming doctors, bankers, lawyers and academics. Thus, by 1900 Jews played an active and visible part in the cultural, economic and financial life of Germany. Most saw themselves as loyal Germans. Many no longer identified with a separate Jewish community: some intermarried with Germans and converted to Christianity. In 1910 the 600,000 practising Jews who lived in the *Reich* constituted about one per cent of the population.

 KEY TERM

Anti-Semitism Hatred of Jews.

Belief in race struggle

During the late nineteenth century anti-Semitism became increasingly racial rather than religious. As early as the 1850s French Count Joseph Arthur de Gobineau argued that races were physically and psychologically different. History, in Gobineau's view, was essentially a racial struggle and the rise and fall of civilisations was racially determined. He claimed that all the high cultures in the world were the work of the Aryan (or Germanic) race and that cultures declined when Aryans interbred with racially 'lower stock'.

Charles Darwin's *On The Origin of Species*, published in 1859, provided further ammunition for the race cause. Although Darwin said nothing about race, his theory of natural selection as a means of evolution was adopted – and adapted – by many scholars. 'Social Darwinists' soon claimed that races and nations needed to be fit to survive and rule. A number of writers claimed that the Germans had been selected to dominate the earth. They therefore needed more land. This would have to be won from other inferior races, most likely the Slavs. Such visions of international politics as an arena of struggle between different races for supremacy were commonplace by 1914.

The growth of anti-Semitism

Militant German nationalists, who believed that the Germans were indeed the master race, were invariably hostile to – and contemptuous of – other races, especially the Jews. Jews came to stand for all that nationalists loathed: liberalism, socialism and pacifism. Pamphleteers, newspaper editors and politicians presented anti-Semitic views to the German public. So did artists and musicians (like Richard Wagner, the famous composer). Among the most prominent anti-Semitic writers was Wagner's son-in-law, Houston Stewart Chamberlain. Son of a British admiral and a German mother, Chamberlain published his most influential work – *Foundations of the Nineteenth Century* – in 1900. He claimed that the Jews were a degenerate race, conspiring to attain world domination and threatening German greatness. His book became a bestseller in Germany, even drawing praise from Wilhelm II.

Economic factors may have encouraged anti-Semitism. Those groups hit by economic and social change (especially peasant farmers and skilled workers) were easily persuaded that Jewish financiers were to blame. Anti-Semitic prejudice was also strong in the higher reaches of society: the court, the civil service, the army and the universities. Thus, anti-Jewish feeling permeated broad sections of German society. In the late nineteenth century anti-Semitic politicians contested elections. Right-wing parties, which espoused anti-Semitism, gained a majority in the *Reichstag* in 1893.

The strength of political anti-Semitism in Germany should not be exaggerated. The success of the nationalist parties in 1893 had little to do with anti-Semitism. Indeed, no major German political party pre-1914 was dominated by anti-Semites and after 1900 the anti-Semitic parties were in steep decline, running out of voters and money. Respectable opinion in Germany remained opposed to anti-Semitism. In 1914 German Jews seemed in less danger than Jews in France or Russia.

SOURCE B

The future Wilhelm II, writing to Emperor William I in 1885 with regard to Adolf Stoecker. Stoecker, an anti-Semitic court chaplain, had been found guilty in a libel case brought by a Jewish newspaper editor and looked set to lose his court position. Quoted in J.C.G. Röhl, *The Kaiser and his Court: Wilhelm II and the Government of Germany*, Cambridge University Press, 1995.

*You will have read and heard of the wholly irresponsible way in which the entire **Judenthum** community of the Reich, with the support of its damned press, has fallen upon poor Stoecker and covered him with insults, slanders and defamation and finally forced him into a monstrous legal case. Now after the judgement of the court, which is unfortunately far too much under Jewish control, a veritable storm of indignation and anger has broken out in all levels of the nation. One cannot believe that in our time, such a heap of vileness, lies and wickedness can be brought together in one place … From all sides … I am receiving letters with the question: 'Does the Emperor know what is going on? Does he realize what the score is? How the Jews – and behind them the Socialists and Progressives – are trying everything to get Stoecker sacked?' One even says the Jews have tried to secure friends in Court circles in order to work on you against Stoecker … O dear grandfather, it is disgusting to observe how in our Christian-German, good Prussian land, the Judenthum, twisting and corrupting everything, has the cheek to attack such men and in the most shameless, insolent way to seek their downfall.*

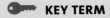

What does Source B suggest about Wilhelm II's views about Jews? **?**

KEY TERM

Judenthum The Jewish community in Germany.

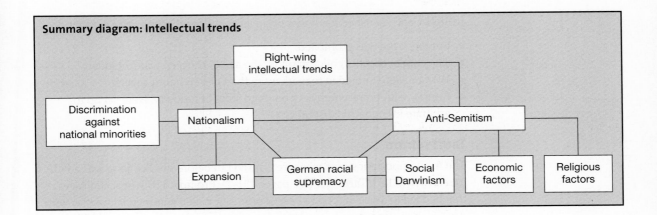

Summary diagram: Intellectual trends

Domestic politics 1890–1914

▶ *What were the main domestic issues in Germany from 1890 to 1914?*

Bismarck's departure in 1890 had repercussions in domestic policy. Wilhelm II was determined to rule the German *Reich* and its powerful constituent state, the military monarchy of Prussia. But while he was often a determining voice, he was not a dictator. He was always obliged to come to an accommodation with the incumbent *Reich* chancellor (whom he appointed), the *Reich* secretaries, the *Reichstag* and the Prussian Parliament, as well as the governments of the other German states. Increasingly too, public opinion, as expressed through political parties, churches, trade unions, special interest groups, pamphlets and books, newspapers and popular demonstrations, acted as something of a brake on his personal influence.

Caprivi's 'new course' 1890–4

Leo Caprivi, a middle-aged soldier with a good administrative record but little political experience, became chancellor in 1890. Wilhelm thought him an amenable character who would do what he was told. In fact, he soon displayed a will of his own. In his first major speech he declared that he was ready to steer a 'new course' that involved a more consultative approach to government and a conciliatory attitude to previously hostile forces. He went out of his way to make concessions to socialists and Poles: the anti-socialist laws were allowed to lapse and teachers in Polish-populated Prussian areas were allowed to use the Polish language.

In 1891 Caprivi pushed a number of social measures through the *Reichstag*:

- Sunday work was prohibited.
- The employment of children under the age of thirteen was forbidden.
- Women were forbidden to work more than eleven hours a week.
- Courts, with representatives from both sides of industry, were set up to arbitrate in industrial disputes.

Tariff reform

The most important single measure Caprivi put before the *Reichstag* was a bill to reform the 1879 Tariff Act (see pages 131–2). Prompted by wheat shortages that had led to a rise in food prices, Caprivi negotiated commercial treaties with Austria, Italy, Russia and a number of smaller states between 1891 and 1894. Germany agreed to reduce tariffs on agricultural imports in return for favourable rates for German manufactured goods.

The Agrarian League

Although most parties supported tariff reform, conservatives opposed it. So did the Agrarian League, formed in 1893. The Agrarian League, which soon had 300,000 members, became an effective and well-organised pressure group. It mounted a virulent anti-Caprivi campaign, denouncing him as a socialist bent on ruining wheat producers. It also agitated for subsidies, import controls and minimum prices to protect German farmers.

The army bill

Caprivi angered the right further by reducing the period of military service from three to two years. He then alienated the left by introducing an army bill that increased the peacetime army strength by 84,000 men. When the army bill was defeated, Caprivi dissolved the *Reichstag*. In the 1893 election, the Conservatives and National Liberals improved their position and the new *Reichstag* passed the army bill.

Caprivi's fall

Wilhelm's enthusiasm for social reform soon cooled. Conservative opposition to the 'new course' reinforced Wilhelm's growing doubts about Caprivi's political suitability. Worried by the SPD's success in the 1893 elections (the party won 44 seats) and frightened by a series of anarchist outrages across Europe, Wilhelm pressed Caprivi to draw up new anti-socialist measures. Aware that the *Reichstag* would not tolerate such a step, Caprivi refused. Wilhelm and Prussian Minister-President Count Eulenburg now devised a bizarre plan to change the constitution, increasing the kaiser's power at the expense of the *Reichstag*, and going on to crush socialism. Caprivi managed to talk Wilhelm out of such a course of action. However, having lost the Kaiser's confidence, Caprivi resigned in 1894.

Prince Hohenlohe 1894–1900

Prince Chlodwig Hohenlohe-Schillingsfürst, the new chancellor, was a 75-year-old Bavarian aristocrat of mildly liberal views. He soon became little more than a figurehead. The government was dominated by men who were more closely in tune with the direction of policy desired by the kaiser.

In 1894–5 the governments in Germany and Prussia took strong action against potential revolutionaries. SPD offices in Berlin were ransacked and party leaders put on trial. Prussians suspected of sympathising with socialism lost their jobs. However, the *Reichstag* rejected all efforts to pass an anti-socialist law. By 1897 a state of deadlock existed between government and *Reichstag*, much as in the last years of Bismarck's rule (see pages 148–9). The government would not introduce legislation acceptable to the *Reichstag* majority, and the majority refused to accept bills presented by the government. In conservative circles there was talk of the former chief of the general staff, General Waldersee, staging a military coup and overthrowing the constitution. Nothing came of this.

What was Waldersee proposing in Source C and why?

SOURCE C

From advice given to Wilhelm II by General Alfred Waldersee in 1897.

In view of the tremendous growth of the Social Democrat movement, it appears to me to be inevitable that we are approaching the moment when the State's instruments of power must measure themselves with those of the working masses. If the struggle is inevitable, the State cannot gain anything by postponing it. I feel that it is in the State's interests not to leave it to the Social Democrat leaders to decide when the great reckoning is to begin. For the moment the State is, with certainty, still strong enough to suppress any rising.

Reorganisation of the government

In 1897:

- Alfred von Tirpitz became navy secretary.
- Count Posadowsky-Wehner became interior minister.
- Bernhard Bülow became foreign minister.

In addition, two long-serving figures, Friedrich Holstein, a senior official in the foreign office, and Johannes Miquel, Prussian finance minister, began to assume even greater prominence. The emergence of this new team coincided with a new policy: *Weltpolitik* (see page 177).

Chancellor Bülow 1900–9

Bülow exerted a strong influence as foreign minister before becoming chancellor in 1900. A competent administrator, he had Wilhelm's trust and effectively handled the *Reichstag*. Mainly interested in foreign policy, he refrained from close contact with the various *Reichstag* parties, hoping not to become too involved in domestic issues.

Social reform

By 1900 it was clear that repressive measures had failed to retard the growth of socialism. Interior Minister Posadowsky resumed, in effect, the policy of the 'new course' (see page 168). He hoped that by extending social welfare benefits, the working class might be reconciled with the state. The new measures included:

- an extension of accident insurance (1900)
- a law making industrial courts compulsory in all large towns (1901)
- an extension of the prohibition on child labour (1903).

Tariffs

The renewal of Caprivi's commercial treaties was an issue of great controversy. While left-wing parties called for lower tariffs to reduce the price of bread, the Agrarian League demanded higher tariffs. Bülow worked successfully for a compromise. By a huge majority, the *Reichstag* restored tariffs to the pre-1892 level. Popular opposition to higher tariffs helped the SPD to win nearly a million extra votes and 26 extra seats in 1903. The Centre Party remained the largest party and continued to hold the balance of power in the *Reichstag*.

Financial problems

The mounting costs of maintaining the army, expanding the navy and running the empire resulted in a large budget deficit. In 1905 Bülow proposed a two-pronged attack on the deficit by proposing an increase in **indirect taxes** and an inheritance tax. The Centre Party and the SPD voted down the indirect taxes, which would have hit ordinary Germans hard. The Conservatives and the Centre Party weakened the inheritance tax so as to make it financially insignificant.

The Hottentot election

Bülow's government was criticised for its handling of a revolt in German South-West Africa in 1904–5. The Hottentot rebels were crushed but subsequent revelations of brutality, corruption and incompetence in the colony encouraged the Centre Party to ally with the SPD and others to vote against the government's proposal to provide extra money for colonial administration.

In 1907 Bülow, determined to bring the Centre Party to heel, dissolved the *Reichstag*. In the ensuing **Hottentot election**, pro-government parties did well, campaigning on a nationalistic, anti-socialist and anti-Catholic ticket. The Conservatives, Free Conservatives, National Liberals and Left Liberals came together in a coalition known as the 'Bülow Bloc'. Bülow removed ministers objectionable to the Bloc. Posadowsky, for example, was dismissed and replaced by Bethmann-Hollweg, a conservative bureaucrat. The Bloc, however, was always fragile. Most Conservatives preferred to co-operate with the Centre Party than ally with the Left Liberals, with whom they had little in common.

The *Daily Telegraph* affair

A major crisis occurred in the autumn of 1908 following an article in Britain's *Daily Telegraph* newspaper in which Wilhelm expressed his wish for closer relations with Britain. *Reichstag* deputies questioned Wilhelm's right to make such important policy statements and there was suddenly clamour for constitutional changes to reduce the kaiser's power. Bülow, who had cleared Wilhelm's article before publication, was in a difficult position. Caught between loyalty to Wilhelm and the demands of the *Reichstag*, he secured a promise from the kaiser that constitutional formalities would in future be properly respected.

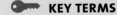

KEY TERMS

Indirect taxes Taxes placed on the sale of goods rather than those collected directly from the taxpayer.

Hottentot election This election was named after native rebels in South-West Africa.

Wilhelm's declaration mollified the opposition and the crisis ended without leading to constitutional change. However, Wilhelm' trust in Bülow had been fatally weakened. He determined to be rid of him. He did not have long to wait. As naval and colonial expenditure continued to mount, the budget deficit rose. To cover the deficit, Bülow introduced a finance bill increasing indirect taxation (opposed by the SPD) and the inheritance tax (opposed by Conservatives). The Centre, keen to have its revenge on Bülow for 1906–7, supported the Conservative stand. When the chancellor's budget proposals were rejected by the *Reichstag* in 1909, Wilhelm secured Bülow's resignation.

Chancellor Bethmann-Hollweg

Theobald Bethmann-Hollweg, a conservative, now became chancellor, even though he had little support in the *Reichstag*. His essential conservatism aligned him to the right-wing parties. Search for broader *Reichstag* support only alienated his natural supporters. The 1912 elections further increased Bethmann-Hollweg's difficulties since there was a distinct shift to the left, with the SPD and a group of Left Liberals winning 110 and 42 seats, respectively. Given that the new *Reichstag* was no longer dominated by the Conservative–Centre Party alliance, Bethmann-Hollweg found it difficult to push government bills through the *Reichstag*.

Serious budgetary problems continued. In 1912–13 the problems of imperial finance and defence came to a head. Both the army and navy submitted major expenditure plans. Fortunately for Bethmann-Hollweg the inheritance tax was finally accepted. Ironically, the tax was still opposed by the Conservatives – who supported the military measures – and supported by Socialists – who disliked military spending but were keen to set the precedent of a property-based tax.

The new tax did not solve the fiscal crisis. By 1914 the *Reich* debt reached 5 billion marks. Given that indirect taxes were unpopular with the left and direct taxes unpopular with the right, there was no easy solution.

The Prussian constitution

Although Conservatives were losing support in the *Reichstag*, in the Prussian *Landtag* their position was virtually unassailable. They controlled the upper chamber and usually had a majority in the lower house, which was still elected by the outmoded three-class system (see pages 50–1). In 1908 the SPD won 23 per cent of the vote in the Prussian elections but won only seven seats. The Conservatives, with sixteen per cent of the vote, won 212 seats. This glaring injustice led to increasing demands for reform.

The SPD

In 1912 the SPD became the largest party in the *Reichstag*. However, its deputies remained divided between orthodox Marxists, who maintained their revolutionary agenda, and moderates, who believed that the party's role was to fight for the improvement of conditions by peaceful means within the framework of capitalism.

Significantly, in 1913 SPD deputies supported the new taxes that Bethmann-Hollweg introduced to cover increased defence expenditure. While they might resent the injustice of the Prussian franchise, indirect taxes and the high price of food, SPD deputies were aware that most SPD voters were patriotic and concerned about the perceived threat from Russia, France and Britain.

Nationalist associations

After 1912 the various nationalist associations (for example, the Pan-German League and the Navy League) became more vocal in their criticism of the German government for what they regarded as its weakness at home and abroad. By 1914 many extreme nationalists were anti-socialist, anti-Semitic and anti-parliamentarian. Many believed in Germanic superiority and dreamed of a new Bismarck who would be strong and ruthless, unafraid to pursue aggressive policies against enemies at home and abroad. 'The political maelstrom of radical ideologies out of which Nazism would eventually emerge was already swirling powerfully well before the First World War', said historian Richard Evans (1978).

The Zabern affair

Relations between Alsace-Lorraine and the rest of Germany were poor. There was considerable friction between the local populace and garrison troops. At Zabern, a small town in Alsace, a young officer made contemptuous remarks about Alsatian recruits that aroused indignation and led to several demonstrations. During one disturbance in November 1913 the commanding officer ordered his men to clear the streets. In the ensuing mêlée 28 citizens were detained overnight in the barracks. This led to public and official protests: only civilian courts and the police could interfere with the liberty of citizens; the army was acting above the law.

Rather than punish the soldiers concerned, Wilhelm ordered them to be sent away on manoeuvres. The affair rumbled on. The minister of war and Bethmann-Hollweg rejected criticism of the army on the grounds that commanding officers were responsible only to the kaiser and certainly not to the *Reichstag*. The political opposition was so intense that there was a massive vote of no confidence in Bethmann-Hollweg. This had little effect. While the Zabern affair underlined the power of the kaiser, it also showed that he could not altogether ignore public opinion.

The political situation in 1914

In 1914 Germany was still in many respects an authoritarian monarchy. Wilhelm's power to appoint the chancellor enabled him to set the general tenor of government, and he did so, particularly in the period from 1897 to 1908. This coincided with Bülow's political supremacy. Bülow recognised that his own position depended on catering to Wilhelm's personal whims. However, the kaiser's political power was within a constitutional framework. German governments could not ignore the *Reichstag* and had to patch up working majorities in order to pass legislation. The *Reichstag*, with its ever-increasing SPD presence, extended its right to debate government policy. Nor was Wilhelm able to take firm action against his critics. All Wilhelm's more repressive schemes were defeated in the *Reichstag*. While he might dream of using his army to strike against the SPD, he did not dare do so in reality.

It may be that Germany was on the way to evolving into a thoroughly democratic state. Certainly many Germans desired the creation of a genuine parliamentary democracy in which the imperial government was responsible to the *Reichstag*. However, the forces of conservatism were strong. The middle classes, backbone of the empire, were solidly on the side of the Establishment. While most *Reichstag* deputies favoured constitutional change, the vast majority had great respect for the monarchy. In short, while there was political tension and frustration in Germany – as elsewhere in Europe in 1914 – revolution seemed less likely in Germany than elsewhere.

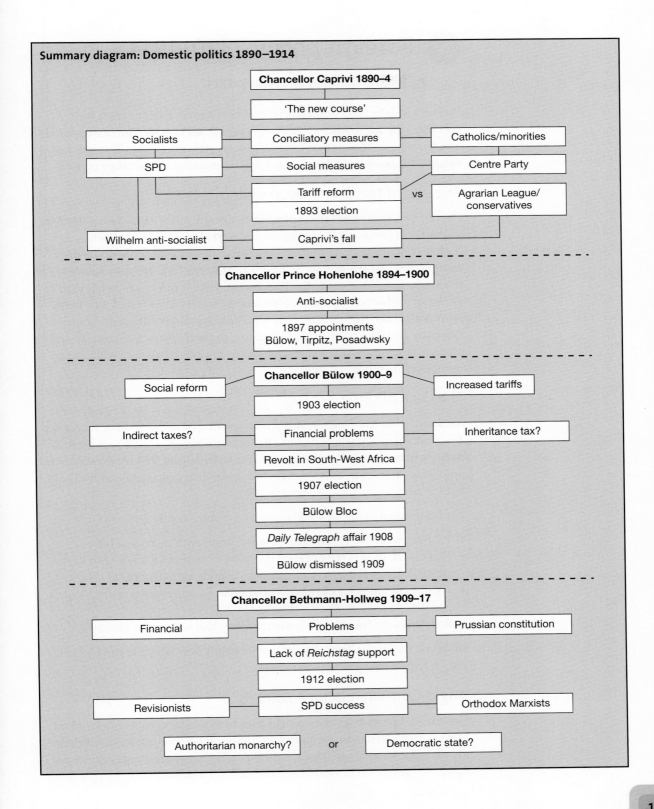

Summary diagram: Domestic politics 1890–1914

Chancellor Caprivi 1890–4

'The new course'

| Socialists | Conciliatory measures | Catholics/minorities |

| SPD | Social measures | Centre Party |

Tariff reform — vs — Agrarian League/conservatives

1893 election

| Wilhelm anti-socialist | Caprivi's fall |

- -

Chancellor Prince Hohenlohe 1894–1900

Anti-socialist

1897 appointments
Bülow, Tirpitz, Posadwsky

- -

| Social reform | **Chancellor Bülow 1900–9** | Increased tariffs |

1903 election

| Indirect taxes? | Financial problems | Inheritance tax? |

Revolt in South-West Africa

1907 election

Bülow Bloc

Daily Telegraph affair 1908

Bülow dismissed 1909

- -

Chancellor Bethmann-Hollweg 1909–17

| Financial | Problems | Prussian constitution |

Lack of *Reichstag* support

1912 election

| Revisionists | SPD success | Orthodox Marxists |

Authoritarian monarchy?   or   Democratic state?

Foreign policy 1890–1914

▶ *Why did Germany go to war in 1914?*

Bismarck's resignation was a crucial event in German foreign policy. By upholding the Triple Alliance (see pages 143–4), seeking friendship with Britain and signing the Reinsurance Treaty (see page 141) with Russia, Bismarck had ensured the isolation of France. After 1890 there was a reorientation of policy.

The end of the Bismarckian system

Chancellor Caprivi had little experience in foreign policy. Thus, Baron Holstein, a senior civil servant in the foreign office, exerted considerable influence. A protégé of Bismarck, Holstein tried to copy the tortuous diplomacy of his mentor – with far less success. In March 1890 Caprivi and Holstein allowed the Reinsurance Treaty to lapse. They believed that it was incompatible with Germany's other commitments, especially to Austria. They feared that, if the terms leaked out, then Austria, Italy and Britain would be estranged from Germany. Bismarck thought the failure to sign the Reinsurance Treaty an act of criminal stupidity, which would push Russia towards an alliance with France. Events were to prove him right.

The Dual Alliance

Annoyed by the growing friendship between Austria and Germany, Russia was also alarmed by Wilhelm's attempts to ingratiate himself with Britain. Fear of isolation drove Russia into the arms of France. In August 1891 the two countries negotiated an entente. This was followed by a military convention in 1892, which laid the basis for the Dual Alliance in 1894.

The significance of the Dual Alliance was not immediately apparent since:

- Wilhelm was soon on excellent personal terms with his cousin Tsar Nicholas II. In 1894 the *Reichstag* approved a commercial treaty with Russia, which did something to restore Russian confidence in Germany.
- For most of the 1890s Germany's position in Europe seemed secure. Austria and Italy were allies. Russia, absorbed in Asia, was friendly.
- Relations with France were better than they had been under Bismarck.

However, the Dual Alliance meant that Germany now faced the prospect of a war on two fronts.

Anglo-German relations 1890–8

Germany's diplomatic position would have been greatly strengthened if it had reached an understanding with Britain. However, German advances to Britain in 1894 came to nothing. Indeed, in 1896 Anglo-German relations deteriorated following Wilhelm's congratulatory telegram to President Kruger for upholding the independence of the Transvaal after the **Jameson Raid**. Wilhelm and his advisers hoped that by bringing pressure to bear on Britain they could draw it closer to the Triple Alliance. But the Kruger telegram simply aroused indignation in Britain.

Weltpolitik

Bismarck thought of Germany as a continental European power. While he had no objection to overseas colonies, he did not regard them as a priority and had no desire to alienate Britain. Bülow and Tirpitz (see page 170) had a different vision of Germany's future. This vision, supported by Wilhelm and many ordinary Germans, was **Weltpolitik**. The decision to pursue *Weltpolitik* after 1897 was a vital moment in German history.

Structuralist historians (see page 161) think that the ruling class embarked on *Weltpolitik* hoping to rally support around the kaiser and divert attention away from the socialist threat at home. (In 1898 the SPD won 27 per cent of the vote in the national elections.) However, the view that *Weltpolitik* was simply a manoeuvre in domestic politics is too simplistic. There were powerful forces at work in Germany that contributed to the new policy:

- Industrialisation had created economic demands for the acquisition of raw materials and markets beyond Europe.
- German nationalists believed that Germany's survival as a leading nation necessitated a more active world policy.
- Pressure groups like the Pan-German League and the Navy League popularised the message of *Weltpolitik* and exerted pressure on the government to pursue the policy to the full.

In reality, *Weltpolitik* was a deliberate attempt to make Germany into a world power on a par with Britain. This meant expanding Germany's navy, creating a large colonial empire and supporting Germany's economic interests across the globe. Wilhelm declared that henceforward no major colonial issue must be decided without Germany having a say in it.

Anglo-German rivalry

The fact that Wilhelm II was a passionate supporter of *Weltpolitik* was crucial. This may have arisen from his love–hate relationship with Britain. Revenging himself on his mother's native land seems to have become something of an obsession with him. (He loathed his mother.) 'The English', he promised, 'will be brought low some day.'

Wilhelm believed passionately that Germany's future lay on the high seas. He was dissatisfied with a fleet only seventh in size in the world when Germany's foreign trade was almost equal to Britain's. Tirpitz was given the task of building the navy. The navy, in Tirpitz's view, was to be a direct challenge to Britain – the lever with which it would be forced to respect Germany. This was a serious

KEY TERMS

Jameson Raid In 1895 Dr Jameson led a force of 470 men into the Transvaal, hoping to spark a revolt which would overthrow President Kruger's Boer government. The raid was a total failure.

Weltpolitik This translates as world policy. The word is used to describe Wilhelm II's efforts to make Germany a great world (as well as European) power.

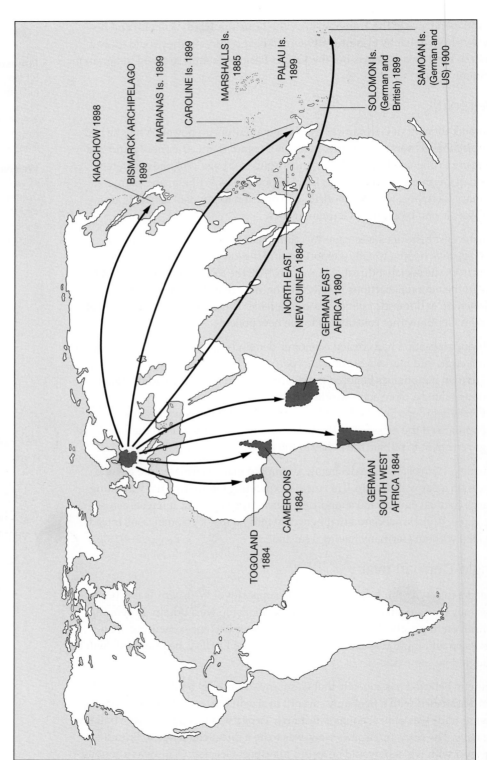

Figure 6.1 *Weltpolitik*: German overseas expansion.

KIAOCHOW 1898

BISMARCK ARCHIPELAGO 1899

MARIANAS Is. 1899

CAROLINE Is. 1899

MARSHALLS Is. 1885

PALAU Is. 1899

SOLOMON Is. (German and British) 1899

SAMOAN Is. (German and US) 1900

NORTH EAST NEW GUINEA 1884

GERMAN EAST AFRICA 1890

TOGOLAND 1884

CAMEROONS 1884

GERMAN SOUTH WEST AFRICA 1884

miscalculation. Britain felt threatened, but was not prepared to be intimidated. Nor would Britain allow Germany to be its equal. Britain's navy and colonies were the basis of its power and security. It seems not to have occurred to Wilhelm or Tirpitz that:

- Germany needed British support against Russia and France.
- Britain might look for support elsewhere.

Naval expansion

In order to gain *Reichstag* support for naval expansion, Tirpitz was instrumental in the creation in 1898 of the Navy League. Supported by financial backing from key industrialists, like Krupp, who had an obvious interest in the construction of a big navy, it soon dwarfed all the other nationalist groups, with a membership in excess of 300,000. The League drummed up popular support for naval expansion. This, in turn, put pressure on the *Reichstag*. The 1898 Naval Bill, which proposed building sixteen major ships, was finally carried by 212 votes to 139. The bill was opposed by some on the right and some on the left: the right thought the money would be best spent on the army; the left opposed any increase in military spending. In 1900 a second bill, which proposed building three battleships a year for the next six years, was passed by a larger majority than the first.

Germany and Britain 1898–1907

Bülow assumed that Britain would be unable to patch up its differences with France (over African territories) and with Russia (over central Asia). Between 1898 and 1901 Britain, concerned at its less than **splendid isolation**, made several approaches to Germany, hoping for some kind of agreement. Germany's reaction was negative. Bülow thought that Britain was seeking cheap insurance in the shape of a continental ally to save it from the effects of its rivalry with Russia. He judged that German interests were best served by remaining on good terms with Russia. The **Boer War** did not help matters. Most Germans sympathised with the Boers. Thus, instead of an alliance, there was a gradual distancing between Britain and Germany.

In 1902 Britain allayed its fears of isolation by signing an alliance with Japan. Then, in 1904 Britain agreed an entente with France. The entente was not a firm alliance, but merely an understanding to settle colonial differences. British Foreign Secretary Lord Lansdowne, who concluded the entente, did not conceive it as anti-German. But this was not the way it was seen by British and German public opinion.

The first Moroccan crisis

Hoping to break the Anglo-French entente, Germany provoked a crisis in Morocco, generally seen as being within the French sphere of influence. In March 1905 Wilhelm landed at Tangiers, and assured the Sultan of Morocco that

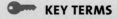

KEY TERMS

Splendid isolation For much of the late nineteenth century, Britain, protected by its navy, had not allied with any major power.

Boer War The conflict in South Africa (1899–1902) between Britain and the Boer republics of the Transvaal and the Orange Free State.

Germany considered Morocco an independent nation, a state of affairs that he would support with all his might.

This was a deliberate challenge to France. Bülow hoped to humiliate France and reveal the flimsy nature of Britain's loyalty to the entente. He miscalculated. At the international conference at Algeciras in January 1906 Britain, France and Russia supported French influence in Morocco. So, too, did Italy, Germany's (supposed) ally. Germany, not France, found itself diplomatically isolated. The Anglo-French entente had stood firm; indeed, thanks to German pressure, it had been strengthened. British leaders were now convinced that Germany represented a threat to European stability and to the security of the British Empire. The Morocco crisis thus ended disastrously for Germany.

The Anglo-Russian entente

In 1907 Britain signed an entente with Russia. This was essentially a colonial agreement, settling differences over Tibet, Persia and Afghanistan: it was not directed at Germany. Nevertheless, the German naval threat and resentment at Germany's blustering diplomatic methods played a part in its signing. Moreover, the very fact of the agreement emphasised Germany's isolation.

The situation by 1907

From 1897 to 1907, as a result of *Weltpolitik*, Germany had added the Chinese port of Kiaochow and a few islands in the Pacific Ocean (1899) to its empire. The diplomatic and strategic consequences of *Weltpolitik* were more important. Maladroit German diplomacy had resulted in Britain aligning itself with France and Russia. German newspapers complained of the ring closing round Germany. There was little substance in the 'encirclement' accusation: the **Triple Entente powers** were banded together for defensive purposes. Nevertheless, Germany's strategic position was much weaker by 1907 than it had been in 1890.

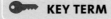

KEY TERM

Triple Entente powers
Britain, France and Russia.

The years from 1907 to 1911

The deterioration in Germany's international standing made it increasingly dependent on one loyal ally, Austria. In Bismarck's day, Germany had restrained Austria from adventurous policies in the Balkans. Now Germany began to underwrite Austrian efforts to preserve its unstable empire.

The 1909 Bosnian crisis

In October 1908 Austria annexed the province of Bosnia-Herzegovina, which it had administered since 1878, even though it had remained nominally under Turkish rule. This move was opposed by Turkey and – more importantly – Serbia, which hoped to incorporate Bosnia in its own state. Russia supported Serbia, a fellow Slav state.

Germany, keen to improve relations with Turkey, did not fully approve Austria's action. Nevertheless, Bülow assured Austrian Foreign Minister Aehrenthal

Figure 6.2 The Balkans 1908–13.

that Germany would support whatever action Austria considered appropriate
against Serbia. In January 1909, when Conrad von Hötzendorf, chief of the
Austrian General Staff, asked his German equivalent Helmuth Moltke (nephew
of Prussian army leader Moltke) what help Austria could expect if it attacked
Serbia and Russia intervened, Moltke replied that Germany would mobilise.
Aehrenthal seriously considered a war against Serbia. Only second thoughts in
Vienna prevented German involvement in a major war over Bosnia.

Russia tried to get Austria to the conference table. Austria refused to attend
unless the powers accepted the annexation. Germany supported this defiant
stand, declaring bluntly in March 1909 that if Russia did not recognise the
annexation it must take full responsibility for the subsequent course of events.
Russia, not ready to risk war, gave way and the crisis ended. Germany's

diplomatic victory was dearly bought. Russia, resentful of its humiliation, drew closer to Britain and France.

Anglo-German naval rivalry

In 1906 Britain launched HMS *Dreadnought*, a vessel that rendered all existing ships obsolete. Tirpitz and Wilhelm grasped eagerly at the possibility of building from what seemed to be a position of equal terms with Britain. Two German naval laws in 1906 and 1908 threatened Britain's naval supremacy. In 1908 the British government, facing massive pressure from public opinion, agreed to build an extra eight 'Dreadnoughts'. Britain and Germany thus became enmeshed in an expensive naval race, which worsened relations between the two countries.

Bethmann-Hollweg recognised that an agreement with Britain to limit naval construction would not only reduce his budget difficulties, but might also loosen Britain's ties to the Triple Entente. However, negotiations with Britain between 1909 and 1911 ended in failure. Wilhelm and Tirpitz refused to make any serious concessions and Britain was determined to preserve its naval supremacy.

SOURCE D

According to Source D, what were the aims of Wilhelm's foreign policy?

In 1910 Wilhelm II explained his vision for the future to David J. Hill, the US ambassador in Berlin. Quoted in J.C.G. Röhl, *Kaiser Wilhelm II*, Cambridge University Press, 2014, p. 125.

We do not want their [the British] colonies nor the dominion of the sea, we only want to have our rights respected. Germany is now almost as rich as England … What we want is an equal chance. They have tried to hold us up as a menace to Europe, but we have menaced no one. They have tried to array Europe against us, but their entente is weakening. As for the Latins, they have had their day. I do not believe the Slavs are to be the leaders of the future. Providence has designs, and it would not be a compliment to Providence to believe that it is to the Slavs and not to the Germanic race that Providence looks for the civilisation of the future. No, it is the Germanic race – we here in Germany, the English and the Americans – who are to lead the civilisation of the world.

The second Moroccan crisis

In 1911 France, in violation of the Algeciras agreement, looked set to establish full control over Morocco. Germany was prepared to accept this, but only in return for being given territory elsewhere in Africa as compensation. German Foreign Minister Alfred von Kiderlen sent the gunboat *Panther* to the Moroccan port of Agadir, ostensibly to protect German nationals, but in reality to remind France that Germany must not be ignored. He increased the tension further by demanding the whole of the French Congo.

Britain stood by France in the face of perceived German bullying. Chancellor of the Exchequer David Lloyd George warned Germany that Britain was ready for war and the British fleet prepared for action. Germany backed down, accepting a narrow strip of the French Congo as compensation for the French protectorate in Morocco. Kiderlen's diplomacy had succeeded only in heightening tensions and confirming the Triple Entente's suspicions of Germany.

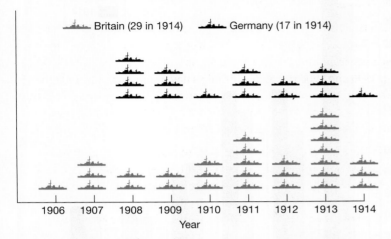

Figure 6.3 The relative numbers of 'Dreadnoughts' built by Germany and Britain 1906–14.

The years from 1911 to 1914

The last three years of peace have been the focus of considerable historical analysis. German historian Fritz Fischer (see page 187) thought that the 'excitement and bitterness of nationalistic opinion over what was seen to be the humiliating outcome of the [Moroccan] crisis were profound and enduring'. He believed that after 1911 there existed a clear continuity of German aims and policies that culminated in war in 1914: a war that was deliberately 'planned'. Fischer's main evidence was a war council of German army and navy chiefs on 8 December 1912. At this meeting Moltke announced that Germany should go to war at the first suitable opportunity and Wilhelm called for increased armaments and talked of a 'racial struggle' with Russia.

Most historians are not convinced by this 'evidence'. In truth, the meeting was a typical piece of theatrical posing and blustering, suggesting a lack of direction at the top rather than a clear indication that Germany was actually planning to unleash a war in 1914. Chancellor Bethmann-Hollweg did not even attend the meeting.

German rearmament

In 1911–12 Bethmann-Hollweg, anxious to reduce naval expenditure, made another attempt to end the naval race with Britain. The negotiations soon stalled: each side felt that the other asked too much and offered too little. The German naval bill of 1912, however, was more modest than Tirpitz had initially proposed. By 1912 the German army had become the main priority in the face of the perceived threat from Russia.

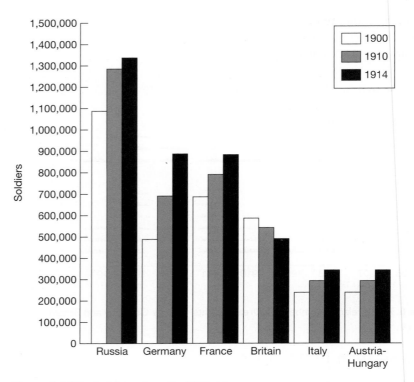

Figure 6.4 The build-up of armies 1900–14.

The Balkans 1912–13

In October 1912 the small Balkan states – Serbia, Greece, Bulgaria and Montenegro – attacked and defeated Turkey. This was a severe blow to Austria:

- It was widely believed in Vienna that the Habsburg Empire could not survive the fall of the Ottomans.
- The dramatic expansion of Serbia, particularly the fear that it might obtain Albania and a foothold on the Adriatic Sea, aroused alarm.

Hötzendorf advocated war to crush Serbia once and for all. However, Count Leopold von Berchtold, who succeeded Aehrenthal as foreign minister in 1912, opposed military action and Germany supported his cautious stance. The Great Powers met in London in 1913 to set the seal of approval on the territorial changes in the Balkans. Germany and Russia actually worked together, the former restraining the Austrians and the latter the Serbs.

German policy hardened, however, when the victorious Balkan states fell out and went to war in the summer of 1913. Austria, alarmed by Serbian incursions into Albania, determined to force the Serbs out. Berchtold was assured by Wilhelm that Germany would stand by Austria. Faced with the prospect of war with Austria, and lacking Russian support, the Serbs pulled out of Albania.

The situation by 1914

In early 1914 Bethmann-Hollweg still saw hopeful signs in Germany's international position. He was encouraged by the extent of Anglo-German co-operation during the Balkan Wars and by the settlement of several colonial disputes. But tension continued to grow. In 1913 Germany increased the peacetime strength of its army from 663,000 to 800,000. France and Russia did likewise, the latter launching a vast rearmament programme. Rearmament was accompanied in all countries by propaganda campaigns to persuade ordinary citizens that the growing risk of war justified additional military spending.

Most Germans believed they were surrounded by enemies. Russia's growing military power was a major fear. German nationalists, who saw war as an inevitable struggle for existence between nations and races, favoured a war of expansion in eastern Europe. Moreover, Germany's leaders were more inclined towards warlike solutions than the leaders of other countries. The German general staff realised that 1914–15 represented the best time for war from the German standpoint. Thereafter, Russia's rearmament programme would make war a more dangerous option.

July 1914

The assassination of Austrian Archduke Franz Ferdinand, heir to the Habsburg throne, and his wife, by Bosnian terrorists at Sarajevo on 28 June 1914 sparked the crisis that led to war. Austrian leaders, aware that the murders had been planned by a secret society that had links with the Serbian government, believed the time had come to settle accounts with Serbia. Germany agreed.

The German 'blank cheque'

Wilhelm pledged full support for Austria, whatever the consequences, to the Austrian ambassador on 5 July. Bethmann-Hollweg confirmed Wilhelm's assurance on 6 July: 'Austria must judge what is to be done to clear up her relations with Serbia. But whatever Austria's decision, she could count with certainty upon it that Germany would stand behind her as an ally.'

Bethmann-Hollweg urged Austria to attack swiftly, hoping that it might destroy Serbia without the crisis developing into a general war. Even so, he recognised the very real danger of a general war breaking out over Serbia. While not necessarily wanting war, he was ready to risk it. He remarked to the Austrian ambassador: 'If war must break out, better now than in one or two years' time, when the Entente will be stronger.'

The Austrian ultimatum

Had Austria acted quickly, war between itself and Serbia might well have been localised. In early July, most European governments were horrified by the Sarajevo assassination. There was some sympathy for Austria, even in Russia. Unfortunately, Austrian reaction was not swift. When it finally came on 23 July, it was in the form of an ultimatum to Serbia. The terms of the ultimatum were so severe that Serbia, emboldened by promises of Russian support, refused to accept them all. When Austria received the reply on 25 July, it broke off diplomatic relations with Serbia.

Crisis

Europe's powers were now faced with a terrible crisis. Britain tried to mediate by calling for an international conference. Significantly, Germany ignored such proposals and privately urged Austria to take military action. Until 27 July there was a reasonable degree of unanimity among German leaders. However, on 28 July Wilhelm, returning from a Norwegian cruise, decided that the Serbian reply ought to be accepted by Austria, who must abandon plans for war. The German foreign office was thoroughly alarmed by Wilhelm's intervention. Bethmann-Hollweg simply passed the proposal to Vienna on 28 July without comment, taking care to suppress the fact that it emanated from the kaiser. Bethmann-Hollweg's overriding concern was Russian mobilisation. If Russia mobilised first, all Germans would unite in what would be perceived as a defensive war against the threat of tsarist aggression. Moreover, Britain might be persuaded to remain neutral.

Mobilisation and war

Austria's declaration of war on Serbia on 28 July was followed by a Russian decision to order partial mobilisation. Moltke knew that once Russia began mobilising, Germany was committed to fight. This was the result of the Schlieffen Plan. Drawn up by Moltke's predecessor, it aimed to counteract the threat of a two-front war by launching a rapid all-out assault in the west in order to defeat France before turning east to face Russia. Thus, as soon as Russia began to mobilise, Germany had to mobilise its own forces. On 30 July Bethmann-Hollweg stated 'that things are out of control and the stone has started to roll'. Military matters now took precedence over diplomatic considerations.

Bethmann-Hollweg informed Russia that unless partial mobilisation was cancelled, Germany would be obliged to order full mobilisation. Russia's partial mobilisation, aimed at bringing diplomatic pressure to bear on Austria, had not been intended as a prelude to war. But in view of Germany's warning, Russia had either to suffer humiliation by cancelling that order or to order full mobilisation to defend itself against a possible German attack. On 31 July Russia opted for full mobilisation.

The German war machine now swung into action. Full mobilisation was ordered and an ultimatum dispatched to Russia demanding cessation of all measures within twelve hours. When Russia refused to comply, Germany declared war on Russia on 1 August. Two days later Germany declared war on France. **German violation of Belgium's neutrality** brought Britain into the war on 4 August.

🔑 **KEY TERM**

German violation of Belgium's neutrality
German troops, in order to get round French defences along the German frontier, invaded Belgium. Britain had pledged itself to protect Belgium's neutrality in 1839.

German responsibility for the First World War

In 1919 Germany was forced to accept responsibility for causing the First World War. By the mid-twentieth century, however, few historians believed that Germany alone was to blame for starting the war. Many, like A.J.P. Taylor, believed that the Great Powers accidentally stumbled into war in 1914. Others thought that the war was largely the result of the international system.

In 1961 Fritz Fischer (in his book *Germany's Aims in the First World War*) claimed that the German government bore the decisive share of responsibility for the start of the war because of its clear desire to achieve a German hegemony over Europe. In 1969 Fischer published *War of Illusions*, in which he suggested that German leaders deliberately planned a war of expansion from 1911. Fischer suggested that the reasons for this aggressive expansionism were to be found less in Germany's international position than in its social, economic and political situation at home. A successful war, the government hoped, 'would resolve the growing social tensions' and consolidate the position of the ruling classes.

Fischer's views generated huge controversy and continue to divide historians. Fischer's critics claim:

- There is little evidence to support the view that German leaders were actively planning an offensive war policy from 1911 onwards.
- The elites did not pursue war as a means of deflecting political opposition and thereby preserving their own threatened position. There was no major domestic crisis in Germany in 1913–14.

It seems fair to say that Germany was by no means the only country to blame for the First World War. Other powers contributed to the general deterioration in the international situation and committed major errors in July 1914. Nevertheless, German leaders must shoulder the major responsibility both for the worsening international atmosphere in the years before 1914 and for the escalation of the July 1914 crisis:

- *Weltpolitik* and the ham-fisted diplomacy which accompanied it had contributed to a marked increase in international tension and to a dangerous deterioration in Germany's strategic position by 1907.
- After 1907 German foreign policy was typified by bluster and brinkmanship.
- From early July 1914, Bethmann-Hollweg adopted a strategy of calculated risk in the hope of winning a diplomatic victory which would weaken the Triple Entente. To achieve this end the July crisis was deliberately escalated and attempts at constructive mediation were torpedoed. The calculated risk was a badly miscalculated risk – another failed exercise in brinkmanship.
- When Russia mobilised in 1914 German leaders had little option, given the Schlieffen Plan, but to accept the challenge. They did so willingly. Many accepted the nationalist rhetoric about an inevitable showdown between Slavs and Germans.

Thus, German leaders, especially Bethmann-Hollweg and Wilhelm, failed to do what they might have done to prevent war. This was because they were convinced that war was probably unavoidable, and that it was in Germany's interest to wage it at a time, and on terms, most favourable to itself. In truth, it was Germany's ill-considered actions that made war inevitable.

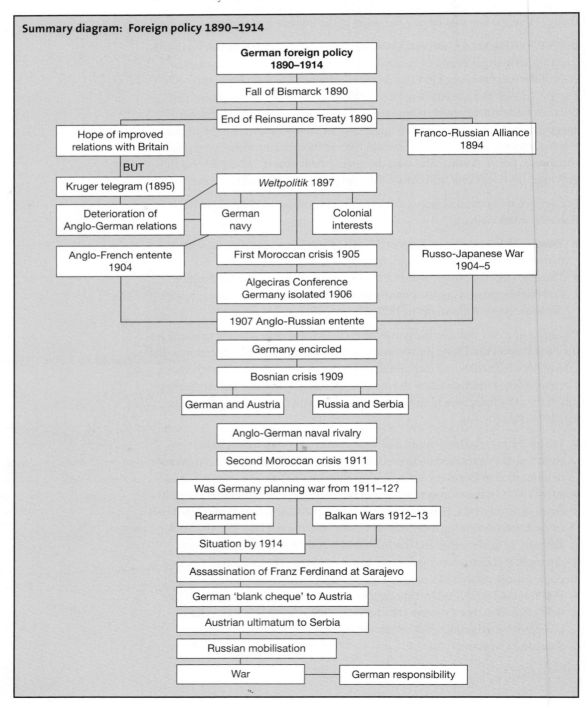

Summary diagram: Foreign policy 1890–1914

6 Key debate

▶ *To what extent did Wilhelm II rule Germany from 1890 to 1914?*

The exact nature of Wilhelm II's role within the German political system after 1890 continues to be debated. Some historians consider him to have ruled almost as an absolute monarch. Others believe that his power was much more limited and claim that the *Reichstag* was starting to really flex its muscles.

EXTRACT 1

From J.C.G. Röhl, *Kaiser Wilhelm II*, Cambridge University Press, 2014, pp. xx–xxi.

Wilhelm II was anything but a silent spectator of the momentous events of his lifetime. From his accession in the so-called Year of the Three Kaisers in 1888 until his abdication and flight to the Netherlands on 9 November 1918 he ruled the German Reich and its hegemonial constituent state, the powerful military monarchy of Prussia, not only as its figurehead but in a very direct and personal manner ... at the centre of power, and above all in the conduct of personnel, military, foreign and armaments policy, Kaiser Wilhelm's was very much the determining voice until the decision to go to war in 1914 – a decision in which he took a leading part.

EXTRACT 2

From M. Kitchen, *A History of Modern Germany 1800–2000*, Blackwell, 2006, p. 179.

The greater the importance of the federal government the greater the power of the Reichstag. [Wilhelm's] government needed a Reichstag majority in order to push through its legislation, and it could not get that majority without the support of the Centre Party. Above all it needed the Reichstag to agree both to how the money was spent and how it was to be collected. The budgetary rights of the Reichstag were strengthened as the fiscal burden increased. Nothing could be done without making compromises and concessions with and to this Catholic party. The Centre Party thus became the most powerful party of the Reichstag, and its strength and importance enhanced that of parliament. The Reichstag proved to be a reliable partner for the government and an increasing number of bills were first discussed by the parties and then introduced in the Reichstag rather than in the Bundesrat.

> **Evaluate the interpretations in both Extracts 1 and 2. Explain which you think is a more convincing explanation of who ruled Germany from 1888 until 1914.** ?

The case for Wilhelm having considerable power

- The constitution gave Wilhelm massive powers.
- He was determined to rule as well as reign. He declared, 'I am the sole master of German policy and my country must follow me wherever I go.'
- He showed that he intended to rule when he dismissed Bismarck in 1890.

- He appointed all the chancellors after Bismarck. They were his servants. When they displeased him, they were dismissed.
- He appointed all the generals, admirals, ministers and ambassadors.
- He had a central role in decision-making throughout his reign. This was particularly so with regard to foreign and military matters.
- He supported the ambitious naval and world power policies that proved disastrous for Germany.
- He played a major role in deciding that Germany should go to war in 1914.

The case for Wilhelm having only limited power

- The German constitution gave considerable powers to the chancellor, the *Reichstag,* the *Bundesrat* and state governments.
- The *Reichstag,* which voted on the money necessary for the government to operate, was growing in power.
- Neither Wilhelm nor his chancellors had much control over the *Reichstag.*
- The German press had considerable freedom.
- The government often responded to rather than manipulated public opinion.
- Wilhelm was weak and indecisive: he was unable to determine a coherent and co-ordinated policy.
- Wilhelm spent a great deal of time on social and ceremonial duties. He did not have command of the detail of the government's work.
- *Junkers,* civil servants, diplomats and army officers were the real leaders of Germany.
- Wilhelm did not control events in July 1914. He tried to stop Austria going to war with Serbia on 28 July – to no effect.

Chapter summary

Kaiser Wilhelm II's long reign was to end with the disaster that was the First World War. It is debatable to what extent he was responsible for that disaster. While he had massive potential powers and intended to rule as well as reign, he was always obliged to come to an accommodation with the *Reichstag*, the Prussian Parliament and the governments of the various German states. Given that he spent a great deal of time on social and ceremonial duties, he was forced to rely on his chancellors: Caprivi, Hohenloe, Bülow and Bethmann-Hollweg. However, the chancellors were his servants: he appointed and dismissed them all. Neither domestic nor foreign policy went according to Wilhelm's – or anyone else's – plan. In Germany the socialists grew in strength, becoming the largest party in the *Reichstag* by 1912. Germany's failure to resign the Reinsurance Treaty resulted in the Russian–French alliance while Wilhelm's support for *Weltpolitik*, especially his expansion of the German fleet, alienated Britain. Thus, by 1914 Germany was surrounded by potentially hostile powers and increasingly dependent on Austria. The German government, while not necessarily wanting war, bore a great deal of responsibility for the start of the First World War in 1914.

Refresher questions

Use these questions to remind yourself of the key material covered in this chapter.

1 To what extent did Wilhelm's personality shape the history of imperial Germany?

2 How powerful was the *Reichstag*?

3 How powerful were the elites?

4 Why was Germany so successful economically?

5 To what extent did German nationalism change in the late nineteenth and early twentieth centuries?

6 How strong was anti-Semitism in Germany by 1914?

7 How successful was Caprivi's 'new course'?

8 What were Bülow's aims?

9 What were Germany's main domestic issues in the years 1909–14?

10 Was the failure to renew the Reinsurance Treaty a major mistake?

11 How and why did *Weltpolitik* emerge as government policy?

12 Why was *Weltpolitik* seen as a threat to Britain?

13 How skilful was German diplomacy after 1897?

14 Was Germany planning a war after 1911?

15 Why did Germany go to war in 1914?

Question practice

INTERPRETATION QUESTION

1 Evaluate the interpretations in both of the passages and explain which you think is a more convincing explanation of the role of Wilhelm II in governing Germany from 1888 to 1914.

PASSAGE A

From J.C.G. Röhl, *Kaiser Wilhelm II*, Cambridge University Press, 2014, p. xv.

Kaiser Wilhelm II, imperious, impulsive, imbued with antiquated notions of the divine right of kings and of Prussia/Germany's God-given trajectory to greatness, while at the same time insecure and hypersensitive to perceived slights to his imperial dignity or his dynastic mission, was arguably the very last person who should have been entrusted with the immense powers of the Hohenzollern military monarchy at such a critical juncture in Germany's and Europe's history. Nevertheless, he stood at the apex of the Kaiserreich's policy-making pyramid for thirty years, from his accession at the premature death from cancer of his father in June 1888 to his ignominious flight into exile in the Netherlands in November 1918. All the generals and admirals, chancellors, ministers and ambassadors who served under him were appointed by him and dependent on his 'All-Highest favour' while in office. Wilhelm followed events at home and abroad with a nervous intensity that on occasions bordered on insanity, issuing orders and covering diplomatic dispatches with often furious diatribes, which have survived in their thousands in the archives. His own words and deeds mark him out as in many respects a forerunner of Hitler, not least in his vitriolic anti-Semitism in exile. And it was of course he, Prussia's Supreme War Lord, who, having on several occasions beforehand urged the Austrians to attack Serbia, gave the fateful order on the night of 3–4 July 1914 that led to disaster.

PASSAGE B

From H. Kurtz, *The Second Reich: Kaiser Wilhelm II and his Germany*, Macdonald Library, 1970, p. 120.

It was the resurrection of a fake-Kaiser leading the Reich under God and Bismarck that had corrupted him as a human being – the artifice of sham absolute power that, in his case, turned him into an accomplished and very producible actor. Throughout his reign, he received the thunderous applause of his subjects, while abroad his posturing and oratorical aggressions came to be regarded as political facts of consequence and moment. Critical contemporaries called the whole spectacular and disruptive business his 'personal rule', but the exact applicability of the term may be doubted. The strings in everything that mattered were usually pulled by other people. In the Bülow era particularly, his worst qualities were deliberately pushed into the foreground by that superficial and unscrupulous manipulator of power politics who drove the Kaiser into courses which Wilhelm's instincts told him were false and wrong. The whole ill-conceived artifice resulted, to the point of caricature, in a distortion of the function of politics in a modern and thriving state.

Off-stage, the story was different. Beneath the gorgeous and theatrical apparition of the last German Kaiser, a more human, simple and sensible figure becomes sometimes visible, a more friendly spectre all but stifled under the Imperial purple … It is absurd to call a man like him criminal or guilty.

CHAPTER 7

War and revolution 1914–19

The outbreak of war in 1914 was greeted with enthusiasm in Germany. Virtually everyone thought the war would be short and victorious. However, the conflict degenerated into a war of attrition on a scale without precedent. Millions of men were killed or badly wounded. In 1918, in the wake of military defeat, Wilhelm II abdicated and the Second Empire gave way to the Weimar Republic. Why did Germany fail to achieve victory? How did the war affect Germany? How revolutionary were the events of 1918–19? These questions will be examined by looking at the following themes:

★ Germany at war 1914–16

★ Germany defeated 1917–18

★ The German Revolution 1918–19

★ Establishment of the Weimar Republic

Key dates

1914		Battle of the Marne
1916	**Feb.–Aug.**	Battle of Verdun
	July–Nov.	Battle of the Somme
1917	**Feb.**	Unrestricted submarine warfare reintroduced by Germany
	April	USA entered the war
1918	**March**	Treaty of Brest-Litovsk
	Mar.–July	German offensive on the Western Front

1918	**July–Nov.**	Allied counteroffensive
	Oct.	Prince Max appointed chancellor
	Nov. 9	Abdication of Wilhelm II
	Nov. 11	Armistice between Allies and Germany
1919	**Jan.**	Spartacist revolt
	Jan.	Election of National Assembly
	June	Treaty of Versailles

1 Germany at war 1914–16

▶ *Why did the First World War last so long?*

In 1914 political differences in Germany were submerged in the wave of patriotic fervour. All the political parties promised their support for the war. SPD leaders, who tended towards **pacifism**, could not ignore the fact that most of their supporters wanted to defend the fatherland against perceived Allied aggression.

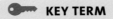

KEY TERM

Pacifism Opposition to war on principle.

On 4 August 1914 Wilhelm, addressing the *Reichstag*, insisted that Germany had done all it could to avoid war and now drew its sword with a clear conscience. 'I know no parties any more, only Germans', he declared. All the party leaders agreed to a political truce for the duration of the war. The *Reichstag* unanimously passed **war credits** and then adjourned, leaving the conduct of the war to the government.

KEY TERM

War credits Financial bills, enabling the war to be funded.

The Schlieffen Plan

Germany's military leaders had long recognised the danger of fighting a two-front war. The Schlieffen Plan had been devised as a way to counter the threat (see Figure 7.2 on page 196). Although attractive in theory, the final draft of the plan was flawed in several ways:

- The invasion of Belgium brought Britain into the war.
- The plan assumed (incorrectly) that it would take Russia many weeks to mobilise its forces. As the bulk of its army moved west, Germany was largely unprotected from Russian attack.

Nevertheless, the Schlieffen Plan came close to success. In August 1914 French troops, hoping to recover Alsace-Lorraine, were mown down by German machine guns and artillery in the Battle of the Frontiers. Meanwhile 1.5 million German troops pushed through Belgium. However, not everything went well for the Germans:

- The Belgians and the 160,000-strong British Expeditionary Force (BEF) slowed down the German advance.
- The First Army under General Alexander von Kluck lost contact with the Second Army and a gap appeared between them. Instead of moving around Paris to the west, Kluck veered southeast to regain contact. Meanwhile French troops from Lorraine were rushed to defend Paris.

Battle of the Marne

On 5 September the French struck at Kluck's exposed flank. The fighting, involving over 2 million men, is known as the Battle of the Marne. Moltke, chief of the German general staff, lost his nerve and ordered his troops to retreat to the Aisne river. Although the French had won a vital battle, they were unable to exploit it. Meanwhile Erich Falkenhayn replaced Moltke.

Both sides now tried to outflank each other in a race for the Channel ports – crucial if Britain was to maintain easy communication with France. Dogged resistance at the first Battle of Ypres ensured that the Allies retained control of the key ports. After this, both sides dug in and by the end of 1914 a system of trenches ran for 600 km from the English Channel to Switzerland.

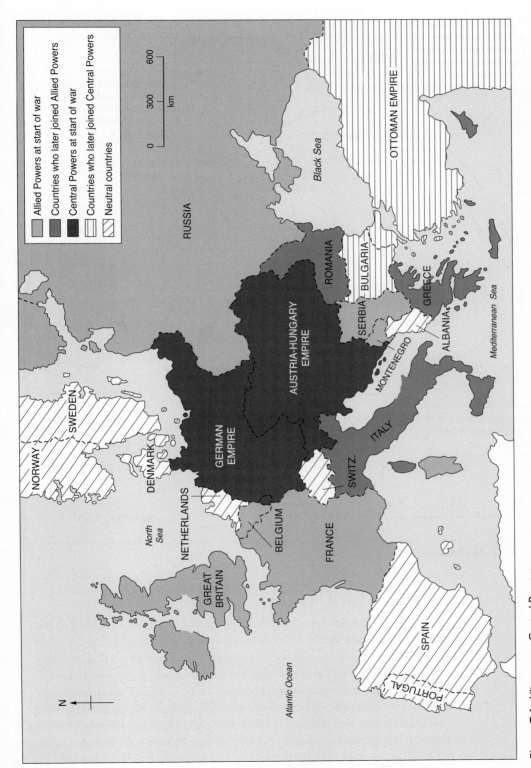

Figure 7.1 Allies versus Central Powers.

Legend:
- Allied Powers at start of war
- Countries who later joined Allied Powers
- Central Powers at start of war
- Countries who later joined Central Powers
- Neutral countries

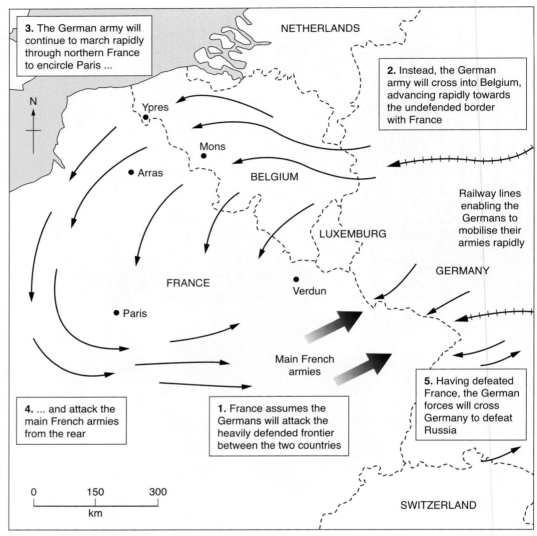

Figure 7.2 The Schlieffen Plan.

Labels on the map:

3. The German army will continue to march rapidly through northern France to encircle Paris ...

2. Instead, the German army will cross into Belgium, advancing rapidly towards the undefended border with France

Railway lines enabling the Germans to mobilise their armies rapidly

5. Having defeated France, the German forces will cross Germany to defeat Russia

4. ... and attack the main French armies from the rear

1. France assumes the Germans will attack the heavily defended frontier between the two countries

Main French armies

NETHERLANDS

Ypres

Mons

Arras

BELGIUM

LUXEMBURG

GERMANY

FRANCE

Verdun

Paris

SWITZERLAND

N

0   150   300
km

The Eastern Front in 1914

In late August, Russian forces invaded East Prussia. Wilhelm, disturbed by the invasion, persuaded Moltke to send two divisions from France to the east. This was a mistake: the move weakened the armies in the west at a crucial moment, and the troops arrived too late to have any influence on the outcome in East Prussia. German forces in the east, commanded by General Paul Hindenburg and his Chief of Staff Erich Ludendorff, were able to deal with the Russian threat. One Russian army was defeated at Tannenburg and a few days later the other was beaten at the Masurian Lakes. By September East Prussia was cleared of Russian troops. These victories made Hindenburg and Ludendorff popular heroes.

SOURCE A

German troops 'digging in' in 1914.

Why were the German soldiers in Source A 'digging in' in 1914?

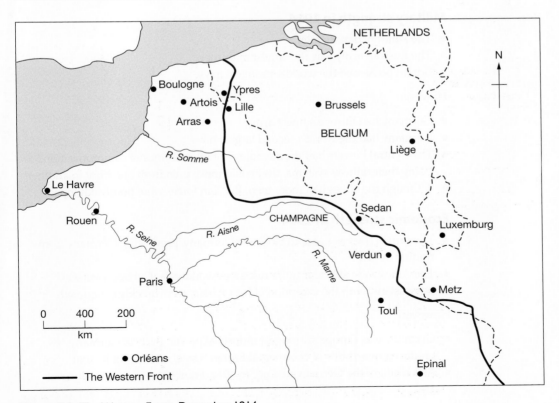

Figure 7.3 The Western Front, December 1914.

Table 7.1 Material resources in 1913

	Germany	Austria-Hungary	Central Powers	France	Russia	Britain	Entente	USA	Entente and USA
Population (millions)	66.9	52.1	119.0	39.7	175.1	44.4	259.2	97.3	356.5
Iron and steel production (millions of tonnes)	17.6	2.6	20.2	4.6	4.8	7.7	17.1	31.8	48.9
Percentage of world manufacturing output	14.8	4.4	19.2	6.1	8.2	13.6	27.9	32.0	59.9

Source: Paul Kennedy, *Rise and Fall of the Great Powers: Economic Change and Military Conflict from 1500 to 2000*, Random House, 1987.

Allied and Central Power strength

Given that both sides had failed to win a quick victory and that both were of similar strength, it was always likely that the war would be lengthy.

Military strength in 1914

- The Allies had more men.
- The Russian army was the largest in Europe.
- Britain possessed the world's strongest navy.

However:

- Germany had Europe's finest army.
- Germany had the world's second largest navy.
- The Central Powers had the advantage of interior lines of communication. Using their railway systems, they could move men from one front to another.
- Although the Allies had more men, Russian forces were poorly equipped.

Economic strength in 1914

- The British fleet was able to blockade Germany, preventing Germany from trading by sea.
- The Allies were able to acquire resources worldwide. German overseas possessions, with the exception of East Africa, were quickly conquered.

However:

- Germany was Europe's strongest industrial power. By 1914 Germany produced two-thirds of continental Europe's steel and half of its coal.
- As a result of the German advance in 1914, France lost its main industrial area.

Figure 7.4 The war in eastern Europe.

The nature of the land war

By the end of 1914 it was clear that the increased range, volume and accuracy of firepower provided by the magazine rifle, the machine gun and heavy artillery made defence stronger than ever before. On all fronts, but especially on the Western Front, both sides dug in. The trench systems became more elaborate as the war progressed. In general, the Germans adapted better to trench warfare. They made better use of barbed wire, developed better machine guns and built huge bunkers deep enough to withstand the heaviest artillery pounding.

SOURCE B

German gunner Lieutenant Adolf Spemann, writing on the Somme front on 1 November 1914, quoted in Max Hastings, *Catastrophe: Europe Goes to War 1914*, William Collins, 2013, p. 533.

In this beautiful autumn light, the view across the plain is really pleasant, despite its uniformity. But everything is messed up, the landscape seamed for miles by ribbons of trenches and dugouts; one thinks of it as a single trench line stretching from Dunkirk to Verdun. The whole plain looks dead and empty … a few cows graze the fields; over there on enemy territory, you can see peasants ploughing and an occasional vehicle. Tomorrow Thiepval church steeple is to be demolished. It is a long-standing aiming-point for French gunners, and thus endangers the whole position. Steeples are favoured observation posts, and thus special artillery targets. Charges are being laid in Pozieres tower, too, to be detonated immediately in the event of an enemy barrage. Amid all the devastation before our eyes, we give hourly thanks that we brought this war into the enemy's territory. If this was our homeland, how would those beasts treat it?

> ? What does Source B tell us about the nature of the war in November 1914?

The war at sea

Given that Britain and Germany had spent millions constructing powerful navies, a great naval battle seemed inevitable in 1914. It did not happen. The Germans were unwilling to risk their High Seas fleet against the (larger) British Grand Fleet. Britain, therefore, dominated the seas, imposing a tight blockade on German ports.

The main German naval threat came from the **U-boat**. This had not been envisaged before 1914. (Germany had only 30 U-boats in 1914.) German U-boats concentrated on sinking merchant ships, hoping to starve Britain into surrender. In February 1915 Germany declared the waters around Britain a war zone and announced that all shipping would be sunk without warning.

While the U-boats inflicted serious damage on Allied shipping, they also sank neutral ships. The USA, Britain's greatest trading partner, protested. The sinking of the liner *Lusitania* in May 1915, resulting in the loss of over 1100 lives (including 128 Americans), led President Woodrow Wilson to issue an ultimatum to Germany. Rather than risk war with the USA, Bethmann-Hollweg

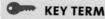

KEY TERM

U-boat *Unterseeboot*: German for submarine.

agreed to abandon unrestricted submarine warfare. Tirpitz resigned in protest. However, Germany continued building U-boats so that, if needs be, it could conduct a more deadly campaign in the future.

The domestic impact of the war

Despite the failure to secure a quick victory, dissident views were few in 1914–15. Lulled into a false sense of security by official propaganda, most Germans remained confident of eventual victory. Until mid-1916 Bethmann-Hollweg faced little opposition from the public or the *Reichstag*. He did his best to keep the SPD loyal, fearing internal chaos if he failed to do so. This meant keeping secret his expansionist war aims: he knew that the SPD opposed 'wars of conquest'.

Military rule

As the war progressed Germany's military leaders were able to interfere in political and economic affairs, with only a limited degree of accountability. Army leaders justified intervention on the grounds of military necessity. Wilhelm II exerted little control. His self-confidence seemed to desert him with the onset of war. Despite being supreme warlord, he was kept in the dark about military developments.

Mobilisation

The German government tried to ensure that all its citizens contributed to the war effort:

- Thirteen million men in total were called up to serve in the armed forces from 1914 to 1918: twenty per cent of the population.
- Armies demanded men, but so did industry and agriculture. Substitute workers, particularly young women, helped Germany to cope with its labour shortage.

The economic front

Faced with the consequences of the British blockade, the German government tried to reorganise its economic production. Although economically strong, Germany was far from self-sufficient. It lacked cotton, rubber, nitrates, petroleum, copper, nickel and tin. It was also dependent on imported fertilisers, fats and oils – all essential if Germany's population was to be adequately fed. As early as August 1914 Germany established a War Raw Materials Department. This soon exercised vast power: directing labour, controlling the railways, introducing rationing and price controls, and allocating resources to industries competing for scarce raw materials. Scientists tried to produce substitute materials for goods of which Germany was lacking.

In the short term the measures taken to regulate Germany's war economy were reasonably successful. However, two crucial economic weaknesses threatened to erode Germany's capacity to continue the war:

- Germany had a huge financial deficit pre-1914 and once war started it soared. Bethmann-Hollweg's government, rather than raise taxes, simply printed money. This fuelled **inflation**.
- The blockade, a series of poor harvests, problems of transportation, shortage of chemicals for fertilisers and mass conscription led to a serious decline in grain production. In January 1915 bread rationing started, to be followed by the rationing of virtually every foodstuff.

Stalemate: 1915

For the most part, Germany remained on the defensive on the Western Front, defeating a series of unsuccessful French and British assaults.

In 1915 Germany and Austria launched a major offensive in the east. Breaking through enemy lines, they forced the Russians into headlong retreat. By September, German forces occupied Poland, Lithuania and Latvia. This success ensured that the reputations of Hindenburg and Ludendorff remained sky-high.

The stalemate continues: 1916

In 1916 there were efforts by both sides to achieve victory.

Verdun

Believing that the war could only be won in the west, Falkenhayn decided to attack Verdun, the pivotal point in the French defence system. Gambling on French determination to defend the place at any cost, Falkenhayn hoped to suck French forces into Verdun, bleed the French army 'white' and break France's will to resist. The German attack was launched in February: 1400 guns fired over 100,000 shells an hour on French positions. France rose to the bait, pouring forces into Verdun. German artillery wreaked terrible damage: some 315,000 French soldiers died in five months. However, more and more German troops were sucked into the fighting and they too suffered heavy casualties, 281,000 men.

Battle of the Somme

In an effort to help the French at Verdun, Britain attacked on the River Somme. On the first day of the battle (1 July) Britain suffered 60,000 casualties. The fighting continued for another five months. Hundreds of thousands of men died on both sides. Allied forces advanced a maximum of ten kilometres.

The Brusilov offensive

In June 1916 Russian commander Brusilov launched a major offensive. His forces broke through the Austrian lines and made great advances. However, Russian attacks against the Germans were less successful. Romania joined the war on the Allied side but was swiftly forced to surrender.

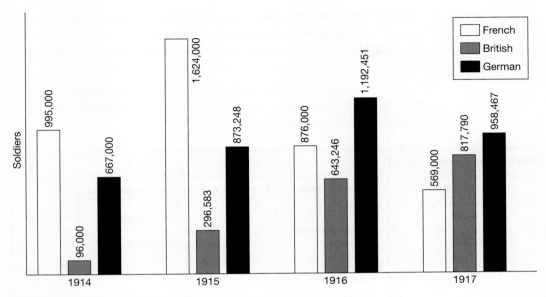

Figure 7.5 Losses on the Western Front 1914–17.

Battle of Jutland

In 1916 the German fleet ventured out of port and met the Royal Navy in the Battle of Jutland. Some 250 ships were involved. Although the German fleet sank more British ships (fourteen to eleven) and killed more British sailors (6000 to 2500), it was heavily outnumbered and retreated back to port, where it stayed until 1918.

Hindenburg and Ludendorff

Bethmann-Hollweg, keen to shore up his own political position by winning popular support, decided to dismiss Falkenhayn. On 29 August 1916 Hindenburg and Ludendorff were appointed chief of the general staff and quartermaster-general, respectively, and given joint responsibility for the conduct of military operations. Far from strengthening his position, Bethmann-Hollweg soon found that his and Wilhelm's authority had been decisively weakened, since neither of them enjoyed the popular backing of Hindenburg and Ludendorff. By the simple expedient of threatening resignation, the two generals exerted a powerful influence over events – political, economic and military.

The Auxiliary Service Act

Hindenburg and Ludendorff tried to mobilise German resources more thoroughly than before:

- Ludendorff ordered a systematic economic exploitation of the enemy areas occupied by German troops.

- The Auxiliary Service Act (December 1916) enabled the government to control the labour of all males between seventeen and 60.
- A Supreme War Office was set up and given wide powers over industry and labour.

The measures did not prevent serious shortages of coal and transport over the winter of 1916–17. Nevertheless, there was a recovery in iron and steel output and a huge increase in munitions production.

Summary diagram: Germany at war 1914–16

	The Western Front	**The home front**	**The naval war**	**The Eastern Front**
1914	Schlieffen Plan Battle of the Marne Stalemate	German unity War Raw Materials Department Economic mobilisation		Battle of Tannenburg Battle of Masurian Lakes
1915		Effect of blockade Financial deficit Inflation	Unrestricted submarine warfare *Lusitania* US ultimatum Germany backed down	German success: occupation of Poland, Latvia and Lithuania
1916	Verdun The Somme	Hindenburg and Ludendorff became 'the silent dictators' The Auxiliary Services Act	*Sussex* sunk US ultimatum Germany backed down Battle of Jutland	Brusilov offensive

2 Germany defeated 1917–18

▶ *Why was Germany defeated in 1918?*

Table 7.2 Material and human resources 1917

	Central Powers	Allied Powers
Actives and reserves	10,610,000	17,312,000
Field artillery	14,730	19,465
Heavy artillery	9,130	11,476
Machine guns	20,042	67,276
Aeroplanes	1,500	3,163

Source: Fritz Klein *et al.*, *Deutschland im Ersten Weltkrieg*, Leipziger Universitätsverlag, 1968–9.

Revolution in Russia

Inflation, food shortages and high casualties led to revolution in Russia in March 1917. Tsar Nicholas II abdicated. The liberal politicians who led the new Provisional Government proved no more capable than the tsar in terms of waging war and Russia quickly disintegrated into anarchy. The chief beneficiary of this situation was the Bolshevik Party, an extreme Marxist group, led by Vladimir Lenin. Hindenburg and Ludendorff, while hating Lenin's Marxist ideals, arranged for him to travel back to Russia from Switzerland across Germany. He lived up to German expectations, overthrowing the Provisional Government in November and taking Russia out of the war.

The USA joins the war

At the start of 1917 Hindenburg and Ludendorff, unaware that Russia was on the point of revolution, believed that Germany was losing the war. Given that German civilians were being slowly starved into surrender while German armies were being worn down by attrition, Germany's military leaders decided that the U-boat was the last hope of victory. Aware that the reintroduction of unrestricted submarine warfare might well bring the USA into the war, they gambled that the U-boats would starve Britain into surrender before significant US military aid reached Europe.

On 1 February 1917, therefore, Germany commenced unrestricted U-boat warfare, sinking without warning all ships in Allied waters. President Wilson immediately severed diplomatic relations with Germany. US politicians and newspapers urged a declaration of war. Wilson hesitated. Then, in March a telegram from the German Foreign Secretary Arthur Zimmermann to the German minister in Mexico was intercepted by British intelligence and published in the USA. Hoping to persuade Mexico to ally with Germany, Zimmermann promised Mexico the US states of Texas, New Mexico and Arizona. The telegram caused a wave of anti-German sentiment in the USA.

The March revolution in Russia removed a further political obstacle to US entry into the war: the war now did seem like a struggle between autocracy and democracy. On 2 April Wilson asked the US Congress to declare war on Germany. On 6 April Congress obliged.

American entry into the war gave the Allies a huge morale boost. The resources of the world's greatest economic power would now be mobilised on their behalf. However, it would take many months before the USA was able to mobilise its forces. This gave the Central Powers some hope of victory.

Allied and Central Power problems in 1917

The war on the Western Front went disastrously for the Allies:

- In April–May, a large part of the French army mutinied. Order was restored but the French army now adopted a defensive policy.
- In July, British forces launched the Battle of Passchendaele. The four-month offensive resulted in over 500,000 British casualties.
- Russia no longer posed a serious military threat. Germany was thus able to transfer thousands of men to the west.
- In October, German and Austrian forces defeated Italian troops at Caporetto, forcing the Italians into a headlong retreat.
- The U-boat gamble came close to success. In April one out of four ships leaving British ports was sunk. Britain was threatened with starvation.

But by late 1917 the Central Powers also had problems:

- Greece joined the Allies.
- The Turks faced a serious Arab revolt.
- At sea, Britain adopted the convoy system. Fewer ships were sunk. The U-boat gamble had failed.

Table 7.3 Percentage indices of real wages 1913–18 (1913 = 100%)

Year	Railwaymen	Printers	Miners	Civil servants
1913	100.0	100.0	100.0	100.0
1914	97.2	97.2	93.3	97.2
1915	79.7	77.3	81.3	77.3
1916	69.2	60.6	74.4	58.9
1917	63.9	49.4	62.7	48.6
1918	83.9	54.1	63.7	55.0

German civilian morale

On the domestic front the impact of war slowly but remorselessly affected the lives of ordinary Germans, weakening morale. Cold weather and a poor potato crop led to a disastrous food and fuel crisis over the winter of 1917–18. Severe malnutrition and infectious diseases made life, for most, truly miserable. Many workers resented being forced to work even longer hours as a result of the Auxiliary Service Law. The result was that social discontent grew markedly.

Considerable anger was harboured against industrialists who were making vast profits from the war. In 1917 the 'left' organised an increasing number of strikes. The 'right' blamed Jews and socialists for all of Germany's problems.

The July 1917 crisis

As popular disillusionment with the conduct of the war increased, so did dissent in the *Reichstag*. Socialists, with National Liberal support, succeeded in establishing a *Reichstag* committee to consider constitutional reform. Bethmann-Hollweg, hoping to maintain unity, persuaded Wilhelm to promise reform of the Prussian franchise system, to the consternation of conservatives.

By 1917 it was impossible to overlook the widening gulf between those who sought a 'peace without victory' and those who believed that only a 'victorious peace' would legitimate the sacrifices already made. In June 1917 left-wing parties made it clear that they would vote against war credits if Bethmann-Hollweg did not support 'peace without victory'. He refused, thus losing the support of the *Reichstag*, which he had enjoyed since 1914.

Ludendorff refused to work any longer with a man who supported political change and who had lost control of the *Reichstag*. Bethmann-Hollweg was forced to resign in July. His resignation was not a victory for the *Reichstag*. *Reichstag* deputies did not appoint his successor or use the crisis to force negotiations for peace. Most felt that it was unpatriotic to divide the nation. The July crisis

SOURCE C

Wilhelm (centre) studying maps alongside Hindenburg (left) and Ludendorff (right).

Examine Source C. Why do you think the photograph was taken?

simply gave the Supreme Command an opportunity to assert its superiority. George Michaelis, an insignificant Prussian administrator who had impressed Ludendorff during a brief interview, became the new chancellor. Michaelis had no intention of sharing power with the *Reichstag*.

On 19 July the *Reichstag* passed a peace resolution by 212 votes to 126. 'The *Reichstag* strives for a peace of understanding and permanent reconciliation of peoples. Forced territorial acquisition and political, economic and financial oppressions are irreconcilable with such a peace.' The resolution, supported by SPD, Radical and Centre Party deputies, had no influence on Germany's military leaders, who remained committed to winning a victorious peace.

Michaelis and Hertling

On 1 November 1917 Michaelis, who had shown much dithering and little initiative, was dismissed. Wilhelm, without consulting Hindenburg and Ludendorff, chose Count Hertling, an elderly Bavarian aristocrat, as his successor. Hertling disliked parliamentary government, but appreciated the need for consulting the parties. He promised to support the peace resolution and to reform the Prussian franchise. However, the decisive factor was the attitude of the Supreme Command. Ludendorff, busy with preparations for the 1918 offensive, hoped that Hertling's conciliatory measures could keep the home front quiet long enough for Germany to win the war.

The right

Radical nationalists, alarmed by the peace resolution, founded the Fatherland Party in September 1917. Heavily subsidised by industrialists, the party demanded annexations east and west, and supported military rule. It soon claimed it had over a million members. (It probably had fewer than 500,000.)

The left

By 1917 German socialists were seriously divided. Most SPD deputies, unwilling to damage the war effort, were prepared to work with the other parties. However, a number of radical socialists opposed collaboration with the capitalist German state. In April 1917, 42 SPD deputies formed a new party, the Independent Social Democratic Party (USPD). The USPD was committed to an immediate peace without annexations. The remaining 68 SPD deputies reconstituted themselves as the Majority Socialist Party, with Friedrich Ebert (see page 215) as chairman.

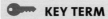 **KEY TERM**

Revolutionary shop stewards Working-class activists who tried to organise mass action in the factories of Berlin in an attempt to end the war.

The USPD was loosely associated with two other groups, the Spartacus League and the **revolutionary shop stewards**. The League, founded by a small group of socialist intellectuals and led by Karl Liebknecht and Rosa Luxemburg, had no mass following. The revolutionary shop stewards, by contrast, had considerable grass-roots influence. The League and the shop stewards believed that working people must use the war to destroy capitalism and inaugurate world revolution.

Strike action

In January 1918 some 400,000 Berlin workers went on strike. The strike spread quickly to other cities. The strikers' demands, influenced by the revolutionary shop stewards, were political as well as economic: they included democratic government and 'peace without victory'. The authorities acted firmly, placing large plants under military control, prohibiting public meetings and arresting a number of socialist leaders. Significantly, Majority Socialists and most official trade union leaders opposed the strike. The shop stewards quickly backed down and called off the strike.

The Treaty of Brest-Litovsk

In March 1918 the new Bolshevik government in Russia agreed to make peace with Germany. By the terms of the Treaty of Brest-Litovsk, Russia lost its Polish territories, Lithuania, Courland, the Ukraine, Estonia, Latvia and Finland: a third of its population and agricultural land. Russia also had to pay 3 billion roubles in reparations. The *Reichstag* approved the treaty by a large majority, even though it was a clear repudiation of the 1917 peace resolution. Only the

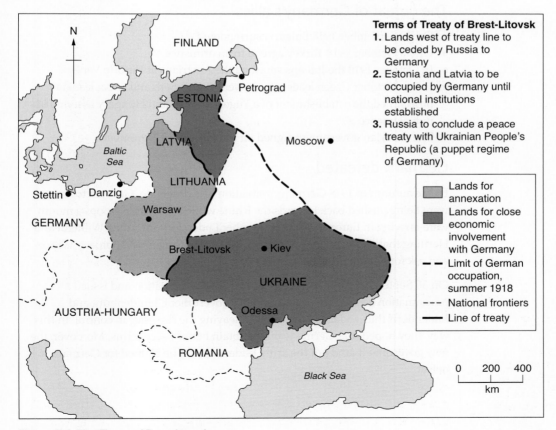

Figure 7.6 The Treaty of Brest-Litovsk.

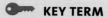

Fourteen Points These were President Wilson's main war aims. Wilson hoped to prevent future wars by eliminating secret alliances and frustrated nationalism, and by establishing a League of Nations.

USPD voted against it. Success in the east made Germany deaf to President Wilson's proposals for peace in January 1918: his **Fourteen Points**.

The German spring offensive 1918

Germany's main advantage in early 1918 was that it no longer had to fight a two-front war. But Germany's allies were a source of serious concern and huge US forces would soon help the Allies. The German High Command therefore launched a great offensive in March 1918, its troops smashing through British lines and driving British forces back 65 km. Further German offensives followed and by June German forces were within 60 km of Paris. However, the German army did not possess sufficient manpower to exploit the breakthrough and the advance ground to a halt.

In July, the Allies successfully counterattacked. On 8 August (Ludendorff later termed it the German army's 'black day') British forces broke through the German lines at Amiens. Morale in the German army began to crumble and there were large numbers of desertions. The Allied advance continued through early September, ensuring that Germany lost all the gains made in the spring.

The defeat of Germany's allies

- On 30 September 1918 Bulgaria surrendered.
- On 30 October 1918 Turkey agreed to an armistice.
- In October 1918 the Italians smashed the Austrians at Vittorio Veneto.
- In late October Czech leaders took over Prague, Serb and Croat leaders proclaimed the establishment of a Yugoslav state, and Hungary asserted its independence.
- The Austrian government signed an armistice on 3 November.

Germany defeated

By the autumn of 1918 Germany's situation was desperate. German troops were being pushed back towards the Rhine while 300,000 US troops a month were arriving in Europe. On 29 September Ludendorff informed Wilhelm and Hertling that the war was lost. Consequently, Hertling must approach Wilson and ask for an immediate armistice.

On 30 September, Wilhelm accepted Hertling's resignation and issued a proclamation establishing parliamentary government. Hindenburg and Ludendorff thus abdicated their power, leaving the *Reichstag* in control. In this way, they hoped that Germany might obtain better peace terms. Moreover, the new government (and not the army leaders) would be blamed for Germany's defeat.

Summary diagram: German defeated 1917–18

	The Western Front	The home front	The naval war	The Eastern Front
1917	French mutiny Battle of Passchendaele	'Turnip' winter hardship July crisis Peace Resolution Bethmann resigned Chancellor Michaelis Chancellor Hertling	Unrestricted submarine warfare US entered war U-boat success Convoy system established	March Revolution Bolsheviks seized power Peace negotiations
1918	German spring offensive US troops arriving German offensive stalled Allied advance	Left-wing unrest Strikes Hertling resigned Parliamentary democracy established	Britain not starved into surrender	Treaty of Brest-Litovsk German troops moved to Western Front
September–October: Bulgaria, Turkey and Austria-Hungary surrendered				

③ The German Revolution 1918–19

▶ *Why did the 1918–19 German Revolution fail?*

The six months from October 1918 to March 1919 witnessed turbulent revolutionary activity across Germany. There were several different revolutions, each with its own aims and agenda.

Constitutional reform

On 1 October Wilhelm asked **Prince Max of Baden**, a moderate conservative, to form a government. Max's government, which included representatives from the Majority Socialists and the Left Liberals, was stunned when told the seriousness of Germany's position. When Max raised objections to an immediate request for an armistice, Wilhelm told him: 'You have not been brought here to make things difficult for the Supreme Command.'

Thus, Max (on 3 October) wrote formally to President Wilson asking for an armistice and a peace based on the Fourteen Points. Several weeks of secret negotiation followed. The main obstacle to peace was the kaiser, whose removal from power Wilson insisted on as a precondition for an armistice.

Meanwhile Max's government introduced a series of reforms that turned Germany into a parliamentary monarchy:

- The three-class franchise was abolished in Prussia.
- The kaiser's powers over the army were curtailed.
- The chancellor and the government were made accountable to the *Reichstag*.

At this point, Ludendorff recovered his nerve. Morale among front-line soldiers had not collapsed and the Allied advance seemed to have run out of steam. He thus issued an order (without consulting Max) to army commanders calling on all ranks to resist a humiliating surrender. Max was appalled. He told Wilhelm that he must choose between Ludendorff and the cabinet. On 26 October Ludendorff resigned and fled to Sweden. The next day Max reiterated Germany's wish for an armistice, emphasising that the military authorities were at last subject to the civilian government.

How important was the *Reichstag*?

In a three-week period, power had been transferred peaceably from the kaiser to the *Reichstag*. The changes were essentially a 'revolution from above'. Nevertheless, much of what occurred resulted from *Reichstag* demands for the creation of a government responsible to the *Reichstag*.

Most Germans paid little heed to the hugely important (but ill-publicised) reforms. After all, Wilhelm remained kaiser, a prince was still chancellor, and the war continued. Nor did the *Reichstag* behave as if the changes represented a turning point in German history. It adjourned on 5 October and did not meet until 22 October, when it again adjourned until 9 November. These were hardly the actions of an institution that wished to shape events.

The revolutionary situation

By late October a revolutionary situation existed in Germany. Four years of privations had eroded the old relationship between ruler and subject. The shock of looming military defeat, after years of optimistic propaganda, radicalised popular attitudes. Germans were only too ready to blame Wilhelm for their country's misfortunes. Once the public became aware that Wilson regarded Wilhelm as an obstacle to peace, pressure for his abdication grew rapidly. Many south Germans blamed Prussia for Germany's misfortunes. Some Bavarians pressed for independence.

The Kiel mutiny and revolution

On 29 October rumours that the German fleet was going to be sent out on a last do-or-die mission against the Royal Navy led to a mutiny among the sailors at Wilhelmshaven. The mutiny rapidly spread to Kiel and other ports. On 4 November dockworkers and soldiers in Kiel joined the mutinous sailors and set up workers' and soldiers' councils, on the 1917 Russian **soviet** model. Although Independent Socialists were in close touch with some mutineers, this was more a spontaneous protest movement than a politically led mutiny. The sailors' councils were not disloyal to the government. On the contrary, they asked for representatives to come and listen to their grievances. The government sent a Majority Socialist who promised better conditions and reassured the sailors that there would be no 'suicide offensive'.

News of the Kiel mutiny fanned the flames of discontent across Germany. By 8 November, workers' and soldiers' councils had been established in most major cities. The councils demanded peace and assumed control of local food supplies and services. In Bavaria the Wittelsbach dynasty was deposed and an independent socialist republic was proclaimed by Kurt Eisner. There was little resistance. The time seemed ripe for a remodelling of society and a clean break with the imperial past.

Divisions among the revolutionaries

The revolutionary wave which swept Germany was not a united force:

- Majority Socialists upheld democracy and favoured moderate reforms. They totally rejected Bolshevik-style communism.
- Spartacists and shop stewards believed that Germany should follow a similar road to Russia. They campaigned for a socialist republic, based on the workers' and soldiers' councils, which would smash the institutions of imperial Germany.
- The USPD was between the two extremes. It demanded radical social and economic change to complement political reform. Its influence was curtailed by factional squabbles.

Left-wing socialists tried to drive forward the workers' revolution by organising strikes and demonstrations by workers. The situation appeared menacing to many Germans, alarmed by what they perceived as 'Russian solutions' being put forward for German problems. However, many of the councils were controlled by moderate socialists who were anxious to maintain law and order and ensure

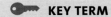

KEY TERM

Soviet A council of workers, peasants and soldiers.

the functioning of local services at a time of crisis. In most cases the councils coexisted uneasily with pre-revolutionary bodies.

Wilhelm II's abdication

On 7 November Majority Socialist leaders threatened to withdraw support from the government unless Wilhelm abdicated and socialists were given greater representation in the cabinet. When Max failed to persuade Wilhelm to abdicate, the socialist ministers **Philipp Scheidemann** and Otto Bauer resigned and the party agreed to call a general strike. Majority Socialist leaders took this step reluctantly. Their hand was forced by the revolutionary shop stewards, who had already called a strike for 9 November in protest against the arrest of some of their leaders.

Thus, on 9 November most workers went on strike. A deputation of socialists, headed by Ebert and Scheidemann, called on Max. They informed him that the local garrison in Berlin was on their side and that a new democratic government must be formed at once. Max hesitated no longer. At noon he announced Wilhelm's abdication. By now even Hindenburg and General Groener (who had succeeded Ludendorff in October 1918 as deputy chief of the general staff) realised that the kaiser must go. Abandoned by his generals, Wilhelm accepted the reality of the situation and fled to the Netherlands. Later on 9 November Max resigned and announced the formation of a new government, to be led by Ebert.

The German Republic

Ebert issued his first proclamation on 9 November, signing himself 'imperial chancellor', a title chosen to emphasise continuity between his government and that of Max. This device conferred some semblance of legitimacy on the new government and helped to rally the officer corps and the civil service behind it, as did the fact that Ebert's government confirmed the old officials in power. Ebert declared that the goal of the government was to bring peace. He hoped to stabilise the political situation sufficiently to enable elections to take place as soon as possible for a National Assembly. This body would then draw up a new constitution. His main worry was that the extreme left would gain the upper hand. He was determined to prevent the descent into civil strife.

Ebert was under no illusions about his government's weak position. Its authority did not extend with certainty beyond Berlin, and it was not even accepted in all parts of the capital. Furthermore, he knew that the revolutionary shop stewards were planning to set up a provisional government, based on the workers' and soldiers' councils. To forestall this, Ebert decided to offer the USPD seats in the government.

The USPD was deeply divided. While moderates favoured acceptance, the left opposed collaboration with Ebert and demanded that the workers' and soldiers'

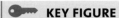
KEY FIGURE

Philipp Scheidemann (1865–1939)

A leading SPD politician. During the German Revolution, he proclaimed Germany a republic on 9 November 1918. He later became the second chancellor of the Weimar Republic, staying in power for just 127 days.

Friedrich Ebert

1871	Born, the son of a tailor; he became a saddler and entered politics through his trade union activities
1905	Elected secretary to the SPD's central committee
1912	Elected to the *Reichstag*. His hard work behind the scenes was partly responsible for the SPD's success in the elections
1913	On the death of August Bebel, he was elected joint leader of the SPD alongside the more radical Hugo Haase
1918–19	Effective leader of Germany. Ensured the defeat of the left-wing socialists and elections to a Constituent Assembly
1919	Became the first president of the Weimar Republic
1925	Died of a ruptured appendix

Ebert was not a great orator or charismatic leader. His skills lay in other directions. He was a calm, patient and subtle negotiator, more concerned with improving the lot of the working class by evolutionary rather than revolutionary change. During the war, he worked with other left-wing parties, hoping to push the kaiser's administration towards an acceptance of parliamentary democracy. As well as a democrat, Ebert was a patriotic German who lost two sons during the war. By 1918–19 he was effective leader of Germany.

Radical critics at the time and since have accused Ebert of betraying the interests of workers and of ensuring the failure of the revolution by allying with the forces of conservatism. But Ebert had no wish to preside over chaos. Like most SPD leaders, he was suspicious of the extreme left. Given the situation in 1918–19, he had little option but to rely on the forces of reaction. In the context of 1918–19, Ebert had a sensible set of political and economic goals. He aimed to end the war, to maintain law and order and (most importantly) to establish parliamentary democracy. In the event, he achieved most of his goals – at least in the short term.

councils should assume full power. By 21 votes to 19 the Independents finally decided to accept Ebert's offer. To appease their left wing they insisted on a number of concessions:

- Only socialists must be included in the government.
- The government must declare that all power resided in the councils.
- Elections to the National Assembly must be delayed until the revolution was consolidated.

Reluctantly Ebert accepted the conditions. Therefore, on 10 November a new government, the Council of People's Commissars, was formed. It consisted of three SPD members and three USPD members; Ebert and Hugo Haase, the USPD leader, acted as co-chairmen.

The workers' and soldiers' councils

On 10 November elections to form workers' and soldiers' councils were held in all the factories and garrisons in Berlin. At a mass meeting of the councils, the delegates approved the new government by a huge majority. An executive committee was elected to manage the affairs of the Berlin councils. This committee, which consisted of seven Majority Socialists, seven Independents and fourteen soldiers (many of whom were not socialists), began negotiations with the government to define the precise relationship between the two bodies.

The armistice

The change in government did not change the Allied attitude to Germany. In November 1918 German troops still controlled most of Belgium and huge areas of eastern Europe. Allied leaders feared that Germany intended to use the armistice as a breathing space before resuming the war. The armistice terms were designed to remove Germany's ability to fight:

- German troops had to withdraw beyond the Rhine. German territory on the left bank of the river was to be occupied.
- Germany had to surrender its U-boats, much of its surface fleet and its air force.
- Germany had to repudiate the Treaty of Brest-Litovsk.
- The blockade of Germany would continue until a final peace treaty had been signed.

The armistice terms were hugely resented in Germany. Nevertheless, the political situation made continuation of the war impossible. On 11 November the socialist government agreed to the terms and the First World War ended.

Germany had suffered 6,193,058 military casualties in the war, 2,044,900 of whom had died. A further 624,000 civilian deaths could be attributed to the war.

Germany: November 1918 to January 1919

Relations between the Majority Socialists and Independents remained tense. A key issue was the authority of the workers' and soldiers' councils. Ebert viewed the councils with suspicion as a possible rival to parliamentary government. He therefore did his utmost to speed up the calling of the National Assembly.

The Independents were not opposed to this: most believed in parliamentary democracy. But whereas the Majority Socialists maintained that the revolution was over, the Independents believed that the gains of the revolution must be consolidated before the assembly met. They believed that the councils, the embodiment of the revolutionary will of the people, should supervise the implementation of a crash programme of socialism: the nationalisation of key industries, the breaking-up of the great landed estates, and the democratisation of the civil service, the judiciary and the army.

As the weeks passed Ebert's position grew stronger. Permanent officials co-operated willingly enough with him, regarding him as Max's legitimate successor. They would not work with the executive committee of the councils.

The Ebert–Groener pact

On 10 November General Groener (Ludendorff's successor) telephoned Ebert. The general agreed to support the government in return for Ebert's promise to resist Bolshevism and to preserve the officers' authority against the councils. Ebert's critics, both at the time and since, have claimed that this 'pact' was proof that he betrayed the revolution. However, Ebert never made any secret of his distaste of Bolshevik revolution. His understanding with Groener was a reasonable precaution to protect his government against violence from the extreme left.

The Stinnes–Legien agreement

On 15 November the Stinnes–Legien agreement further strengthened Ebert's position. (Hugo Stinnes was an industrialist and Carl Legien a trade union leader.)

- The trade unions agreed not to interfere with private ownership.
- Employers guaranteed full legal recognition to trade unions.
- Workers' councils (which were to be introduced into all large factories) could help to regulate wages and working conditions.
- An eight-hour working day was introduced.

This agreement, quickly endorsed by the government, did much to satisfy workers' grievances.

The All-German Congress of Workers' and Soldiers' Councils

The All-German Congress of Workers' and Soldiers' Councils met in Berlin from 16 to 21 December. Over 300 of the 500 delegates supported the Majority Socialists and only 90 the USPD. Delegates passed resolutions demanding the nationalisation of key industries and the **democratisation of the army**.

Nevertheless, most delegates wanted Germany to be a parliamentary democracy. On 19 December Congress approved by a huge majority the government decision to hold elections to the National Assembly on 19 January. In the meantime, it agreed that power should be vested in the government.

The resignation of the Independent Socialists

On 23 December the sailors' division, which had come from Kiel to defend the government, was ordered to evacuate its quarters in the former royal palace. The disgruntled sailors barricaded themselves in the palace. Faced with a direct challenge to its authority, the government – on Christmas Eve – ordered a regular army division to attack the palace. Failing to dislodge the sailors, the troops withdrew. Violence quickly spread to other parts of Berlin. Fortunately for Ebert, the sailors agreed to leave the building once the question of their back pay – the real cause of the action – was settled.

The Independents were incensed by Ebert's action, undertaken without their knowledge. On 29 December the three Independent ministers, already frustrated by the slow progress towards socialism and suspicious of the ties between Ebert and the army, resigned. While Ebert now had a freer hand in the government, he also faced growing opposition from the streets.

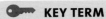 **KEY TERM**

Democratisation of the army Officers would be elected by the men and the regular army would be replaced by a people's militia.

? How, according to Source D, did the SPD hope to win the support of the electorate in the forthcoming elections to the National Assembly?

SOURCE D

The programme of the SPD, 29 December 1918, quoted in J. Hiden, *The Weimar Republic*, Longman, 1996, p. 73.

To the German people! Workers! Soldiers! Citizens! Citizenesses! The Independents have left the government. The remaining members of the Cabinet vacated their posts so that the Central Council could have a wholly free hand. The latter unanimously re-instated them. The crippling disunity is at an end. The Reich government is reconstructed and united. It professes but one principle: the well being, the survival, the indivisibility of the German Republic above all party interest ... And now for our programme. At home: To prepare for the National Assembly, urgently attend to feeding the people, initiate socialisation ... deal severely with war profiteering, to create jobs and support the unemployed, improve dependants' relief, to develop the people's army with all means and to disarm unauthorised personnel. Abroad: To achieve peace as quickly and as favourably as possible and to restaff the foreign representations of the German Republic with men imbued with the new spirit. That is the broad outline of our programme prior to the National Assembly.

The Spartacist rising

On 1 January 1919 the Spartacists broke with the USPD and founded the German Communist Party. Led by Liebknecht and Luxemburg, the communists declared that the National Assembly would be an organ of counter-revolution and called instead for government by workers' and soldiers' councils. On 6 January a revolutionary committee of 53 communists and shop stewards was set up. It issued a proclamation deposing Ebert and announcing the establishment of a revolutionary government. At the same time armed communists occupied newspaper offices and various public buildings in Berlin.

Faced with this challenge, the government first tried to negotiate with the Spartacist leaders, to no effect. It thus had little option but to turn to the army. Groener, in addition to using regular units, recruited hundreds of right-wing ex-soldiers, organised into *Freikorps* units. The *Freikorps* were only too willing to suppress communist activity. By 15 January the Spartacist revolt was crushed after savage street fighting. Liebknecht and Luxemburg were shot while in police custody.

The events of January 1919, especially the murder of Liebknecht and Luxemburg, ensured the implacable hostility of the Marxist left towards the Majority Socialists (who again called themselves the SPD) and the new parliamentary republic. In March 1919 the USPD came out in favour of government by workers' councils. Many Independents agreed with the communists that Ebert had sold his soul to the conservative forces of imperial Germany.

SOURCE E

Barricades in Berlin during the 1919 Spartacist rising.

Further bloodshed

In February widespread strikes were organised by communists and in some towns there was sporadic street fighting. In March, the communists called for a general strike. Again Berlin became the scene of fighting; again the *Freikorps* were sent in. By mid-March 1919 order had been restored at the cost of over 1000 dead.

Bavaria

The elections to the Bavarian parliament in mid-January 1919 resulted in an overwhelming defeat for Eisner's Independents: they won only three seats. On the way to opening the first session of the new Parliament in February, Eisner was murdered by a right-wing fanatic. Disorder broke out and the new coalition government, led by Majority Socialists, fled from Munich, leaving the city in the hands of Independents and communists. On 9 April the communists, brushing aside the Independents, set up a soviet republic. The coalition government called on a local *Freikorps* unit for help. The army and *Freikorps* restored order in Munich after some days of savage fighting. Hundreds of communists were shot.

> Examine Source E. Do you think the men in the picture are *Freikorps* or Spartacists? Explain your reasoning. **?**

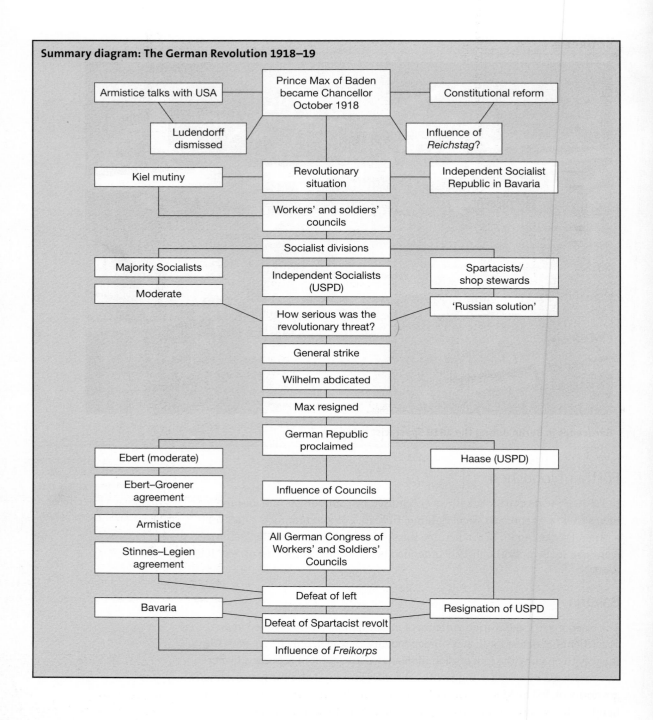

Summary diagram: The German Revolution 1918–19

Armistice talks with USA — Prince Max of Baden became Chancellor October 1918 — Constitutional reform

Ludendorff dismissed — Influence of *Reichstag*?

Kiel mutiny — Revolutionary situation — Independent Socialist Republic in Bavaria

Workers' and soldiers' councils

Socialist divisions

Majority Socialists — Independent Socialists (USPD) — Spartacists/shop stewards

Moderate — How serious was the revolutionary threat? — 'Russian solution'

General strike

Wilhelm abdicated

Max resigned

German Republic proclaimed

Ebert (moderate) — Haase (USPD)

Ebert–Groener agreement — Influence of Councils

Armistice

Stinnes–Legien agreement — All German Congress of Workers' and Soldiers' Councils

Bavaria — Defeat of left — Resignation of USPD

Defeat of Spartacist revolt

Influence of *Freikorps*

Establishment of the Weimar Republic

▶ *What problems did the Weimar Republic face?*

The elections for the National Assembly took place on 19 January 1919. Most political parties took the opportunity to re-form themselves. New names did not hide the fact that there was considerable continuity in the structure of the party system. The Nationalists were essentially an amalgamation of the old conservative parties. The liberals remained divided between left (the Democrats) and right (the People's Party).

The 1919 election results

Eighty-three per cent of those eligible to vote (including women) turned out to vote. The SPD won 165 seats (38 per cent of the vote) and the USPD 22. The Centre won 91 seats, the Democrats 75, the Nationalists 44 and the Populists 19.

On 10 February Ebert was elected first president of the Republic by 277 votes to 51. He immediately asked the SPD to form a government. The SPD found allies in the Centre and Democrat parties. Over 75 per cent of the electorate had voted for these three parties, all of which were committed to the new republic. The election was a clear repudiation of the extreme right and left. The new government was headed by Chancellor Scheidemann and consisted of six Social Democrats, three Centrists and three Democrats. Given the unsettled conditions in Berlin, the new Assembly met in the picturesque town of Weimar.

The Weimar constitution

The Assembly's main task was to draw up a constitution. Largely the work of Hugo Preuss (a Democrat), the Weimar constitution attempted a careful balance of political forces:

- Germany was to be a republic, its sovereignty based on the people.
- It remained a federal rather than a unitary state.
- The central government would control direct taxation, foreign affairs, the armed forces and communications.
- The states retained their powers over education, police and the churches.

At national level Germany was to be governed by a president, a *Reichstag* and a *Reichsrat*. *Reichstag* deputies were to be elected every four years by all men and women over the age of twenty. A system of **proportional representation** was introduced, ensuring that all German views would be represented in the *Reichstag*. The chancellor and his ministers had to possess the *Reichstag's* confidence and were obliged to resign when they forfeited it. The *Reichstag* was to initiate and approve legislation.

 KEY TERM

Proportional representation This system of voting ensures that a party receives the same percentage of seats as votes received.

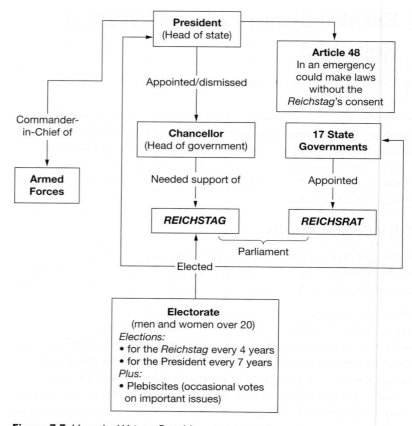

Figure 7.7 How the Weimar Republic was governed.

The *Reichsrat* was to be composed of delegates from the German states. Each state was represented according to its population, except that no state was allowed to have more than two-fifths of the seats: this was designed to prevent Prussian dominance. The *Reichsrat* could veto *Reichstag* legislation; its veto, in turn, could be overridden by a two-thirds vote of the *Reichstag*.

The president, directly elected by the people for seven years, was supreme commander of the armed forces, convened and dissolved the *Reichstag*, and appointed the chancellor and the *Reich* government. In the event of an emergency, Article 48 provided the president with the authority to suspend civil rights and to take whatever action was required to restore law and order by the issue of presidential decrees.

The Weimar constitution guaranteed German people personal liberty, equality before the law, freedom of movement, expression and conscience, and the right of association.

On 31 July 1919 the new constitution was passed by 262 votes to 75. Only the USPD and the right were in opposition. The adoption of the black, red and gold revolutionary flag of 1848 enraged right-wing nationalists.

The peace settlement

In January 1919 Allied leaders assembled in Paris to make peace with the defeated Central Powers. The main decisions were taken by the 'Big Three': US President Woodrow Wilson, British Prime Minister David Lloyd George and French Prime Minister Georges Clemenceau. The peacemakers faced huge problems:

- The map of Europe as it had existed in 1914 had been swept away. There was political and economic chaos across much of central and eastern Europe.
- There was the fear that Bolshevism might spread westwards from Russia.

The 'Big Three' held different views about how to ensure a durable peace settlement. Clemenceau wanted Germany punished and its power permanently reduced. Wilson was primarily concerned with establishing a just and lasting system of international relations. Lloyd George, not wanting to leave an embittered Germany, was inclined to leniency. Germany was not allowed to participate in the peace negotiations. On 7 May German delegates were handed a document consisting of 440 articles. They were told that they had three weeks to consider it and to formulate counterproposals.

The Treaty of Versailles

Scheidemann's government lodged its objections at considerable length but to little effect. On 19 June the cabinet rejected the treaty and Scheidemann resigned. The new government, led by Gustav Bauer, knew that rejection of the treaty was not really an option. Germany was in no state to fight a new war, a war which might result in Germany being divided up or losing even more territory. Accordingly, the *Reichstag* sanctioned the signing of the treaty (see Figure 7.8 for its main terms). This took place on 28 June 1919 in the Hall of Mirrors at Versailles – the same place in which the German Empire had been proclaimed in 1871.

Opposition to the Treaty of Versailles

On no other political issue were Germans so united as in the condemnation of the Treaty of Versailles. It was seen as a humiliating **diktat**, at variance with the Fourteen Points. If **self-determination** was the guiding principle, Germans found it incomprehensible that Germans in Austria, Danzig, Posen (Poznań) and West Prussia, Memel, Upper Silesia, the Sudetenland and the Saar were all placed under foreign rule. Germans, convinced that they had fought a war of self-defence, found it impossible to accept the war guilt clause and regarded reparations as totally unfair.

Historians today are not convinced that Germany was treated over-harshly. The application of self-determination was not as unfair as many Germans believed. Virtually all of the German territory lost (with the exception of Danzig and the Polish Corridor) was justified on the grounds of nationality. More Poles were left under German rule than Germans under Polish rule. The only outright violation

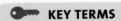

KEY TERMS

Diktat An imposed settlement allowing for no negotiations.

Self-determination The right of people to decide their own form of government.

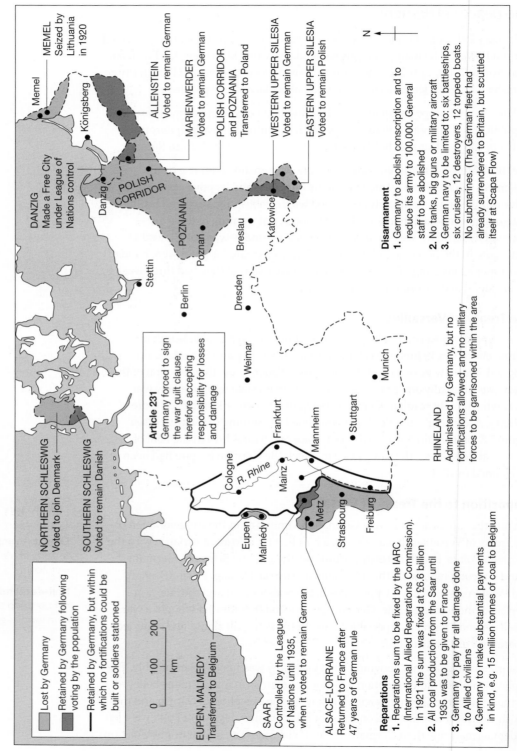

Figure 7.8 The Treaty of Versailles.

MEMEL
Seized by
Lithuania
in 1920

ALLENSTEIN
Voted to remain German

MARIENWERDER
Voted to remain German

POLISH CORRIDOR
and POZNANIA
Transferred to Poland

WESTERN UPPER SILESIA
Voted to remain German

EASTERN UPPER SILESIA
Voted to remain Polish

DANZIG
Made a Free City
under League of
Nations control

Disarmament
1. Germany to abolish conscription and to
   reduce its army to 100,000. General
   staff to be abolished
2. No tanks, big guns or military aircraft
3. German navy to be limited to: six battleships,
   six cruisers, 12 destroyers, 12 torpedo boats.
   No submarines. (The German fleet had
   already surrendered to Britain, but scuttled
   itself at Scapa Flow)

Article 231
Germany forced to sign
the war guilt clause,
therefore accepting
responsibility for losses
and damage

NORTHERN SCHLESWIG
Voted to join Denmark

SOUTHERN SCHLESWIG
Voted to remain Danish

RHINELAND
Administered by Germany, but no
fortifications allowed, and no military
forces to be garrisoned within the area

Lost by Germany

Retained by Germany following
voting by the population

Retained by Germany, but within
which no fortifications could be
built or soldiers stationed

EUPEN, MALMEDY
Transferred to Belgium

0   100   200
       km

SAAR
Controlled by the League
of Nations until 1935,
when it voted to remain German

ALSACE-LORRAINE
Returned to France after
47 years of German rule

Reparations
1. Reparations sum to be fixed by the IARC
   (International Allied Reparations Commission).
   In 1921 the sum was fixed at £6.6 billion
2. All coal production from the Saar until
   1935 was to be given to France
3. Germany to pay for all damage done
   to Allied civilians
4. Germany to make substantial payments
   in kind, e.g. 15 million tonnes of coal to Belgium

Memel

Königsberg

Danzig

POZNANIA

Poznań

Breslau

Katowice

Stettin

Berlin

Dresden

Weimar

Munich

Frankfurt

Mannheim

Stuttgart

Cologne

R. Rhine

Mainz

Metz

Strasbourg

Freiburg

Eupen

Malmédy

N

of self-determination was the Allied refusal to permit the union of Austria and Germany. Had they done so, Germany would have ended the war with more territory and 6 million more people. Despite German claims to the contrary, the treaty was not radically different from the Fourteen Points (in so far as they applied to Germany).

The treaty's territorial provisions were mild compared with the Treaty of Brest-Litovsk (see page 209). Germany lost 13.5 per cent of its territory and ten per cent of its population. Yet it remained a formidably strong economic power. Reparations – fixed in 1921 at £6600 million – were a significant, but not impossibly heavy burden. The sum was not unreasonable given the destruction visited on Belgium and France by German armies.

Arguably, the treaty produced the worst of all worlds: too severe to be permanently acceptable to most Germans, and too lenient to constrain Germany. After 1919 every German government would do its best to overthrow the treaty. The peace settlement would last only as long as the victorious powers were in a position to enforce it on resentful Germans. However, in fairness to the peacemakers, it should be stressed that it is hard to conceive of any peace treaty acceptable to the Allied powers and to their electorates in 1919 that the Germans would not have found humiliating. In the circumstances it may be that the Treaty of Versailles was a rational attempt at marrying principle and pragmatism in a dramatically altered world.

Economic problems

- The First World War impoverished Germany. Between 1913 and 1919 the national debt had risen from 5000 million marks to 144,000 million marks.
- In 1919 real national income was two-thirds of what it had been in 1913.
- Manufacturing output was 30 per cent lower in 1919 than in 1914.
- A large trade deficit and the difficulties of readjusting a war economy to the requirements of peace were not helped by reparation payments and the loss of important industrial regions.
- The Allied blockade, which did not end until the signing of the Treaty of Versailles, worsened an already dire food supply situation.

Financial problems

Germany's finances were a shambles. Rather than increase taxation, Germany had financed the war through short-term loans and by printing money. Between 1914 and 1919 the value of the mark against the dollar had fallen from 4.20 marks to 14.00 marks and the price of basic goods had increased three- to four-fold. The situation did not improve with the coming of peace. By early 1920 a dollar was worth 100 marks. Narrowing the massive gap between government income and expenditure, thereby bringing about the control of inflation, could only be achieved by increasing taxation and/or by cutting expenditure. Neither of these options was attractive.

Political problems

The fact that there were so many political parties, all obtaining a percentage of the seats in the *Reichstag*, meant that German governments were dependent on coalitions. Most parties were fairly narrowly based, on a class, religious or regional basis. Politicians were often too closely tied to their particular political ideology to find it easy to co-operate with other parties. Between 13 February 1919 and 30 January 1933 there were to be no fewer than twenty different cabinets. This made for weak government.

The threat from the left

In the eyes of the left, the new Germany looked remarkably like the old. The kaiser was gone but the imperial institutions, run by men with imperial mentalities, remained. The structure of German society was hardly affected by the revolution. The old elites – industrial barons, great landowners, the civil service, army officers – retained their power. There was to be no nationalisation of industry or massive land redistribution. The radical left were thus bitterly disappointed with the outcome of the revolutions of 1918–19. Nor was the suppression of workers' uprisings in 1919 forgotten or forgiven by the extreme left. The Communist Party, which received support (and orders) from Russia, remained a threat to the new Republic's stability.

The threat from the right

Ebert's willingness to compromise with the old order did not endear him to those regretted its passing. Right-wing political forces totally rejected the Weimar system and democratic principles. They demanded strong government, vied with each other to attack the Treaty of Versailles settlement, and had considerable success in propagating the notion that the German army had been 'stabbed in the back' in 1918 by the 'November Criminals': pacifists, socialists, communists and Jews.

The right was divided between conservatives and radicals. Many conservative supporters of the Nationalist party hoped to bring back the kaiser. Conservatives continued to exert influence in a number of key institutions, not least the army, civil service, judiciary and education system, all of which were preserved in much their old form.

After 1918 there were numerous radical right-wing groups, which had little sympathy with the conservatives. These groups – nationalistic, anti-democratic, anti-socialist and anti-Jewish – wanted to smash the new Republic. Ex-soldiers, especially those who had fought in the *Freikorps* units, were particularly attracted to the radical right. In September 1919 an obscure corporal joined the small right-wing German Workers' Party in Munich. The obscure corporal was Adolf Hitler.

Summary diagram: Establishment of the Weimar Republic

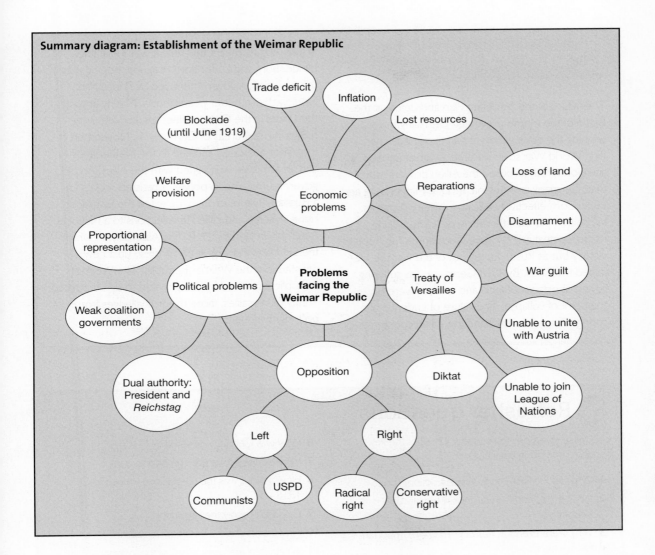

Chapter summary

The failure of the Schlieffen Plan and defeat at the Battle of the Marne prevented Germany from winning the quick victory it had expected. The First World War soon became a war of attrition, a situation which favoured the Allied powers rather than Germany and Austria. In 1916 Hindenburg and Ludendorff effectively became military dictators. Wilhelm II played little role in decision-making. Russia's defeat in 1917 gave Germany some hope of victory but as Russia pulled out of the war the USA joined the Allies. By 1918 Germany was suffering severe shortages of food and its allies were on the point of collapse. The failure of Ludendorff's spring offensive in 1918 and the Allied counterattack in July–August meant that defeat was inevitable. Hindenburg and Ludendorff resigned, hoping that the new civilian government, led by Prince Max, would achieve better peace terms. Mutiny among the sailors in the German fleet sparked left-wing risings in many areas of Germany. In November the kaiser abdicated and fled to the Netherlands and an armistice was signed with the Allies. An SPD government came to power. It resisted moves for a Russian-style revolution, defeated the Spartacist rising in Berlin and called for elections to a National Assembly in January 1919. The Assembly, in which the SPD was the largest party, drew up a new constitution: the Weimar Republic. The Weimar Republic, tarnished by being forced to sign the hated Treaty of Versailles, faced major challenges from both right and left.

Refresher questions

Use these questions to remind yourself of the key material covered in this chapter.

1 Why did the First World War last so long?

2 What impact did the war have internally on Germany?

3 Why were events in Russia in 1917–18 important for Germany?

4 Why did the USA join the war?

5 Why were Germans divided on the issue of making peace?

6 Why was Germany defeated in 1918?

7 Why did the November revolution occur?

8 How serious was the revolutionary threat in 1918–19?

9 Did Ebert betray the revolution?

10 How harsh was the Treaty of Versailles?

11 What were the weaknesses of the Weimar constitution?

12 How serious were the economic and political problems facing the Weimar Republic in 1919?

Question practice

THEMATIC ESSAY QUESTIONS

1 Assess the view that German nationalism changed from being a left- wing to a right-wing force in the course of the nineteenth century.

2 Assess the impact of free trade on the forging of a united Germany in the period from 1789 to 1914.

3 'Bismarck was a much more successful manager of German nationalism than either Metternich or Kaiser Wilhelm II.' How far do you agree with this view?

4 'The process of German unification was essentially a process of Prussian expansionism.' How far do you agree with this view?

5 'The Napoleonic Wars were the most important turning point in the development of German nationalism.' How far do you agree with this view?

6 'Prussian economic growth was the most important factor in the growth of German nationalism.' How far do you agree with this view?

7 'Nationalist feeling in Germany was weaker in the period to 1848 than in the period after 1848.' How far do you agree with this view of the period 1789–1919?

8 'Economic developments did more to hinder German nationalism than encourage it.' How far do you agree with this view of the period 1789–1919?

9 'War was the most important factor in the creation of a united Germany.' How far do you agree with this view of the period 1789–1919?

10 'Bismarck did more than any other ruler or minister to develop German nationalism in the period 1789–1919.' Assess this view.

11 'Germany was no more united in 1919 than it was in 1789 or 1848.' How far do you agree?

OCR A level History

Essay guidance

In the OCR Unit Y314 The Unification of Germany and the Challenge of Nationalism, there are two elements:

- The thematic essay which will require you to consider developments over approximately 100 years. You will answer two essays from a choice of three.
- The in-depth interpretation element where you will comprehend, analyse and evaluate the ways in which the past has been interpreted by historians.

Essay skills

There are a number of skills that you need to develop to reach the higher levels in the marking bands:

- Understand the wording of the question.
- Plan a thematic answer to the question set.
- Write a focused opening paragraph.
- Avoid irrelevance and description.
- Write analytically and thematically.
- Make comparisons within the themes, showing similarity and difference across the whole period.
- Write a conclusion that reaches a supported judgement based on the argument in the main body of the essay.

The skills are made very clear by both mark schemes, which emphasise that the answer must:

- focus on the demands of the question
- be supported by accurate and relevant factual knowledge
- be analytical and well structured
- reach a supported and developed judgement about the issue in the question
- demonstrate evidence of well-developed synthesis across the whole period.

These skills are the same as those you have developed for essay writing in Units 1 and 2.

However, in this unit there is a significant emphasis on *synthesis* across the whole period.

Understanding the wording of the question

To stay focused on the question set, it is important to read the question carefully and focus on the key words and phrases. Unless you directly address the demands of the question you will not score highly. Remember that in questions where there is a named factor you must write a good analytical paragraph about the given factor, even if you argue that it was not the most important.

Types of AS and A level questions you might find in the exams	The themes you might consider in answering them
1 Assess the impact of industrialisation on the development of German nationalism in the period 1789–1919.	You should weigh up the impact of industrialisation, both its positive and negative impacts, against other factors in the development of German nationalism: • German nationalists and individuals • military factors • foreign policy.
2 '1815 was the most important turning point in the course of German nationalism.' How far do you agree with this view of the period 1789–1919?	You might consider the relative importance of 1815 by comparing it with other events in the development of: • political nationalism • social nationalism • economic nationalism • cultural nationalism.
3 Assess the view that wars were the main factor in the unification of the German people in the period 1789–1919.	You should consider a range of factors, including the positive and negative impact of wars, that brought about unification. These may include: • economy • individuals • culture.

Types of AS and A level questions you might find in the exams	The themes you might consider in answering them
4 'Continuity rather than change characterised the nature of German nationalism throughout the period 1789–1919.' How far do you agree with this view?	You might consider whether the dominant aims and ideas of German nationalists remained the same throughout the period. You might consider some of these themes: • The creation and development of a united nation and the *Grossdeutschland* or *Kleindeutschland* debate. • The impact of intellectual developments. • The role of Prussia. • The impact of economic developments. • Radical nationalism. • The impact of people.

Planning an answer

Many plans simply list dates and events – this should be avoided as it encourages a descriptive or narrative answer, rather than an analytical answer. The plan should be an outline of your argument; this means you need to think carefully about the issues you intend to discuss and their relative importance before you start writing your answer. It should therefore be a list of the themes or issues you are going to discuss and a comment on their relative importance in relation to the question.

For question 3 in the table, your plan might look something like this:

- Opening paragraph: war was not only the factor and had positive and negative impacts on unification; importance varied during the period.
- War important: the Napoleonic Wars gave impulse to nationalism but only in a minority; gave control to Austria so it limits nationalism. War against Austria important as removes obstacle, but limits Germany to *Kleindeutschland*. War against France

established empire, but it could be argued that the war of 1870 did not unite Germany as it was no more than a Prussian takeover.

- Economy: a vital role as it provides materials that allow successful wars in 1860s and *Zollverein* helps drive Austria out, therefore it also limits the idea that wars were the most important factor. Idea of 'coal and iron'.
- Individuals: the roles of Metternich, Bismarck and Wilhelm II. The repressive policies of Metternich helped create nationalism. Bismarck and his role in the 1860s. Wilhelm and expansionist/radical nationalism.
- Culture: provides early basis but limited to intellectuals, later ideas of a Pan-German League, but also limits as religious and cultural divisions in the north/south.
- Conclusion: wars brought physical unity/geographical unity, but *Kleindeutschland* only possible because of situation exploited by Bismarck and economic power.

The opening paragraph

Many students spend time 'setting the scene'; the opening paragraph becomes little more than an introduction to the topic – this should be avoided. Instead, make it clear what your argument is going to be. Offer your view about the issue in the question – war played an important role, but it also impacted on the nature of Germany that emerged, *Kleindeutschland* – and then introduce the other issues you intend to discuss. In the plan it is suggested that war was an important factor, particularly in the 1860s. This should be made clear in the opening paragraph, with a brief comment as to why – this was because it resulted in geographical unity, albeit *Kleindeutschland*, but success was only possible because of economic strength and the diplomatic skill of Bismarck. This will give the examiner a clear overview of your essay, rather than it being a 'mystery tour' where the argument becomes clear only at the end. You should also refer to any important issues that the question raises. For example:

War played a crucial role in the unification of the German people throughout the period[1]. Wars were crucial in creating a feeling of nationalism and uniting the people[2]. The Napoleonic Wars helped to create initial feelings of patriotism and nationalism, while the wars of the 1860s brought about the geographical unity of Germany, and in 1914 war, initially at least, further united the country. However, war also helped to limit unification, particularly in the 1860s, when it led to the creation of a Kleindeutschland, and in 1918, when the nation was again divided geographically[3].

1 The opening sentence offers a clear view about the factor in the question.
2 This sentence offers the view that war had a positive impact on the development of nationalism throughout the period.
3 This sentence provides a balance and suggests that it was also a limiting factor.

The answer could then go on to raise other factors and provide an overview of the role they played across the whole period.

Avoid irrelevance and description

The plan will hopefully stop you from simply writing all you know about the reasons for unification and force you to weigh up the role of a range of factors. Similarly, it should also help prevent you from simply writing about the military events of the war. You will not lose marks if you do that, but neither will you gain any credit, and you will waste valuable time.

Write analytically

This is perhaps the hardest, but most important skill you need to develop. An analytical approach can be helped by ensuring that the opening sentence of each paragraph introduces an idea, which directly answers the question and is not just a piece of factual information. In a very strong answer it should be possible to simply read the opening sentences of all the paragraphs and know what argument is being put forward.

If we look at question 1, on the impact of industrialisation on the development of nationalism

(see page 230), the following are possible sentences with which to start paragraphs:

- Industrialisation played a pivotal role in creating Prussian dominance and providing the raw materials by which it could win military victories in the 1860s.
- Although industrialisation paved the way for military victories in the 1860s, it also limited the development of German nationalism as it excluded Austria and thwarted the ambitions of those nationalists who wanted a *Grossdeutschland*.
- Industrialisation helped to create urbanisation and socialism, which created an alternative loyalty to patriotism and nationalism.
- Industrialisation encouraged the kaiser to develop a radical nationalism through a populist foreign policy which had a negative impact as it led to defeat in the First World War and divided Germany.

You would then go on to discuss both sides of the argument raised by the opening sentence, using relevant knowledge about the issue to support each side of the argument. The final sentence of the paragraph would reach a judgement on the role played by the factor you are discussing in the development of German nationalism. This approach would ensure that the final sentence of each paragraph links back to the actual question you are answering. If you can do this for each paragraph you will have a series of mini-essays, which discuss a factor and reach a conclusion or judgement about the importance of that factor or issue. For example:

Industrialisation played a pivotal role in creating Prussian dominance and providing the raw materials by which Prussia could win military victories in the 1860s[1]. The military strength by which Prussia was able to defeat Austria at Sadowa in 1866 and France at Sedan was the result of 'coal and iron' rather than 'blood and iron'. There was major development of industries such as Krupps, which was founded in 1811 and grew from a single foundry to a vast complex, employing some 2000 people by 1861. Together with the creation of the *Zollverein*, major industries allowed the Prussian economy to develop and provide large sums of revenue from customs, which could be used to expand the military. This economic growth was aided by a new rail network, which gave them not only an economic but also a strategic advantage**[2]**. The dynamics of the economy helped to reduce the influence of Austria. The struggle between Austria and Prussia for control of the *Zollverein* helped to destroy Austria's attempts to reduce Prussia to a secondary role. The gap between the two was further widened by economic depression. Austria's exclusion from the *Zollverein*, and Prussia's dramatic economic growth between 1820 and 1850, were therefore crucial in creating Prussian dominance and led to the resultant *Kleindeutschland* that emerged in 1871**[3]**.

1 A clear view about the impact of industrialisation is offered.
2 This view is explained and supported by evidence from across the early part of the period.
3 This is then linked to how it helped to exclude Austria and cement Prussia's dominance and create a united Germany.

The answer could go on to argue that this industrialisation also had a limiting impact as it helped to exclude Austria and resulted in the creation of a *Kleindeutschland*, as opposed to a *Grossdeutschland*.

The conclusion

The conclusion provides the opportunity to bring together all the interim judgements to reach an overall judgement about the question. Using the interim judgements will ensure that your conclusion is based on the argument in the main body of the essay and does not offer a different view. For the essay answering question 2 (see page 230), you can decide what was the most important turning point in the course of German nationalism, but for questions 1 and 3 you will need to comment on the importance of the named factor – industrialisation or war – as well as explain why you think a different

factor is more important, if that has been your line of argument. Or, if you think the named factor is the most important, you would need to explain why that was more important than the other factors or issues you have discussed.

In reaching a judgement for question 2 you might conclude:

*1815 was important politically in the course of German nationalism because of the consequences of the Congress of Vienna, which reduced the number of states in Germany**[1]**. However, it was not as important as the 1866 victory over Austria as it gave Prussia control over the future of Germany, whereas 1815 had given Austria control and the opportunity under Metternich to repress nationalism**[2]**. Nor was 1815 as important as the defeat of France, which unified the north and south states, whereas 1815 had simply reduced the number of states in the German Confederation. Although it could be argued that 1815 played a role in the development of nationalism, militarily 1866 was more important than 1815, but in political and geographical terms the defeat of France was a greater turning point**[3]**.*

1 Summarises why the named turning point might be seen as significant.
2 Explains why other possible turning points are more important in terms of particular themes.
3 Reaches an overall judgement, which weighs up the possible turning points against a range of themes.

Interpretations guidance

For each of the in-depth interpretation elements, three topics are listed in the specification and a question will be set on *one* of the topics. The three topics for the Challenge of German Nationalism 1789–1919 are:

- 1848/9 Revolutions.
- Nationalism and Unification 1867–71.
- Wilhelmine Germany and the growth of Nationalism 1884–1914.

Although this is an A level paper it is not a historiography paper. The aim of this element of the unit is to develop an awareness that the past has been interpreted in different ways. The question will require you to assess the strengths and limitations of the two interpretations of an issue related to one of the specified in-depth topics. The interpretations will always be from historians and will not be primary sources.

You should be able to place the interpretation within the context of the wider historical debate on the key topic. However, you will not be required to know the names of individual historians associated with the debate or to have studied the specific books of any historians.

There are a number of skills you will need to develop if you are to reach the higher levels in the mark bands:

- Remain focused on the question throughout the answer.
- Assess and evaluate the two interpretations in the wider context of the historical debate about the issue.
- Apply your knowledge of the topic to the interpretations in order to evaluate their strengths and weaknesses.
- Ensure that you consider both interpretations.
- Reach a supported judgement as to which interpretation you think is more convincing.

Approaching the question

It might be helpful to think of a four-paragraph structure:

- In the first paragraph, explain the interpretations in the two passages and place them in the wider debate.
- In the second paragraph, apply your own knowledge in interpretation A to evaluate the validity of its view about the issue in the question. In doing this, your own knowledge should be used to analyse the strengths and weaknesses of the view in the interpretation.
- Repeat the second point, but for interpretation B.
- In the final paragraph, reach a supported and balanced judgement as to which view you think is more convincing.

You do not need to evaluate the provenance of the interpretation and therefore comments on the author and his or her background will not gain marks.

The questions set will be similar to the following:

> Evaluate the interpretations in both of the passages and explain which you think is a more convincing explanation of the impact of the Luxemburg crisis.
>
> (30 marks)

PASSAGE A

Once again, with the Luxembourg [sic] Crisis, Bismarck applied what had always been a basic political tactic, the use of a foreign crisis to achieve domestic objectives. Bismarck probably did think a war with France inevitable and may even have underestimated the influence of the peace party at the French court at this time, but neither Napoleon III nor he were for the moment ready to fight it. The constitution of the North German Confederation was not yet fully accepted, the south German states were by no means itching for a fight on the side of Prussia, nor was Bismarck keen to bring large numbers of potentially disaffected Catholics into the north German state prematurely. When the Luxembourg crisis was submitted to a conference of European powers in May 1867, Bismarck went out of his way to conciliate France by agreeing to the neutralization of Luxembourg and the withdrawal of Prussian troops from the fortress.

(From E. Feuchtwanger, *Bismarck*, 2002.)

PASSAGE B

In the spring of 1867, Bismarck exploited tensions in the set piece known as the Luxembourg [sic] Crisis. He first secretly encouraged Napoleon III to satisfy his wishes through the annexation of Luxembourg. Bismarck then leaked news of Napoleon's plans to the German press, knowing that these would prompt a wave of nationalist outrage. He then posed publicly as the German statesman bound by honour and conviction to execute the will of his people. The crisis was resolved by an international conference that guaranteed Luxembourg's status as an independent principality, but it could easily have led to a declaration of war, as Bismarck himself was aware. Here again, Bismarck showed himself to be the master of manipulation, who could blend underhand dealings and public posturing, high diplomacy and popular politics, with great skill.

(From C. Clark, *Iron Kingdom: The Rise and Downfall of Prussia*, 2006.)

In answering the question, the opening paragraph could consider the views of the two interpretations and place them in the context of the debate. For example:

The Luxemburg crisis of 1867 should be seen in the context of Bismarck's aims. The two interpretations raise the crucial issue of whether in 1867 he was happy with the expansion of Prussia or whether he was looking to use the crisis to provoke a war with the French and defeat them in order to complete the unification.

The opening places the passages in the wider context of the debate about the 1867 crisis and the aims of Bismarck during that crisis.

Passage A puts forward the view, particularly in the last part of the passage, that Bismarck went out of his way to placate France it suggests that Bismarck was not ready for unification with the southern states as the North German Confederation was not fully accepted and the southern states were not keen on fighting on the side of Prussia at that point.

The next part explains Passage A in relation to the issue raised in the question and supports its view by summarising part of the interpretation. The answer could then go on to consider the view put forward in Passage B and might suggest that Bismarck is looking to use and manipulate the tensions the crisis created and would have welcomed a war that might have developed from it. The answer could then go on to evaluate Passage A as follows:

Feuchtwanger is correct to emphasise how Bismarck used foreign crises to achieve domestic aims, and in this instance by invoking nationalism he was able to strengthen a fragile North German Confederation and increase Prussian influence over 'Germany'[1]. The crisis helped to create stronger national feeling and even hysteria, which it could be argued would also be useful when, as the interpretation suggests, the inevitable war with France did break out. The interpretation also rightly states that Bismarck was not ready for war, as was shown in his comments to a British journalist in September 1867, when he spoke of his wish for peace[2].

1 The opening sentence puts forward the view that the interpretation is correct to emphasise how Bismarck used foreign crises for domestic purposes and uses the need to strengthen the North German Confederation to support the claim. More precise detail of this could have been given, or other examples of where he did this, to strengthen the response.
2 Once again, there is evaluation and this time the claim that the interpretation is correct is supported by some very precise detail.

In evaluating this passage the response might have gone on to consider the position and attitude of the south German states. The response might also consider the weaknesses of the passage and might suggest that some of Bismarck's claims were simply propaganda to reassure nations such as Britain. A strong answer would reach an overall judgement, perhaps in the final sentence of the paragraph, about the validity of the views in the interpretation.

The answer should then consider the strengths and weaknesses of Passage B before writing a concluding paragraph which brings together the two interim judgements to reach an overall judgement as to which view is more convincing.

In the conclusion it might be argued:

Although Passage A is correct to argue that the internal problems within North Germany and the divisions between the north and south states did mean that Bismarck wanted to avoid war in 1867[1], Passage B is more convincing as it acknowledges that the crisis could have resulted in war and it was used cynically by Bismarck to increase Prussian influence over the rest of the German states and therefore lessen some of the fragility mentioned in Passage A[2].

1 The answer reaches a judgement, initially about Passage A, and supports the judgement.
2 The judgement is developed and the answer explains why, despite the strengths of Passage A, Passage B is more convincing and again supports the claim.

Edexcel A level History

Essay guidance

Edexcel's Paper 2, Option 2D.2: The Unification of Germany, *c*.1840–71 is assessed by an exam comprising two sections:

- Section A tests the depth of your historical knowledge through source analysis (see page 241 for guidance on this).
- Section B requires you to write one essay from a choice of two from your own knowledge.

The following advice relates to Paper 2, Section B. It is relevant to A level and AS level questions. Generally, the AS exam is similar to the A level exam. Both examine the same content and require similar skills; nonetheless, there are differences, which are discussed below.

Essay skills

In order to get a high grade in Section B of Paper 2 your essay must contain four essential qualities:

- focused analysis
- relevant detail
- supported judgement
- organisation, coherence and clarity.

This section focuses on the following aspects of exam technique:

- understanding the nature of the question
- planning an answer to the question set
- writing a focused introduction
- deploying relevant detail
- writing analytically
- reaching a supported judgement.

The nature of the question

Section B questions are designed to test the depth of your historical knowledge. Therefore, they can focus on relatively short periods, or single events, or indeed on the whole period from *c*.1840 to 1871. Moreover, they can focus on different historical processes or 'concepts'. These include:

- cause
- consequence
- change/continuity
- similarity/difference
- significance.

These different question focuses require slightly different approaches:

Cause	1 How far was Bismarck's diplomacy responsible for the unification of Germany in the years 1862–71?
Consequence	2 To what extent was the failure of the 1848–9 German Revolution a direct consequence of the mistakes of the Frankfurt Parliament?
Continuity and change	3 'Prussia's military victory against Austria in 1866 was dependent on economic developments in both countries after 1840.' How far do you agree with this statement?
Similarities and differences	4 'Bismarck's success against France in 1870–1 echoed his success against Austria in 1866.' How far do you agree with this statement?
Significance	5 'The rise of Prussia was the most significant result of the failure of the 1848–9 German revolutions'. How far do you agree with this statement?

Some questions include a 'stated factor'. The most common type of stated factor question would ask how far one factor caused something. For example, the first question in the table asks: 'How far was Bismarck's diplomacy responsible for the unification of Germany in the years 1862–71?' In this type of question you would be expected to evaluate the importance of 'Bismarck's diplomacy' – the 'stated factor' – compared to other factors.

AS and A level questions

AS level questions are generally similar to A level questions. However, the wording of AS questions will be slightly less complex than the wording of A level questions.

A level question	AS level question	
To what extent did Bismarck's success from 1862 to 1871 depend on the errors and misjudgements of others?	To what extent did Bismarck's success from 1862 to 1871 depend on the errors and misjudgements of Napoleon III?	The A level question focuses on 'others', whereas the AS question focuses specifically on the errors and misjudgements of Napoleon III
'The German revolutions in 1848 resulted, at least in part, from social and economic crisis.' How far do you agree with this statement?	How far were economic problems in the German states responsible for the outbreak of revolution in 1848?	The AS question asks how far economic problems led to the 1848 revolutions. The A level question asks you to make a more complex judgement: was there a social as well as an economic crisis (as opposed to just problems)?

To achieve the highest level at A level, you will have to deal with the full complexity of the question. For example, if you were dealing with question 4, about Bismarck's success against France in 1870–1, you would have to compare his dealings with France (say between 1866 and 1870) with his dealings with Austria (say between 1862 and 1866) and decide whether there were any similarities.

Planning your answer

It is crucial that you understand the focus of the question. Therefore, read the question carefully before you start planning. Check the following:

- The chronological focus: which years should your essay deal with?
- The topic focus: what aspect of your course does the question deal with?
- The conceptual focus: is this a causes, consequences, change/continuity, similarity/difference or significance question?

For example, for question 3 you could point these out as follows:

'Prussia's military victory against Austria[1] in 1866 was dependent on economic developments in both countries[2] after 1840[3].' How far do you agree with this statement?

1 Topic focus: Prussia's military success in 1866.
2 Conceptual focus: continuity/change.
3 Chronological focus: 1840–66.

Your plan should reflect the task that you have been set. Section B asks you to write an analytical, coherent and well-structured essay from your own knowledge, which reaches a supported conclusion in around 40 minutes.

- To ensure that your essay is coherent and well structured, it should comprise a series of paragraphs, each focusing on a different point.
- Your paragraphs should come in a logical order. For example, you could write your paragraphs in order of importance, so you begin with the most important issues and end with the least important.
- In essays where there is a 'stated factor', it is a good idea to start with the stated factor before moving on to the other points.
- To make sure you keep to time, you should aim to write three or four paragraphs plus an introduction and a conclusion.

The opening paragraph

The opening paragraph should do four main things:

- answer the question directly
- set out your essential argument
- outline the factors or issues that you will discuss
- define key terms used in the question – where necessary.

Different questions require you to define different terms, for example:

A level question	Key terms
To what extent was the policy of 'blood and iron' the main reason for the unification of Germany by 1871?	Here it is worth defining 'blood and iron'
'Bismarck was a ruthless opportunist who was able to manipulate any diplomatic incident to his advantage in the years 1862–71.' How far do you agree with this statement?	In this example, it is worth defining 'ruthless opportunist'

Here's an example introduction in answer to question 2 in the table on page 237: 'To what extent was the failure of the 1848–9 German Revolution due to the mistakes of the Frankfurt Parliament?'

The Frankfurt Parliament, which came about because of the 1848 German Revolution, was ultimately to disappoint the hopes of the revolutionaries[1]. Its failure to create a united, constitutional Germany was, in part, due to its own mistakes[2]. However, it may be that, given the situation in Germany in 1848–9, the Frankfurt Parliament never stood much chance of success[3].

1 The essay starts by referring to words used in the question.
2 The sentence accepts that mistakes were made.
3 Finally – and with the help of the key word 'however' – the essential argument is stated.

The opening paragraph: advice

- Don't write more than a couple of sentences on general background knowledge. This is unlikely to focus explicitly on the question.
- After defining key terms, refer back to these definitions when justifying your conclusion.
- The introduction should reflect the rest of the essay. Don't make one argument in your introduction, then make a different argument in the essay.

Deploying relevant detail

Paper 2 tests the depth of your historical knowledge. Therefore, you will need to deploy historical detail. In the main body of your essay your paragraphs should begin with a clear point, be full of relevant detail and end with explanation or evaluation. A detailed answer might include statistics, proper names, dates and technical terms. For example, if you are writing a paragraph about the Prussian–German army in 1870 you might include some discussion as to what extent it was a Prussian–German force, some information about the work of General Moltke, chief of the general staff, and War Minister Roon, and statistics about the army's strength in 1870.

Writing analytically

The quality of your analysis is one of the key factors that determines the mark you achieve. Writing analytically means clearly showing the relationships between the ideas in your essay. Analysis includes two key skills: explanation and evaluation.

Explanation

Explanation means giving reasons. An explanatory sentence has three parts:

- a claim: a statement that something is true or false
- a reason: a statement that justifies the claim
- a relationship: a word or phrase that shows the relationship between the claim and the reason.

Imagine you are answering question 1 in the table on page 237: 'How far was Bismarck's diplomacy responsible for the unification of Germany in 1862–71?' Your paragraph on Bismarck's diplomatic skill should start with a clear point, which would be supported by a series of examples. Finally, you would round off the paragraph with some explanation:

Therefore, Bismarck's diplomacy was a major factor in bringing about German unification[1] because[2] it helped to isolate his enemies and ensure that the Prussian army could defeat both Austria and France[3].

1 Claim.   2 Relationship.   3 Reason.

Make sure of the following:

- The reason you give genuinely justifies the claim you have made.
- Your explanation is focused on the question.

Reaching a supported judgement

Finally, your essay should reach a supported judgement. The obvious place to do this is in the conclusion of your essay. Even so, the judgement should reflect the findings of your essay. The conclusion should present:

- a clear judgement that answers the question
- an evaluation of the evidence that supports the judgement
- finally, the evaluation should reflect valid criteria.

Evaluation and criteria

Evaluation means weighing up to reach a judgement. Therefore, evaluation requires you to:

- summarise both sides of the issue
- reach a conclusion that reflects the proper weight of both sides.

So, for question 2 in the table on page 237: 'To what extent was the failure of the 1848–9 German Revolution a direct consequence of the mistakes of the Frankfurt Parliament?', the conclusion might look like this:

In conclusion, the Frankfurt Parliament undoubtedly made a number of crucial mistakes[1]. Clearly, it failed to act decisively, becoming more a talking shop than an institution set upon leading Germany forward, and remained seriously divided about its precise aims from start to finish[2]. However, lacking an effective administration, an army to carry out its decisions and a popular mandate, it never stood much chance of success. Once the rulers of Austria and Prussia had regained control of their territories, the Parliament was doomed to defeat[3]. Therefore, the failure of the revolutions in Austria and Prussia was ultimately far more important in ensuring the failure of the German Revolution than the mistakes of the Frankfurt Parliament[4].

1 The conclusion starts with a clear judgement that is geared to the question.
2 This sentence considers the Frankfurt Parliament's mistakes.
3 The conclusion also considers evidence to suggest that the Parliament's failure was not due simply to its mistakes.
4 The essay ends with a final judgement that is supported by the evidence of the essay.

Sources guidance

Edexcel's Paper 2, Option 2D.2: The Unification of Germany, *c.*1840–71 is assessed by an exam comprising two sections:

- Section A tests the depth of your historical knowledge through source analysis.
- Section B requires you to write one essay from a choice of two from your own knowledge (see page 237 for guidance on this).

The following advice relates to Paper 2, Section A. It is relevant to A level and AS level questions. Generally, the AS exam is similar to the A level exam. Both examine the same content and require similar skills; nonetheless, there are differences, which are discussed below.

The questions in Paper 2, Section A are structured differently in the A level and AS exams.

AS exam	Full A level exam
Section A: contains one compulsory question divided into two parts.	Section A: contains a single compulsory question worth 20 marks. The question asks you to evaluate the usefulness of two sources for a specific historical enquiry.
Part a) is worth 8 marks. It focuses on the value of a single source for a specific enquiry.	
Part b) is worth 12 marks. It asks you to weigh the value of a single source for a specific enquiry.	Together the two sources will comprise about 300–400 words.
Together the two sources will comprise about 300–400 words.	
Questions will start with the following stems: a) Why is Source 1 valuable to the historian for an enquiry about … b) How much weight do you give the evidence of Source 2 for an enquiry into …	Questions will start with the following stem: How far could the historian make use of Sources 1 and 2 together to investigate …

Edexcel style questions

AS style question

a) Study Sources 1 and 2 before you answer this question. Why is Source 1 valuable to the historian for an enquiry into the causes of the Franco-Prussian War 1870–1?

Explain your answer using the source, the information given about it and your own knowledge of the historical context.

b) How much weight do you give the evidence of Source 2 for an enquiry into Bismarck's attitude to France in 1867?

Explain your answer using the source, the information given about it and your own knowledge of the historical context.

A level style question

Study Sources 1 and 2 before you answer this question.

How far could the historian make use of Sources 1 and 2 together to investigate the causes of the Franco-Prussian War?

Explain your answer using both sources, the information given about them and your own knowledge of the historical context.

Sources 1 and 2

SOURCE I

From Count Helmuth von Moltke, the Prussian chief of staff 1870–1, *The Franco-Prussian War*, **published in Germany in 1891.**

A Napoleon on the throne of France was bound to justify his pretensions by political and military successes. Only temporarily was the French nation contented by the victories of its armies in remote fields of war; the triumphs of the Prussian armies excited jealousy, they were regarded as arrogant, as a challenge; and the French demanded revenge for Sadowa …

[The French] army was by no means in thorough preparedness for a great war, but in the temper of the nation, the Spanish succession question furnished an opportune pretext on which to go to war. The French Reserves were called out on July 15th, and, as if the opportunity for a rupture was on no account to be let slip, only four days later the French declaration of war was presented at Berlin.

SOURCE 2

From a long interview which Bismarck gave to a British journalist in September 1867.

There is nothing in our attitude to annoy or alarm France … there is nothing to prevent the maintenance of peace for ten or fifteen years, by which time the French will have become accustomed to German unity, and will consequently have ceased to care about it.

I told our generals this spring, when they endeavoured to prove to me, by all sorts of arguments that we must beat the French, if we went to war then, 'I will still do all I can to prevent war; for you must remember, gentlemen, a war between such near neighbours and old enemies as France and Prussia, however it may turn out, is

only the first of at least six; and supposing we gained all six, what should we have succeeded in doing? Why, in ruining France certainly, and most likely ourselves into the bargain. Do you think a poor, bankrupt, starving, ragged neighbour is as desirable as a wealthy, solvent, fat, well-clothed one? France buys largely from us, and sells us a great many things we want. Is it in our interests to ruin her completely?' I strove for peace then, and I will do so as long as may be; only, remember German susceptibilities must be respected, or I cannot answer for the people – not even for the King!

Understanding the questions

- To answer the question successfully you must understand how the question works.
- The question is written precisely in order to make sure that you understand the task. Each part of the question has a specific meaning.
- You must use the source, the information given about the source and your own knowledge of the historical context when answering the question.

Understanding the AS question

a) Why is Source 1 valuable to the historian for an enquiry[1] into the causes of the Franco-Prussian War 1870–1[2]?

1 You must focus on the reasons why the source could be helpful to a historian. Indeed, you can get maximum marks without considering the source's limitations.

2 The final part of the question focuses on a specific topic that a historian might investigate. In this case: 'the causes of the Franco-Prussian War 1870–1'.

b) How much weight do you give the evidence of Source 2[1] for an enquiry[2] into Bismarck's attitude to France in 1867[3]?

1 This question focuses on evaluating the extent to which the source contains evidence. Therefore, you must consider the ways in which the source is valuable and the limitations of the source.
2 This is the essence of the task: you must focus on what a historian could legitimately conclude from studying this source.
3 This is the specific topic that you are considering the source for: 'Bismarck's attitude to France in 1867'.

Understanding the A level question

How far[1] could the historian make use of Sources 1 and 2[2] together[3] to investigate the causes of the Franco-Prussian War[4]?

Explain your answer using both sources, the information given about them and your own knowledge of the historical context[5].

1 You must evaluate the extent of something, rather than giving a simple 'yes' or 'no' answer.
2 This is the essence of the task: you must focus on what a historian could legitimately conclude from studying these sources.
3 You must examine the sources as a pair and make a judgement about both sources, rather than simply making separate judgements about each source.
4 The final part of the question focuses on a specific topic that a historian might investigate. In this case: 'the causes of the Franco-Prussian War'.
5 This instruction lists the resources you should use: the sources, the information given about the sources and your own knowledge of historical context that you have learnt during the course.

Source skills

Generally, Section A of Paper 2 tests your ability to evaluate source material. More specifically, the sources presented in Section A will be taken from the period that you have studied: *c.*1840–71, or be written by people who witnessed these events. Your job is to analyse the sources by reading them in the context of the values and assumptions of the society and the period that produced them.

Examiners will mark your work by focusing on the extent to which you are able to:

- Interpret and analyse source material:
  - At a basic level, this means you can understand the sources and select, copy, paraphrase and summarise the source or sources to help answer the question.
  - At a higher level, your interpretation of the sources includes the ability to explain, analyse and make inferences based on the sources.
  - At the highest levels, you will be expected to analyse the source in a sophisticated way. This includes the ability to distinguish between information, opinions and arguments contained in the sources.
- Deploy knowledge of historical context in relation to the sources:
  - At a basic level, this means the ability to link the sources to your knowledge of the context in which the source was written, using this knowledge to expand or support the information contained in the sources.
  - At a higher level, you will be able to use your contextual knowledge to make inferences, and to expand, support or challenge the details mentioned in the sources.
  - At the highest levels, you will be able examine the value and limits of the material contained in the sources by interpreting the sources in the context of the values and assumptions of the society that produced them.
- Evaluate the usefulness and weight of the source material:
  - At a basic level, evaluation of the source will be based on simplistic criteria of reliability and bias.
  - At a higher level, evaluation of the source will be based on the nature and purpose of the source.
  - At the highest levels, evaluation of the source will be based on a valid criterion that is justified in the course of the essay. You will also be able to distinguish between the value of different aspects of the sources.

Make sure your source evaluation is sophisticated. Avoid crude statements about bias, and avoid simplistic assumptions such as that a source written immediately after an event is reliable, whereas a source written years later is unreliable.

Try to see things through the eyes of the writer:

- How does the writer understand the world?
- What assumptions does the writer have?
- Who is the writer trying to influence?
- What views is the writer trying to challenge?

Basic skill: comprehension

The most basic source skill is comprehension: understanding what the sources mean. There are a variety of techniques that you can use to aid comprehension. For example, you could read the sources included in this book and in past papers:

- Read the sources out loud.
- Look up any words that you don't understand and make a glossary.
- Make flash cards containing brief biographies of the writers of the sources.

You can demonstrate comprehension by copying, paraphrasing and summarising the sources. However, keep this to the minimum as comprehension is a low-level skill and you need to leave room for higher-level skills.

Advanced skill: contextualising the sources

First, to analyse the sources correctly you need to understand them in the context in which they were written. Moltke was writing, with the benefit of hindsight, two decades after the Franco-Prussian War. Bismarck was speaking to a British journalist, and probably trying to reassure the British public that he was a peacemaker, not a warmonger. The sources reflect this. Your job is to understand the values and assumptions behind the source.

- One way of contextualising the sources is to consider the nature, origins and purpose of the sources. However, this can lead to formulaic responses.

- An alternative is to consider two levels of context. First, you should establish the general context. In this case, Sources 1 and 2 refer to a period in which relations between France and Prussia were uneasy – at best. Secondly, you can look for specific references to contemporary events or debates in the sources. For example:

Sources 1 and 2 both refer to Franco-Prussian relations. Source 1, written many years after 1870, blames Napoleon III and the French public for the war of 1870–1. Note the reference to the battle of Sadowa and the Spanish succession question. Source 2 is from 1867: the year of the Luxemburg crisis. Note that Bismarck declares he does not wish to alarm France. However, note also the veiled threats in the interview: the fact that Prussian generals were confident of defeating France; and Bismarck's declaration that if France ignores German susceptibilities, the German people or King William might force him to go to war.

Use context to make judgements

- Start by establishing the general context of the source:
  - Ask yourself, what was going on at the time when the source was written, or the time of the events described in the source?
  - What are the key debates that the source might be contributing to?
- Next, look for key words and phrases that establish the specific context. Does the source refer to specific people, events or books that might be important?
- Make sure your contextualisation focuses on the question.
- Use the context when evaluating the usefulness and limitations of the source.

For example:

Source 1 is valuable to a historian investigating the origins of the Franco-Prussian War because it shows General von Moltke's view of why the war came about. Moltke, the Prussian chief of staff who prepared the Prussian army for war, seems to have no doubt that Napoleon III and the French people were totally responsible for the war. This was the official Prussian line in 1870: it was still the official German line in 1891. Source 2 is valuable because it shows Bismarck's view of Franco-Prussian relations in 1867. He presents himself as a man of peace. But Bismarck's words cannot necessarily be taken at face value. He was fully aware that he was speaking to a British audience and wanted to allay British fears about Prussian warlike intentions, reducing the chance of a British alliance with France. He thus sought to present himself and his policies in a favourable light. Of course, it may be that Bismarck really did have pacific intentions with regard to France in 1867. The Luxemburg crisis was resolved and the years 1867–70 were peaceful. It is far from certain that Bismarck wanted – or deliberately planned – a full-scale war with France in 1870. The Spanish succession crisis and the Ems telegram enabled him to manipulate the situation – a situation he had not initially created. While he had clear aims, the exact means of achieving them were left to short-term decisions based on the situation at the time. He was not essentially a warmonger. For Bismarck, wars were a risky means to an end. He was not necessarily disguising his true feelings in the 1867 interview.

Glossary of terms

Absolute rule   A state where a single person or group has total power.

Anarchist   A person whose ideal society is one without government of any kind. Late nineteenth-century anarchists often sought to bring about such a condition by terrorism.

Ancien régime   The old feudal order in France.

Anti-Semitism   Hatred of Jews.

Austrian Empire   Included much of what is today Austria, Hungary, Poland, the Czech Republic, Slovakia, Croatia and northern Italy.

Boer War   The conflict in South Africa (1899–1902) between Britain and the Boer republics of the Transvaal and the Orange Free State.

Bonapartist   Supportive of the Bonaparte family. Although Napoleon Bonaparte had been defeated in 1815, many French people regarded his rule with great nostalgia.

Bourgeoisie   The upper and middle classes who owned the capital and the means of production and who (Marx claimed) exploited the workers.

Breech-loading needle gun   This gun, which loaded at the breech rather than the barrel, could fire seven shots a minute. It could also be fired lying down rather than standing up.

Bundesrat   The Federal Council, comprising 58 members nominated by state assemblies. Its consent was required in the passing of new laws.

Bureaucracies   Systems of administration.

Cartel   An association of manufacturers who come to a contractual agreement about the level of production and the scale of prices and maintain a monopoly.

Chassepot **rifle**   A breech-loading rifle, named after the man who invented it.

Civic Guard   A military force composed of ordinary people, not professional soldiers.

Civil disobedience   Refusal to obey state laws and regulation.

Cleansing the Augean stables   A difficult and dirty task. (According to Greek legend, it was one of the labours of the hero Hercules.)

The Communist Manifesto   Karl Marx's book supported the idea of class revolution. It encouraged workers everywhere to unite.

Concordat   An agreement between the Vatican and a government.

Constitution   A set of rules by which a state is governed.

Constitutional monarch   A king or queen whose powers are limited by a constitution and who usually rules in co-operation with an elected parliament.

Continental blockade   Napoleon's trade boycott of British goods. Introduced in 1806, its aim was to force Britain to make peace with France.

Cortes   The Spanish Parliament.

Counter-revolution   A subsequent revolution (usually by conservative forces) counteracting the effect of a previous one.

Crimean War   A war fought by Britain, France and Turkey against Russia between 1854 and 1856. Most of the fighting was in the Crimea – a southern part of Russia. The war ended with Russia's defeat.

Democratisation of the army   Officers would be elected by the men and the regular army would be replaced by a people's militia.

Deutschland über Alles   This means 'Germany above the others'. It eventually became Germany's national anthem, the words being set to a popular melody by eighteenth-century composer Joseph Haydn.

Diet   An assembly or parliament.

Diktat   An imposed settlement allowing for no negotiations.

Divine right of kings   The notion that kings are God's representatives on earth and thus entitled to full obedience from their subjects.

Duchies   States ruled by a duke.

Dynastic   Ruled by the same family.

Entente   A friendly understanding rather than a binding agreement.

Executive   The power or authority in government that carries laws into effect.

Federal   A government in which several states, while independent in domestic affairs, combine together under a central authority.

Federation   A group of states joined together in some form of union.

Feudal system   A system of social organisation prevalent in much of Europe in the Middle Ages. Powerful lords owned most of the land.

Fig-leaf of despotism   Something intended to cover the fact that Germany was ruled by an authoritarian government.

Fourteen Points   These were President Wilson's main war aims. Wilson hoped to prevent future wars by eliminating secret alliances and frustrated nationalism, and by establishing a League of Nations.

Franchise   The right to vote.

Fraternity   Brotherhood and companionship.

Free trade   Unrestricted trade without protective import duties.

German National Association (*Deutscher Nationalverein*)   A political organisation in the German Confederation from 1859 to 1867. It was formed by moderate democrats who wanted a liberal, parliamentary *Kleindeutsch* Prussian-led national state.

German violation of Belgium's neutrality   German troops, in order to get round French defences along the German frontier, invaded Belgium. Britain had pledged itself to protect Belgium's neutrality in 1839.

Great Powers   Europe's strongest nations in 1814–15 were Britain, Russia, Austria, Prussia and France. The first four countries had allied together to defeat France.

Gross national product   The total value of all goods and services produced within a country.

Grossdeutschland   A greater Germany that would include the German-speaking provinces of the Austrian Empire.

Habsburg   The ruling family of the Austrian Empire.

Hanseatic towns   A league of German commercial cities mainly on the Baltic Sea coast.

Hottentot election   This election was named after native rebels in South-West Africa.

Indirect taxes   Taxes placed on the sale of goods rather than those collected directly from the taxpayer.

Inflation   An excessive increase in the supply of money that results in a decline in its purchasing power.

Jameson Raid   In 1895 Dr Jameson led a force of 470 men into the Transvaal, hoping to spark a revolt which would overthrow President Kruger's Boer government. The raid was a total failure.

Jesuit order   A Catholic order of militant priests founded in 1534 by Ignatius Loyola.

Judenthum   The Jewish community in Germany.

July Revolution in Paris   In 1830 the reactionary King Charles X of France was overthrown and replaced by the more liberal Louis-Philippe.

Junkers   The conservative landed aristocracy of Prussia.

Kleindeutschland   A little Germany that would exclude Austria.

Kulturkampf   A struggle for culture or a struggle for civilisation. In Germany, the struggle was between the state and the Catholic Church.

Landwehr   A reserve army, made up of men who are partially but not necessarily fully or recently trained.

Lobby groups   Particular groups who campaign to persuade politicians to pass legislation favouring their interests.

Luther's stand against the Pope   In 1517 this German religious leader protested against a number of practices of the Catholic Church, leading to a bitter religious divide. Martin Luther's followers became known as Protestants.

Martial law   The exercise of military power by a government in time of emergency, with the temporary suspension of ordinary administration and policing.

Marxist historians   Historians who accept the ideas of Karl Marx and believe that history is essentially about class conflict.

Marxist programme   The plan of those who supported the ideas of Karl Marx. Marxists believed that leaders of the proletariat must work to overthrow the capitalist system by (violent) revolution.

Minimum programme   The name given to the plans of moderate socialists who were opposed to violent revolution.

Multinational Austrian Empire   The Austrian Empire contained people of many different nationalities. Although a relatively small minority, the Germans were the dominant ethnic group within the Empire.

National guard   A national guard was supposed to be a force of the people. It was thus less under the control of the monarch.

Nationalisation   Government ownership.

Nationalism   The belief in – and support for – a national identity and the desire for the nation's success.

Nationalist   Someone who favours or strives after the unity, independence, interests or domination of a nation.

North Italian War   In 1859 French Emperor Napoleon III supported Piedmont against Austria. Piedmont was seeking to increase its influence in northern Italy at Austria's expense. Austria was defeated.

Orthodox Church   The Greek or Eastern Christian Church.

Ottoman Empire   The Turkish Empire, which was ruled by the Ottoman family.

Pacifism   Opposition to war on principle.

Pan-German League   Formed in 1893, the League was a right-wing nationalist movement. It supported German expansion both in Europe and worldwide.

Pan-Slavist   Someone who supported the union of all Slav peoples.

Potato blight   A destructive disease of the potato caused by a parasitic fungus.

Principalities   States ruled by a prince.

Proletariat   The exploited industrial workers who (Marx claimed) would triumph in the last great class struggle.

Proportional representation   This system of voting ensures that a party receives the same percentage of seats as votes received.

Protectionist   Favouring the protection of trade by having duties on imports.

Reactionary   Opposing political or social change and wanting to revert to past conditions.

Realpolitik   The term is used to describe the ruthless and cynical policies of politicians, like Bismarck, whose main aim was to increase the power of a state.

Regent   A ruler invested with authority on behalf of another.

Reich   The German word for empire.

Reichsbank   A national German bank which dealt mainly with the German government and with other banks, for example, regulating interest rates and managing the national debt.

Reichstag   The National Parliament, elected by all males over 25 years of age.

Reparations   Money that a country is forced to pay to the victor after defeat in war.

Republican   Of, or favouring, a government without a monarch.

Revolutionary shop stewards   Working-class activists who tried to organise mass action in the factories of Berlin in an attempt to end the war.

Satiated power   A nation satisfied with its strength and position.

Second German Empire   The first empire was the Holy Roman Empire, established by Charlemagne. The second empire was the one established by Bismarck.

Secular   Non-religious and non-spiritual: civil, not ecclesiastical.

Self-determination   The right of people to decide their own form of government.

Septennates   The arrangement whereby military spending was agreed for seven years.

Serfs   Peasants who are forced to remain on the land and work for a landowner.

Slavs   People who regard themselves to be of the same ethnic group and whose language is Slavonic. Slavs include Russians, Czechs, Serbs and Bulgarians.

Sovereignty   Supreme power.

Soviet   A council of workers, peasants and soldiers.

Splendid isolation   For much of the late nineteenth century, Britain, protected by its navy, had not allied with any major power.

Standing army   A state's main military force. The army usually supported the government against revolutionary activity.

Status quo   The existing condition or situation.

The Straits   The Bosphorus and Dardanelles, which link the Black Sea with the Mediterranean Sea.

Tariffs   Import duties, intended to raise money or protect domestic industry and agriculture from foreign competition.

Tenant farmers   Farmers who rented their land from a landowner.

Tithes   A tax paid to the Church; in theory, a tenth of a person's earnings.

Triple Entente powers   Britain, France and Russia.

U-boat   *Unterseeboot*: German for submarine.

Universal suffrage   A system that allows everyone over a certain age to vote.

Volk   The German word translates as people or folk but the concept goes beyond that, implying that the (German) *volk* are almost mystically united and are superior to other groups.

Vorparlament   Usually translated as 'pre-parliament', but it is better thought of as 'preparatory parliament', which was preparing the way for the real parliament.

War credits   Financial bills, enabling the war to be funded.

Weltpolitik   This translates as world policy. The word is used to describe Wilhelm II's efforts to make Germany a great world (as well as European) power.

Wilhelmine Germany   The period from 1888 to 1918 when Wilhelm II was kaiser.

Zollverein   The Prussian Customs Union.

Further reading

There are scores of excellent books on German history in the period covered by this book. It is impossible for most students to consult more than a few of these. However, it is vital that you read some. It is a common complaint of all history examiners that candidates do not read widely enough. The following suggestions are meant to serve as a guide.

General textbooks

M.S. Anderson, *The Ascendancy of Europe 1815–1914* (Longman, 1999)

A bit long-in-the-tooth but the fact that it is still in print says a great deal

J.A.S. Grenville, *Europe Reshaped 1848–1878* (Fontana, 2000)

Obviously limited in scope time-wise but good for the period it covers

L.C.B. Seaman, *From Vienna to Versailles* (Routledge, 1990)

A short but sweet account of European developments from 1815 to 1919

A.J.P. Taylor, *The Struggle for Mastery in Europe 1848–1918* (Clarendon Press, 1965)

A masterly, if dated and often controversial, book

General texts on Germany

D. Blackbourn, *The Fontana History of Germany 1780–1918* (Fontana, 1997)

A good book on the entire period

J. Breilly, editor, *Nineteenth-century Germany: Politics, Culture and Society 1780–1918* (Bloomsbury Academic, 2001)

A useful collection of essays

W. Carr, *A History of Germany 1815–1990* (Edward Arnold, 1991)

This remains one of the best general histories of the period

C. Clark, *Iron Kingdom: The Rise and Downfall of Prussia 1600–1947* (Penguin, 2007)

The definitive history of Prussia

M. Fulbrook, *German History since 1800* (Edward Arnold, 1997)

A solid and reliable introduction to German history

M. Kitchen, *A History of Modern Germany 1800–2000* (Blackwell, 2006)

Probably the best general textbook now available on modern Germany

Texts on German unification

J. Breuilly, *The Formation of the First German Nation-state 1800–1871* (Macmillan, 1996)

A very good read

W. Carr, *The Origins of the Wars of German Unification* (Longman, 1991)

This is a really good book if you can still get hold of it

T. Nipperdey, *German History from Napoleon to Bismarck 1800–1866* (Princeton University Press, 1996)

An excellent history of the situation in Germany pre-1866

J. Sperber, *Germany 1800–70: The Short Oxford History of Germany* (Oxford University Press, 2004)

Well-organised and suitably concise

Texts on Bismarck

L. Abrams, *Bismarck and the German Empire 1871–1918* (Routledge, 1995)

A recommended read on Bismarck post-unification

E. Crankshaw, *Bismarck* (Macmillan, 1981)

This is not a straightforward narrative and needs a basic knowledge and understanding of Bismarck's life for it to make sense

E. Feuchtwanger, *Bismarck* (Routledge, 2002)

Tautly written and thoroughly researched

J. Steinberg, *Bismarck: A Life* (Oxford University Press, 2012)

A deeply researched but still accessible guide to Bismarck

A.J.P. Taylor, *Bismarck: The Man and Statesman* (New English Library, 1974)

This is entertainingly written but is not entirely reliable

B. Waller, *Bismarck* (Blackwell, 1997)

This is a very useful review of Bismarck's life and achievements

D.G. Williamson, *Bismarck and Germany, 1862–1890* (Routledge, 1995)

A good introduction to Bismarck's career

Texts on Imperial Germany

V.R. Berghahn, *Imperial Germany 1871–1914* (Oxford University Press, 1994)

This deals largely with social, economic and cultural developments

C. Clark, *Kaiser Wilhelm II: A Life in Power* (Penguin, 2009)

A critical and illuminating review of Wilhelm's life

C. Clark, *The Sleepwalkers: How Europe Went to War in 1914* (Penguin, 2013)

A stimulating, if controversial, study of how Germany and Europe stumbled into war in 1914

F. Fischer, *Germany's Aims in the First World War* (W.W. Norton, 2007)

A controversial read but worth dipping into

S. Lee, *Imperial Germany 1871–1918* (Routledge, 1998)

A good introduction

A. Mombauer, editor, *The Origins of the First World War: Diplomatic and Military Documents* (Manchester University Press, 2013)

Probably the most authoritative documentation on the decisions that led to the First World War

W.J. Mommsen, *Imperial Germany 1867–1918* (Edward Arnold, 1995)

Another well-written and comprehensive text

J. Retallack, *Imperial Germany 1871–1918: The Short Oxford History of Germany* (Oxford University Press, 2008)

A well-written book, very much on a par with Sperber's book in the same series

J.C.G. Röhl, *Kaiser Wilhelm II* (Cambridge University Press, 2014)

Easily the best short history of Wilhelm II's life

J.C.G. Röhl, *Wilhelm II, The Kaiser's Personal Monarchy* (Cambridge University Press, 2001)

Probably a little too detailed for most readers

Index